HEGEL, LITERATURE
AND THE PROBLEM OF AGENCY

Hegel's *Phenomenology of Spirit* has attracted much attention recently from philosophers, but none of the existing English-language books on the text addresses one of the most difficult questions the book raises: Why does the *Phenomenology* make such rich and provocative use of literary works and genres?

Allen Speight's bold contribution to the current debate on the work of Hegel argues that behind Hegel's extraordinary appeal to literature in the *Phenomenology* lies a philosophical project concerned with understanding human agency in the modern world. It shows that Hegel looked to three literary genres – tragedy, comedy, and the romantic novel – as offering privileged access to three moments of human agency: retrospectivity, or the fact that human action receives its full meaning only after the event; theatricality, or the fact that human action receives its full meaning only in a social context; and forgiveness, or the practice of reassessing human action in the light of its essentially interpretive nature.

Taking full account of the authors that Hegel himself refers to (Sophocles, Diderot, Schlegel, Jacobi), Allen Speight has written a book with a broad appeal to both philosophers and literary theorists that positions Hegel as a central figure in both the continental and Anglo-American philosophical traditions.

Allen Speight is Assistant Professor of Philosophy at Boston University.

MODERN EUROPEAN PHILOSOPHY

General Editor

Robert B. Pippin, University of Chicago

Advisory Board

Gary Gutting, *University of Notre Dame*
Rolf-Peter Horstmann, *Humboldt University, Berlin*
Mark Sacks, *University of Essex*

Some Recent Titles:

Frederick A. Olafson: *What Is a Human Being?*
Stanley Rosen: *The Mask of Enlightenment: Nietzsche's Zarathustra*
Robert C. Scharff: *Comte after Positivism*
F. C. T. Moore: *Bergson: Thinking Backwards*
Charles Larmore: *The Morals of Modernity*
Robert B. Pippin: *Idealism as Modernism*
Daniel W. Conway: *Nietzsche's Dangerous Game*
John P. McCormick: *Carl Schmitt's Critique of Liberalism*
Frederick A. Olafson: *Heidegger and the Ground of Ethics*
Günter Zöller: *Fichte's Transcendental Philosophy*
Warren Breckman: *Marx, the Young Hegelians, and the Origins of Social Theory*
William Blattner: *Heidegger's Temporal Idealism*
Charles Griswold: *Adam Smith and the Virtues of the Enlightenment*
Gary Gutting: *Pragmatic Liberalism and the Critique of Modernity*
Allen Wood: *Kant's Ethical Thought*
Karl Ameriks: *Kant and the Fate of Autonomy*
Alfredo Ferrarin: *Hegel and Aristotle*
Cristina Lafont: *Heidegger, Language and World-Discourse*
Nicholas Wolterstorff: *Thomas Reid and the Story of Epistemology*
Daniel Dahlstrom: *Heidegger's Concept of Truth*
Michelle Grier: *Kant's Doctrine of Transcendental Illusion*
Henry Allison: *Kant's Theory of Taste*

HEGEL, LITERATURE AND THE PROBLEM OF AGENCY

ALLEN SPEIGHT
Boston University

CAMBRIDGE
UNIVERSITY PRESS

PUBLISHED BY THE PRESS SYNDICATE OF THE UNIVERSITY OF CAMBRIDGE
The Pitt Building, Trumpington Street, Cambridge, United Kindgom

CAMBRIDGE UNIVERSITY PRESS
The Edinburgh Building, Cambridge CB2 2RU, UK
40 West 20th Street, New York, NY 10011-4211, USA
10 Stamford Road, Oakleigh, VIC 3166, Australia
Ruiz de Alarcón 13, 28014 Madrid, Spain
Dock House, The Waterfront, Cape Town 8001, South Africa

http://www.cambridge.org

First published 2001

Printed in the United States of America

Typeface New Baskerville 10.25/13 pt.   *System* QuarkXPress 4.0 [AG]

A catalog record for this book is available from the British Library.

Library of Congress Cataloging in Publication data
Speight, Allen.
Hegel, literature and the problem of agency / Allen Speight.
p. cm. – (Modern European philosophy)
Includes bibliographical references.
ISBN 0-521-79184-7 – ISBN 0-521-79634-2 (pbk.)
1. Hegel, Georg Wilhelm Friedrich, 1770–1831. Phänomenologie des Geistes.   2.
Literature – Philosophy.   3. Agent (Philosophy)   I. Title.   II. Series.
B2929.S52 2001
193 – dc21   00-059879

ISBN 0 521 79184 7 hardback
ISBN 0 521 79634 2 paperback

To My Father

CONTENTS

Acknowledgments   *page* xi

Introduction   1
  1 Hegel and Post-Kantian Philosophy   2
  2 A New View of Agency   3
  3 Narrativity, Normativity, and Hegel's Appeal
     to Literature   6

1 "Hegel's Novel": The *Phenomenology of Spirit* and the
  Problem of Philosophical Narrative   11
  1 The *PhG*'s Literary Turn   20
  2 Accounting for the "Literary Turn": Narrative and
     the Project of the *Phenomenology*   37

2 Tragedy and Retrospectivity: Hegel's *Antigone*   42
  1 From Moral Luck to Expressive Agency:
     The Origins of an Hegelian "Poetics" of Action   46
  2 The Hegelian Antigone   50
  3 From Tragic Action to Comic Theatricality   65

3 Comedy and Theatricality: Desire, *Bildung,*
  and the Sociality of Agents' Self-Knowledge   68
  1 The Comic Agent   72
  2 The Notion of *Bildung* and Its Importance
     to "Spirit"   76
  3 Hegel's Rameau   78
  4 Philosophy and the Task of Overcoming
     Theatricality   84

4   Forgiveness and the Romantic Novel:
    Contesting the Beautiful Soul   94
    1 From the Categorical Imperative to the Beautiful
       Soul: Kantian and Post-Kantian Attempts at
       Escaping Retrospectivity and Theatricality   102
    2 The Contest of Conscientious Agent and
       Conscientious Judge   109
    3 Jacobi's *Woldemar* and the Narrative Language
       of Forgiveness   112
    4 Hegel and Jacobi   115
    5 Hegel's Appropriation of Forgiveness: From the
       Reconciliation of Spirit to the Possibility of
       Modern Ethical Agency   117

5   From the *Phenomenology* to the *Philosophy of Right:*
    Hegel's Concept of the Will and the Possibility of
    Modern Ethical Life   122
    1 Retrospectivity and Hegel's Concept of the Will   124
    2 Reason, Desire, and Sociality: Hegel's Generative
       Account of the Will   128
    3 Recognitive Identity and Reconciliation in the
       Institutions of Ethical Life   131
    4 Farewell to Literature? The Use of Literary Modes
       in the Project of Modern Ethical Life   133

Selected Bibliography   137
Index   149

ACKNOWLEDGMENTS

The writing of this book was nurtured by the presence at Boston University of a remarkable number of colleagues who share an interest in German Idealism, and I am grateful to all of them, as to my other colleagues, for their encouragement and support. I am grateful also to Boston University's Humanities Foundation for a one-semester leave in the fall semester of 1996 and to Boston University's College of Arts and Sciences for a subvention that helped with the final stages of manuscript preparation. I should also acknowledge a particular debt of gratitude to Brian Jorgensen, who patiently shouldered some administrative burdens that should have been mine while I worked on this book.

This project as a whole owes a great debt to Robert Pippin, the editor of this series, who encouraged over a number of years my reflections on Hegel's use of literature and made valuable suggestions stemming from his own ongoing work on the Hegelian notions of agency and freedom. My original exploration of the question of literature and agency was inspired by Paul Ricoeur, who first suggested that I take a more careful look at Hegel's notion of tragic action and was a reader of my University of Chicago dissertation on that topic. Thanks to Fulbright and DAAD fellowships, I was able to explore the development of Hegel's thought on both tragedy and Romantic literature with Otto Pöggeler at the Hegel-Archiv of the Ruhr-Universität Bochum, where Christoph Jamme and Andreas Grossmann also helped suggest important directions for my research. I am also indebted for suggestions made, at some crucial interludes along the way, by Mark Roche and H. S. Harris.

I'm grateful to the anonymous readers for Cambridge University Press for helpful suggestions concerning the manuscript; to Russell Hahn for copyediting; to Susan Hahn, Pamela Hieronymi, and Judith Norman

for advice on individual chapters; to Margot Stevenson and Jim John-
son for continuing advice and encouragement; to Hannah Hintze for
editorial assistance; to Lydia Moland for indexing; and to my father,
who allowed me to work on parts of this book at home in Virginia.
Finally, to Hallie White, who has been there for me in more ways than I
can even begin to acknowledge here.

INTRODUCTION

The present book takes as its aim the uncovering of a certain *narrative shape* to Hegel's philosophy of agency. Its concern, however, is not with the (unlikely) task of discussing "Hegel as literature," but rather with the sort of narrative Hegel thought required by his *philosophical* interests – in this narrow compass, the interest of an adequate philosophy of human agency.

For Hegel, the question of narrativity and agency loomed largest in writing the *Phenomenology of Spirit* (*PhG*), a riddlingly allusive work whose far-from-obvious narrative structure has, by turns, been characterized as that of a tragedy, a comedy, and (perhaps most frequently) a *Bildungsroman*. What will be of interest here, however, is not a reading that construes the *PhG* as a whole in terms of a single such genre, or even the development of Hegel's own theory of genres, but rather the question of how literary forms may be crucial to the philosophical project concerning agency that Hegel begins to work out in the *PhG*.

The Hegelian argument that will be considered here is, briefly, that literature, in its various forms, gives a *privileged access to action;* that *tragedy, comedy, and the romantic novel* represent a sequence of essential categories for our self-understanding as modern agents; and that these literary modes open up most particularly for Hegel issues of what I will call the *retrospectivity* and *theatricality* of action and of the possibility for an action's *forgiveness*. Such claims about the importance of literature to Hegel's concept of agency in the *PhG* may immediately raise for some the usual suspicions about Hegel's alleged ambitions to a "grand narrative" of history and human endeavor. Yet the study of Hegel, and particularly that of the *PhG*, has recently been reinvigorated in a way that may allow the approach to agency that emerges within it to avoid some of these familiar objections.

1. Hegel and Post-Kantian Philosophy

The reinvigoration of which I speak turns in large part on understanding Hegel's project as an engagement with the implications of an essentially *post-Kantian* philosophical situation, rather than (as many of those who see the "grand narrative" in Hegel's strategy would have it) as some regression into precritical modes of thinking. One way of considering this post-Kantian situation may be glimpsed in John McDowell's notion that Kant's legacy lies in the attempt to supersede a "familiar predicament" of a "typical form of modern philosophy": the problem of the "Myth of the Given" – as McDowell describes it, the tendency to appeal to something "outside the space of concepts" that is "simply received in experience."[1] The difficulty this notion presents is that we cannot expect that an extraconceptual Given – something *outside* the "space of reasons" – could provide us with the *reasons* or warrants that we need for empirical judgments, since relations like implication hold only *within* the "space of reasons." Kant's achievement for getting beyond this myth is, McDowell holds, to see that intuition is not a "bare getting of an extraconceptual Given," but a kind of occurrence or state that already has conceptual content. Receptivity, in other words, "does not make an even notionally separable contribution to the co-operation" between receptivity and spontaneity.[2]

To Hegel and the immediate post-Kantian generation of which he was a part, Kant's philosophical approach both opened up the possibility of getting beyond the difficulty associated with the aspiration for the Given and created, as they saw it, some fresh obstacles to the pursuit of a reconstrued epistemology.[3] The epistemological project that Hegel pursues in response to Kant is one that I will characterize in the following

---

1. John McDowell, *Mind and World* (Cambridge: Harvard University Press, 1994), 6, 110.
2. McDowell, *Mind and World*, 9.
3. McDowell's claim that "the way to correct what is unsatisfactory in Kant's thinking about the supersensible" is "rather to embrace the Hegelian image in which the conceptual is unbounded on the outside" (*Mind and World*, 83) is examined further in Sally Sedgwick, "McDowell's Hegelianism," *European Journal of Philosophy* 5:1 (1997): 21–38, and Robert Stern, "Going Beyond the Kantian Philosophy: On McDowell's Hegelian Critique of Kant," *European Journal of Philosophy* 7:2 (August 1999): 247–269. See also Graham Bird, "McDowell's Kant: *Mind and World*," *Philosophy* 71 (1996): 219–243; Michael Friedman, "Exorcising the Philosophical Tradition: Comments on John McDowell's *Mind and World*," *Philosophical Review* 105:4 (1996): 427–67; Alan Thomas, "Kant, McDowell and the Theory of Consciousness," *European Journal of Philosophy* 5:3 (1997): 283–305; and Henry Allison, "We Can Act Only Under the Idea of Freedom," *Proceedings of the American Philosophical Association* 71:2 (November 1997): 39–50.

chapters as a "corrigibilist" one. Philosophy no longer sees itself as being on a search for an "incorrigible" or indubitable Given, but instead responds to the traditional query of the skeptic in a new way: not by a direct "refutation," but by taking up what Hegel comes to call a "thoroughgoing" or "self-consummating" skepticism – the weighing of all knowledge claims, including the claim of Hegel's system itself, as claims that must count *as appearances,* and the examination of what contradictions may be involved just on the terms of those claims themselves.[4]

The employment of such a strategy with respect to skepticism has been well characterized in terms of a general philosophical move from a Cartesian concern with "certainty" to a Kantian concern with "necessity" – a move, that is, from a concern with the hold that we can have on a particular claim to a concern with the hold that various claims may have on us.[5] Thus the *PhG* construes its project with respect to skeptical doubt as a "highway of despair" – the examination of what certain claims involve just on their own terms and whether, in the light of experience, such claims would necessarily need to be revised in order to be justifiable.

Such a general epistemological project would seem to have consequences for the traditional problems raised in the philosophy of *agency,* as well. Who an agent is and what he takes himself to be doing in his actions are questions that might be construed differently, if in our account of action we can also not rely on a Given.

2. A New View of Agency

How might the post-Kantian concern with getting beyond the separability of conceptual and receptive elements in our experience have a bearing on our understanding of action?[6] I want to sketch here briefly

4. See especially the discussion of skepticism in Robert Pippin, *Hegel's Idealism: The Satisfactions of Self-Consciousness* (Cambridge: Cambridge University Press, 1989), and Terry Pinkard, *Hegel's "Phenomenology": The Sociality of Reason* (Cambridge: Cambridge University Press, 1994). On how Hegel's epistemological project with respect to skepticism meant a more serious engagement for him with *ancient,* as opposed to modern, skepticism, see Michael Forster, *Hegel and Skepticism* (Cambridge, MA: Harvard University Press, 1989).

5. Variations on this formulation may be found in Robert Brandom, *Making it Explicit: Reasoning, Representing and Discursive Commitment* (Cambridge, MA: Harvard University Press, 1994), and Pinkard, *Hegel's "Phenomenology": The Sociality of Reason,* 5–6.

6. McDowell sees the matter in terms of a direct analogy to the famous Kantian claim that "thoughts without content are empty, intuitions without concepts are blind": when it

three large considerations of agency that I claim follow from Hegel's attempt to wrestle with this question and that will be the focus of my subsequent discussion in this book.

To begin with, we might contrast the view that I will be sketching as Hegel's with a voluntarist picture of action, on which the construal of responsibility ordinarily considers separately two items: an agent's prior intention (or "will") and the deed that causally resulted or was put into play, as it were, by the agent. On a "corrigibilist" view of agency, by contrast, an agent's intention, or his understanding of the norm on which he acts, is something that is not artificially separable from the entirety of the action itself. The corrigibilist is thus concerned with a facet of our ordinary experience of agency that the voluntarist is unable to give a sufficient account of: an agent's experience that what she understands herself to *intend* may, for example, change in the course of the action or may be adequately understood only when the action has been completed and seen in its full context.

A corrigibilist approach to agency might be characterized, first of all, then, as an inherently *retrospective* one. Retrospectivity has been of philosophical interest particularly in cases of moral luck, where justification cannot appeal to the isolation of single moral motives, but must take into account as well what observers (and even the agent herself at a later time) would say actually happened in an action. The Hegelian concern with retrospectivity in justification goes much more deeply than the problems raised by cases of moral luck, however. Hegel holds, as I will explore particularly in Chapter 2, a kind of pragmatist view of intentions and norms as defined by their actualization or *use*, and a full account of what those intentions or norms are must remain open to what they involve in practice.[7]

---

comes to actions, we should consider similarly that "intentions without overt activity are idle, and movements of limbs without concepts are mere happenings, not expressions of agency" (McDowell, *Mind and World*, 89–90).

7. The account of agency that I am attributing to Hegel here bears some affinities with that adumbrated by Robert Brandom in his recent book *Articulating Reasons: An Introduction to Inferentialism* (Cambridge, MA: Harvard University Press, 2000). Beginning with the pragmatist claim that it is the *use* of concepts that determines their content, Brandom develops an account of agency that has resonances with each of the three points I outline in this section as essential for Hegel's project of agency in the *PhG*: he takes up the separability issue with the claim that "what is implicit may depend on the possibility of making it explicit" (*Articulating Reasons*, 8–9); rejects, as I would claim that Hegel does, a "Humean" notion of practical reasoning on which *desires* and preferences are assumed to be "intrinsically motivating" (30–31); and finally defends a "rationalist expressivism" (32–35) that requires the sort of recognitive structures defended here.

It is not only the assessment of actions and their justifiability that requires a consideration of the public space in which they are regarded, however. If justification cannot refer to incorrigibly known intentions, it would seem also that desire cannot be regarded as a motivating force in the sense of causing action merely because an agent happens to *have* a given desire. An agent's ability to assure himself that his desire to act is really "his" would seem to require instead some account of desire formation that shows how desires are embedded in a pattern of *norms* or social moves.

But if, for the corrigibilist, accounting for the justification and motivation of action involves such inherently retrospective and social elements, a voluntarist or causalist might reasonably ask here just how it is that an agent can be said to assure himself that *he* is "in" his action so as to have any coherent sense of practical identity at all. Such an agent could have no prospective certainty about the justification of his actions or immediate certainty about his desires such as the causalist/voluntarist view claims to offer. Having put aside the causal account of agency in favor of a more holistic one that does not separate intention and deed, the corrigibilist would need, it would seem, to look to a larger way in which individuals may be "in" their actions – more particularly, to the way in which an action might be *expressive* or revealing of an agent. The expressivity that would be involved on such an account, given the retrospective and social concerns we have seen, could not, of course, be understood as the immediate utterance of an inward "given" or nature; it must itself rather be part of an oscillation of the sort that we have seen between impersonal and personal sides of agency: my view of the norm I am applying in action must be correlated with what that norm turned out to involve in practice; my sense of how I understand myself to be motivated must stand in some relation to what other agents would say is behind actions of such a type.

In such an ongoing dialectic of expressivity, what is "mine" in action would inherently involve certain publicizable or shareable modes of expression that open the action to the *interpretation* of others, and impersonal candidates for judgment of action would involve conflicts just insofar as an agent attempting to act on them would be unable to understand her actions, according to those standards, as her own. The notion of practical identity to emerge from this ongoing process of negotiation and interpretation would thus not represent a natural or given form of identity, but would, rather, be a sort of *recognitive achievement*.

These implications of a corrigibilist approach to agency are important elements of the account I will give of Hegel's project in the *Phenomenology of Spirit:* I will take them up in terms of the *retrospectivity* of accounting for justification and motivation; the socially mediated character or *theatricality* of the context of those accounts; and the construal of practical identity as a recognitive achievement, which is most fully acknowledged in the important Hegelian notion of *forgiveness.* Taken together, these three moments already suggest something about how that enterprise may have a narrative shape – a narrative that becomes more explicit to itself in a retrospective way, that involves a continuing effort to revise the accounts agents can give of justification or motivation, and that recognitively acknowledges how an agent's identity has been expressed through just such a process of revision.

3. Narrativity, Normativity, and Hegel's Appeal to Literature

Such a picture may also begin to suggest the use that an account of agency like Hegel's might make of *literary* narrative. Unlike some contemporary philosophical appropriations of literary works, Hegel's appeal to literature is not grounded simply in a general philosophical concern that the ethical "shape" or moral salience of certain situations may require a novelistic or dramatic "sight" for particulars. Nor is it merely a matter of employing a rhetorical strategy that "engages" or "implicates" a reader in a succession of such particular situations. From what we have seen about the structure of Hegel's argument, the question about narrative that leads him to literature would seem, rather, to be something like this: how to present the expressive connection of an agent to his action in a way that captures the move from a set of considerations that are at first only implicit for an agent until he acts; and that then considers the agent's successive reflections about what was socially embedded in the implicit norms on which he acted and the essentially recognitive character of his identity within that set of norms.

In the *PhG,* this question about capturing the peculiar kind of agentive expressivity I have just sketched comes to the fore in an explicit way in the famous "Spirit" chapter. "Spirit" is, most generally considered, the realm of normativity: it is the place in Hegel's project where agency moves from being understood in terms of putatively impersonal or universal "reasons" to a construal of how agents act on norms embodied in particular forms of social life in which they participate. Thus the shapes of consciousness in Hegel's narrative at this point start to involve a more explicitly historical and cultural context. The questions about how

Hegel is effecting the transition at this point in his narrative are many and complicated: how exactly the new historical and cultural elements enter the narrative, why the move is made from an apparently contemporary concern with the Kantian and post-Kantian moral world at the end of the preceding chapter on "Reason" to the world of ancient Greek "ethical life."

Among the most pressing questions that arise for a reader about the moves Hegel makes here is why a series of famous literary figures seems suddenly to be involved in Hegel's account. Why, for example, does Hegel turn for his sketch of the initial "ethical order" in "Spirit" to Sophocles' *Antigone?* And why are the succeeding moments of "culture" and "conscience" so informed by Diderot's *Rameau's Nephew* and the novelistic figure of the beautiful soul?

Unpacking the answer to these questions will allow us to see more broadly how the issue of agency and narrative expressivity I have described plays out in Hegel's text. The famous appropriations of Antigone, Rameau, and the beautiful soul in the "Spirit" chapter are, as many readers know, only part of Hegel's appropriation of various narrative forms.

In fact, Hegel seems in writing the *PhG* to have drawn on an impressive diversity of narrative sources – from contemporary accounts of atrocities during the French Revolution, to newspaper reviews of current novels and historical monographs on ancient slavery. What makes the *literary* sources of narrative so distinctive within his project is that Hegel conceives that the literary genres in their development tell a story that is essential to the purpose of the *PhG*. What can be seen in the emergence of the literary genres of tragedy, comedy, and the romantic novel is an emerging truth about human agency.[8] Tragedy, particularly

8. One of the questions that will be examined in the following chapters is how Hegel's use of the genres in this narrative of agency in the *PhG* compares to his later "official" genre theory in the *Lectures on Aesthetics*. Central to Hegel's account of the beauty of art or the ideal in the *Aesthetics* is in fact a notion of action or *Handlung* (*Aesthetics: Lectures on Fine Art*, trans. T. M. Knox [Oxford: Clarendon Press, 1975], 217–244). What makes drama the highest of the arts is that it places *acting* human beings before an audience (although it is the actors' *speech*, not their gestures, that is the prime expression of that action). The *Aesthetics* tells the further story of the essential *pastness* of that highest embodiment of the truth about human action in ancient Greek drama – a point at which the *PhG* account both corresponds and differs (see Chapter 4 of this volume).

There are numerous studies that bear on the question of the role that the genres play in the *PhG*. A helpful work on Hegel's later theory of the dramatic genres, as it is developed in the lectures on aesthetics, has recently been published by Mark Roche (*Tragedy and Comedy: A Systematic Study and a Critique of Hegel* [Albany: State University of New York

ancient Greek tragedy in its presentation of fate, opens up the retrospective experience of agency; comedy is seen to involve a self-reflectiveness about the socially mediated or theatrical character of agency – a
dropping of the tragic mask of "givenness," as it were; and the romantic
novel of the beautiful soul, in its concern with resolving the paradoxes
of conscience, articulates a notion of recognitive practical identity that
is most fully achieved in certain novelistic moments of forgiveness.[9]

While the clearest moments of Hegel's presentation of tragic retrospectivity, comic theatricality and novelistic forgiveness are in the three
famous literary appropriations of the "Spirit" chapter, the literary influence on Hegel's presentation of agency in the *PhG* is wider than that.
In Chapter 1, I begin with the puzzle of literature's sudden "eruption"
in the *PhG:* the striking fact that, after the Preface, the book's first half
alludes often to philosophical and religious works, but rarely to literary
works until a burst of quotations and appropriations at a crucial juncture in the middle of the "Reason" chapter. Hegel's narrative argument
about agency, as I show in the first chapter, requires him to make use of
the progression of literary forms I have mentioned not only in the "Spirit"
chapter itself but also for initially setting the stage for Spirit's arrival
(hence the unexplained eruption of the literary in the middle of the
"Reason" chapter that precedes "Spirit") and for giving an account of
why literature was so used (hence a cryptic account of the literary genres
in the "Religion" chapter that follows).

Examining these correlations in Hegel's famous literary borrowings
in the *PhG* not only will give a useful point of access to Hegel's own understanding of agency – and to why a term like "Spirit" is required for
an adequate explanatory account of it – but also may provide a better
understanding of the Hegelian side of certain disputes in contemporary

---

Press, 1998]); see also discussion of the issue in H. S. Harris's commentary to the *PhG,*
Hegel's Ladder, 2 vols. (Indianapolis: Hackett, 1997), vol. I: *The Pilgrimage of Reason;* vol. II:
The Odyssey of Spirit; especially I, 18; I, 29, n. 91; II, 581–3; II, 647–8.

9. Hegel's treatment of conscience and the beautiful soul represents a *recapitulatory* moment
that explicitly looks at how the previous two moments of retrospectivity and theatricality can be taken into account in a modern notion of agency and the self. For an examination of how Hegel's account of this last moment represents an "analytic of significant
action," see J. M. Bernstein, "Conscience and Transgression: The Persistence of Misrecognition," *Bulletin of the Hegel Society of Great Britain* 29 (Spring/Summer 1994): 55–70. In
many ways, the moments I outline here represent a reading-back into the "Spirit" chapter as a whole of the recapitulatory "analytic" of action that Bernstein's insightful article
first suggested to me: the five considerations of agency that he discusses there are (as I
hope will become clear in the following sections) all either explicitly or implicitly taken
up in my account of retrospectivity, theatricality, and forgiveness.

philosophy of literature, particularly with respect to the claims of Romantic irony against the Hegelian "system." For among the many underexplored elements of the *PhG*'s claim that the Science of Spirit it heralds must also "make its appearance" is the evident attempt on its part to enter the significant literary *agon* of the day. The moments we have been discussing, in fact, might be said to represent Hegel's contributions to three such competitions: the first, perhaps with an eye to his Tübingen roommates Hölderlin and Schelling, about how the Greeks and in particular their tragic heroes present an alternative path for modernity; second, perhaps with an eye to Goethe, a translation of a work of cosmopolitan French wit that allows for reflection on the relation between French and German aspects of modernity; and third, certainly with an eye to the inhabitants of the literary circle at Jena – and here most particularly Friedrich Schlegel – an attempt to understand what kind of sociality is implicit in the claims of Romantic individualism and whether Romanticism can produce a genre (as Schlegel appears to have claimed about the novel) that can reach beyond the categories of literary genre entirely.

The account that follows will thus involve close readings of Hegel's famous literary borrowings in the *PhG*, but with an eye to how they help Hegel open up the question of agency in the context of his larger philosophical project. Oddly enough, even among those who have been most interested in the literary quality of Hegel's narrative, there has not been a thorough study of Hegel's actual appropriation of literary works.[10] As is well known, part of the need for such a recovery is due to Hegel himself, who complained that the whole of the *PhG* is "such an interlacing of cross-references back and forth" that the reader may not be able always to see the structural parallels he intends.[11] This project will thus be concerned with re-capturing some of Hegel's intended "interlacings." But, more to the point, as I will claim in the first chapter, Hegel's overall philosophical aims in the *PhG* have only recently been opened up in a way that shows the important lines along which the book may be read as a narrative unity.

In setting out Hegel's argument, I have had it in mind chiefly to make a contribution to understanding the philosophical project of the *PhG* and why that project requires Hegel's appropriation of literary works

---

10. A recent exception is Gustav-H. H. Falke, whose *Begriffne Geschichte* (Berlin: Lukas, 1996) is particularly helpful for its examination of the *PhG*'s use of Romantic sources.
11. Hegel, *Letters,* 80.

and forms as it does. Examining Hegel's project with respect to literature in the *PhG* is the primary concern of Chapter 1, which places my
argument in the context of recent scholarly debate about the interpretation of the *PhG*. But I have also had a more general reader in mind:
a reader who may be interested primarily in how certain literary modes
may open up facets of our experience as modern agents, quite apart
from any specific Hegelian argument concerning them. Thus the considerations of tragedy and moral luck (Chapter 2), theatricality and self-
knowledge (Chapter 3), and the relation of irony and practical identity
(Chapter 4) all concern issues that, I hope, will have a resonance for
contemporary readers that goes beyond an interpretation of the project
of the *PhG*.[12] How much our account, as contemporaries, of such issues
in modern agency might owe to Hegel is a question I address in the conclusion (Chapter 5), which examines Hegel's own later post-*Phenomenology* treatment of freedom and the will in his lectures on the philosophy
of right.

12. On the issue of moral luck, see the now-classic essays by Bernard Williams, *Moral Luck*
(Cambridge: Cambridge University Press, 1981), 20–39, and Thomas Nagel, *Mortal Ques-
tions* (Cambridge: Cambridge University Press, 1979), 24–38. The issue of theatricality
in agency has been of particular interest to recent interpreters of Adam Smith and
Rousseau: see Charles Griswold's *Adam Smith and the Virtues of Enlightenment* (Cambridge:
Cambridge University Press, 1999), 63–70, and Jean Starobinski's *Jean-Jacques Rousseau:
Transparency and Obstruction,* trans. Arthur Goldhammer (Chicago: University of Chicago Press, 1988), 93–96. On the question of irony and practical identity, see the recent
exchange between Raymond Geuss and Christine Korsgaard published in her *Sources
of Normativity* (Cambridge: Cambridge University Press, 1996), 192–3.

"HEGEL'S NOVEL":
THE *PHENOMENOLOGY OF SPIRIT*
AND THE PROBLEM OF
PHILOSOPHICAL NARRATIVE

The narrative shape of Hegel's philosophy of agency has its origins most visibly in the philosophical project of his earliest published book, the *Phenomenology of Spirit*. Readers of Hegel have frequently turned to the *PhG* as a place to begin a consideration of his view of agency, yet there has been anything but a consensus about what the work offers in that regard. Scholars have disagreed about what the book is doing and even about whether it can be said to have a coherent unified philosophical project at all: the scholarly literature concerning Hegel's intentions for the work has had to sort through a series of unusually vexing problems, including evident changes in the book's title, organizational structure, and intended relation to Hegel's *Logic* and the rest of his (newly emerging) philosophical system.[1]

The problem of seeing an overarching unity to the *PhG*'s project was perhaps most famously stated by Rudolf Haym, who claimed that the project he thought was evident at the start of the work (providing a "transcendental-psychological proof" of the reality of absolute cognition) is one that was "confused" by a second order of proof involving a concern with concrete historical data.[2] Readers of the *PhG* since Haym have, in fact, often been drawn into one of two camps: those who have been most concerned to work through the claims to systematic connection particularly implicit in the work's original title ("The Science of the Experience

---

1. On the various issues connected with the *PhG* and its origin, see, among others, Otto Pöggeler, "Die Komposition der Phänomenologie des Geistes," in *Materialen zu Hegels 'Phänomenologie des Geistes'*, ed. Hans Friedrich Fulda and Dieter Henrich (Frankfurt: Suhrkamp, 1973), 329–389, and "Zur Deutung der Phänomenologie des Geistes," *Hegel-Studien* I (1961): 255–294.
2. Rudolf Haym, *Hegel und seine Zeit: Vorlesungen über Entstehung und Entwicklung, Wesen und Wert der Hegelschen Philosophie* (Berlin: Gaertner, 1857), 235, 243.

of Consciousness") and those who have been drawn to the text's "anthropological" concerns with history, social structure, and religion. For many in the former camp, it has been Hegel's later system that must take priority over the *PhG*'s explorations into the realm of the social; many of the latter group have taken greatest interest in the *PhG*'s wealth of anthropological detail (the master-slave dialectic, the account of religion's origins, etc.) because they understand it to be an element that pushes against the structures of the eventual System.

On the textual level, there has been a similar split between readers of the *PhG* who assume the unity of the published enterprise and those (like Haym, Haering, and Pöggeler) who have argued that the book is really a palimpsest, because Hegel encountered difficulty with one project and then attempted to revise the book as a result. The urgent circumstances of the book's completion – it was finished, so Hegel later claimed, during the Battle of Jena – have often been appealed to as the explanation for its lack of coherence.

Quite apart from these considerations of the overall philosophical or textual unity of the work, readers have never failed to find difficulty (or, depending on the case, amusement) with some admittedly peculiar elements of the *form* or style of the *PhG*. The "shapes of consciousness" that the book presents often seem to involve allusions to works and figures that are not directly cited, or for which the reader is not particularly prepared. The "experience" of many of those shapes and the transitions from one to another often seem to be part of an underlying pattern of a sort that has suggested to many a connection with other literary modes. The developmental structure of the various moments has led some (Josiah Royce and many others) to characterize the *Phenomenology* as ultimately a sort of *Bildungsroman*. Hegel's stress in the book's Preface on the "labor of the negative" and the self-destruction experienced in the various moments of the journey has led others to characterize it ultimately in terms of tragedy, while still others construe the brightness of the claims for "absolute knowing" that emerge from out of that tempestuous development as essentially comic.[3]

3. On the *PhG* as *Bildungsroman*, see Josiah Royce, *Lectures on Modern Idealism* (New Haven: Yale University Press, 1919), 147–156; and Judith Butler, *Subjects of Desire* (New York: Columbia University Press, 1987). Among those looking for parallels in the dramatic genres, the "comic" readers may predominate: see, for example, Gary Shapiro, "An Ancient Quarrel in Hegel's *Phenomenology*," *The Owl of Minerva* 17:2 (Spring 1986): 165–180, and William Desmond, *Beyond Hegel and Dialectic* (Albany: State University of New York

Recently, however, there has been a change in the terms of the various disputes about the work's coherence, one that seems to have offered the possibility of refiguring both the debates about the anthropological versus the logical significance of the *PhG* and about the palimpsestic versus the unitary readings of the work as a whole. The new ground that has opened up has been based on a new understanding of the epistemological project of the *PhG* – in particular, how that project can be understood to require some of the famous moves with respect to sociality that previously were separated off by those giving an "anthropological" reading of the text.

This new ground has been prepared by several different kinds of readers, interested in several different angles of the Hegelian project.[4] While these readers do not always share a consensus about the details of the *PhG*'s project, one may nonetheless characterize the set of important new interpretive questions that they have (collectively) opened up in recent years as rooted in a common starting point: the understanding of Hegel's epistemological task as having a certain Sellarsian shape in its concern to resist the appeal of the "Myth of the Given" – the notion that, as McDowell puts it, "the space of reasons, the space of justifications or warrants, extends more widely than the conceptual sphere."[5] The Hegelian epistemological approach that emerges may be said to be "*corrigibilist*" and *social*. It is corrigibilist in the sense that it is not concerned to respond to skeptical query by finding some indubitable (or "incorrigible"), noninferential piece of knowledge from which further inferences can be made, but rather sets out to examine

---

Press, 1992), as well as the claims for the *PhG* as resembling something like *Dante's* notion of "comedy" in Peter Fuss and John Dobbins, "The Silhouette of Dante in Hegel's *Phenomenology*," *Clio* 11:4 (1982): 387–413, and the recent claim by H. S. Harris that "the *Phenomenology* (like Goethe's *Faust*) is a '*human* comedy' that can be compared with Dante's great poem" (Harris, *Hegel's Ladder*, I, 18). Among the "tragic" readers, see Elliott Jurist, "Hegel's Concept of Recognition," *The Owl of Minerva* 19:1 (Fall 1987): 5–22, and "Tragedy In/And/Of Hegel," *Philosophical Forum* 25:2 (Winter 1993): 151–72.

4. I will discuss particularly in this connection the *PhG* interpretations of Robert Pippin (*Hegel's Idealism: The Satisfactions of Self-Consciousness*) and Terry Pinkard (*Hegel's "Phenomenology": The Sociality of Reason*), although I also draw in the argument below on the suggestions about Hegel in John McDowell's *Mind and World* and what I have been able to construe of Robert Brandom's approach to Hegel from *Articulating Reasons: An Introduction to Inferentialism* and "Some Pragmatist Themes in Hegel's Idealism: Negotiation and Administration in Hegel's Account of the Structure and Content of Conceptual Norms," *European Journal of Philosophy* 7:2 (August 1999): 164–189.

5. McDowell, *Mind and World*, 7.

claims to knowledge just on their own terms, treating them as appearances and examining what contradictions emerge from their articulation.[6] Such claims to knowledge are "shapes of consciousness," as Hegel calls them, in which a particular agent or judge understands himself to take certain reasons or norms as authoritative, or necessary. The *PhG* is thus concerned with the moves possible within a certain space of reasons – a space that is, as Pinkard has shown, importantly a *social* space.[7] A large part of the *PhG*'s task is devoted to the question of how I (must) come into that space – a question that it addresses in terms of a notion of *Bildung*, a German word that means literally "formation" and is usually translated in the *PhG* as "culture." The *PhG*'s project is not merely to show what would be required in such a notion of *Bildung*, but actually to *effect* it, to bring about such a transition to awareness of the "space of reasons" for the individual reader. As Forster has put it, the *PhG* has not only an "epistemological" or "metaphysical" task, but also a "practical" or "pedagogical" one,[8] in its acknowledgment that the individual "has the right to demand that Science should at least provide him with the ladder to this standpoint [i.e., the standpoint of the System]" (*PhG* §26).[9]

A reading of the *PhG* that takes into account these important elements of corrigibility and sociality in the book's philosophical project

6. A large part of Hegel's attempt to avoid the problem that the notion of the "Given" implies for modern philosophy involves a reassessment of the most serious challenge that skepticism poses for philosophy. In particular, it is Hegel's attack on the assumptions that he found embedded in modern (Cartesian or Humean) skepticism – most notably its unquestioning stance toward the putatively "incorrigible" knowledge of one's own (current) mental states – that provides much of the animus for the *PhG*'s epistemological strategy. Hegel's interest in combating modern skepticism's reliance on such supposedly incorrigible mental data – what he would call the "immediate" in experience – means also, as Michael Forster has shown (*Hegel and Skepticism*), that the shape of the *PhG* owes a significant amount to Hegel's greater regard for the challenge provided by the method of equipollence in ancient (Pyrrhonist) skepticism.

7. Pinkard adopts the metaphor of "social space" in part from Jay Rosenberg's book *The Thinking Self* (Philadelphia: Temple University Press, 1986). See the discussion of "material" inference and social space in Pinkard, *Hegel's "Phenomenology,"* 7 and 346, n. 12.

8. Michael Forster, *Hegel's Idea of a Phenomenology of Spirit* (Chicago: University of Chicago Press, 1998), 17–125.

9. This and all further references in this volume to the *PhG* are by paragraph number to the translation of A. V. Miller (*Hegel's Phenomenology of Spirit* [Oxford: Oxford University Press, 1977]). On occasion, where indicated, I have offered a translation of my own. I have used the German texts of the *Phänomenologie des Geistes* edited by J. Hoffmeister (Hamburg: Felix Meiner Verlag, 1955) and by Hans-Friedrich Wessels and Heinrich Clairmont (Hamburg: Meiner, 1988).

offers the possibility of a revision in the way that two of the famous old difficulties about the *PhG*'s coherence are usually discussed. To be sure, substantial questions about the *PhG* and its connection to the rest of the system remain for all of those interested in at least some version of the claims outlined here. Yet the hard-and-fast lines of both the anthropological/logical division and the palimpsest/unity division would now appear to be quite altered. With respect to the first, readers like Pippin and Pinkard, for example, have shown how the "anthropological" interest of the *PhG* – the various facets of the *Bildung* it attempts to effect for the individual reading it – actually serves an important part of the epistemological project of Hegel's work as a whole, the need to account for how agents come to make moves within the "space of reasons." And, while there is certainly no general agreement about the unity of the text, understanding Hegel in light of these interpretive issues offers a way of getting at some of the most famous puzzles in the text: in particular, why Spirit makes its sudden and seemingly unannounced appearance as it does. Spirit, on this view, will be construed as a normative realm, a form of self-reflective "social space" in which the concrete historical and cultural issues it brings with it are taken not as elements imposed by Hegel on an original project, but rather as considerations that necessarily emerge from an examination of the insufficiencies involved in other claims to knowledge.[10]

But if this new reading suggests a way of viewing the *PhG* as a project with some philosophical and textual unity, what about the other, quite famous difficulty faced by generations of *PhG* readers – the question of the curious, quasi-literary *form* of the book? As yet, the reassessments that I have been discussing have given only a possible ground for the discussion of this difficulty, since the question about the *PhG*'s literary nature has not as yet been taken up in a direct and detailed fashion. What I shall show here, however, is how these recent reconstructions of the *PhG*'s project have indeed provided a necessary basis for understanding at least some of the important questions about the work's literary character. In what follows, I shall examine the "literary" shape of the *PhG* in light of this reevaluation of its *philosophical* concerns in order to show both how a narrative shape is essential to Hegel's philosophy of agency *and* how the *PhG* cannot finally be read simply *as* a tragedy, comedy, or novel. To the "epistemological," "metaphysical," and "pedagogical" tasks of the *PhG* we must then add an essential and

---

10. Pinkard, *Hegel's "Phenomenology"*, 9.

philosophical *literary* task, one that in fact grows out of Hegel's commitments with respect to the other tasks.[11]

In some ways, this project may seem to fit under a familiar rubric – that of the "ancient quarrel" between poetry and philosophy. But to understand it as such would also miss an important point: part of what Hegel is doing, I will claim, is in fact blurring the lines of such traditional ways of construing the relation between philosophy and literature, so that "fiction" must be seen as having a necessary place within the philosophical project as a whole.

To this bold claim, some of Hegel's readers – particularly those drawn to the systematic claims of his philosophy – may object: doesn't Hegel himself, in the Preface to the *PhG,* explicitly rebuke those who are interested in Plato, for example, because of his "scientifically valueless myths" rather than because of works like the *Parmenides,* which was "surely the greatest artistic achievement of the ancient dialectic" (*PhG* §71)?

Partly because the evident interest among Romantic writers like Friedrich Schlegel in a fusion between philosophy and literature was so great at the time of the *PhG,* Hegel does indeed criticize in the *PhG* Preface the "disorganized" notion of "imagery (*Gebilde*) that is neither fish nor flesh, neither poetry nor philosophy" (*PhG* §68). Yet the very terms of this quotation suggest that, in fact, there might be something that could be called "*philosophical* imagery" – imagery understood, of course, to have a different purpose than the imagery of poetry. And, at the conclusion of the *PhG,* this notion itself seems to return in a recollective way, as Hegel describes the foregoing "succession of Spirits" as a "gallery of images [*Galerie von Bildern*]" (§808).

The importance of literature to the *PhG*'s project, however, is not one of static images, but rather of their *movement* and – as the allusion to the paragraph at the work's end suggests – the ways in which that movement can be "*recollected* " or held together as part of a narrative. What kind of narrative Hegel's "succession of Spirits" comprises is, as was noted earlier, a question that has motivated many different readings of the *PhG* – particularly along lines, as mentioned, that compare it to works of tragedy or comedy or that construe it as a sort of *Bildungsroman.* These readings

---

11. The topic of the *PhG*'s stylistic and formal aspects is, of course, immense. The consideration to be explored here will be primarily one of how Hegel thinks that his narrative must appropriate these traditional literary genres – a circumscribed question, but one that may be revealing for other formal issues about the *PhG.*

are all suggestive, and – as I hope to show – each of them has a *place* within the narrative structure of the *PhG*.

But the *PhG* is, in fact, a work that, as Pinkard and Pippin have said, has no predecessors in its genre.[12] Its status as a narrative sui generis is evident, to begin with, in the fact that, despite the appeal of the many comparisons, it cannot finally, as Robert Pippin has remarked, be read *as* a *Bildungsroman*, but only as a work that is in important respects *like* a *Bildungsroman*.[13] That is to say, the view of Hegelian narrativity that will be defended here will *not* ultimately end in reducing the *PhG*'s project to merely that of a Rortyan sort of "vocabulary exchange" or a Nehamasian notion of "life as literature."[14] Hegel's concern with narrative requires that we consider the claim that what he is examining is a set of shapes that are *necessary* for our self-understanding as modern agents, rather than an account that would understand itself in terms of how we just "go on."

But what *is* literarily important about the peculiar narrative that is the *PhG* is how, in fact, it *appropriates* – without ever *becoming* merely any one of them – each of the three important literary modes (tragedy, comedy, and the novel) we have mentioned. As a sort of *successor narrative* to these forms of literature, the *PhG* shows how the literary modes develop one from the other and finally push forward to a perspective that will go beyond the confines of the literary – a succession that resonates with the famous (or rather infamous) claim of Hegel's later work on aesthetics about the "end of art" in the approach of the scientific age.[15] But the other side of this claim will be equally important for the study we are undertaking: namely, that the sort of narrative Hegel is presenting may *require* its literary predecessors in an indispensable way.

Explaining how these three important literary modes become central to Hegel's project with respect to *agency* is the central task of this book. In making this claim about the literary turn the *PhG* takes, I am not concerned with the (multitude of) ways in which the *PhG* as a whole

---

12. Pinkard, *Hegel's "Phenomenology"*, 1; Robert Pippin, "'You Can't Get There from Here': Transition Problems in Hegel's *Phenomenology of Spirit*," in *The Cambridge Companion to Hegel*, ed. Frederick C. Beiser (Cambridge: Cambridge University Press, 1993), 78.

13. See Robert Pippin, "Hegelianism as Modernism," *Inquiry* 38:3 (September 1995): 315.

14. For a helpful comparison to these strategies of narrativity, see Pippin, *Modernism as a Philosophical Problem* (Oxford: Blackwell, 1991), particularly 42–45, 70–74.

15. For a discussion of the difficulties in interpreting this famous "thesis," see Stephen Bungay, *Beauty and Truth: A Study of Hegel's Aesthetics* (Oxford: Oxford University Press, 1984), 76–89; and J. M. Bernstein, *The Fate of Art: Aesthetic Alienation from Kant to Derrida and Adorno* (University Park: Pennsylvania State University Press, 1992), 72–73.

and various moments within it might be read with interest and imagination *as* literature.[16] Rather, in unpacking the *philosophical* project of
narrative in the *PhG*, I want to show the essential role Hegel has literature play within the larger philosophical purpose of the *PhG*.

The clearest place to begin is perhaps with the most famous set of literary borrowings in the *PhG:* the three great appropriations within the
"Spirit" chapter of Sophocles' *Antigone*, Diderot's *Rameau's Nephew*, and
the Romantic figure of the beautiful soul. As every reader of the *PhG*
knows, these figures shape the development of Spirit in a way that the
"Spirit" chapter itself does not seem explicitly to give an account of. *Why*
does Hegel choose to present the development of Ethical Spirit as essentially an exegesis of a Greek tragedy – and why is the *Antigone* the
tragedy he turns to for this exegesis?

Hegel's literary references outside these famous moments of "Spirit"
do not seem to fit any obvious larger plan, either. The chapter on "Reason," which precedes "Spirit," includes, for example, a quotation from
an early version of Goethe's *Faust* and evident references to Schiller; the
"Religion" section, which follows "Spirit," considers Greek epic, tragedy,
and comedy as moments of the "art-religion."

The engagement with literature in the *PhG*, in other words, would
appear to be quite a haphazard affair. But there is a way of understanding more deeply the structure of the work's literary appropriations, and
in what follows I hope to suggest, if not a "key" to every literary element
of the *PhG*, at least a way of better understanding the role that literature
plays within the philosophical enterprise of the work as a whole.

Briefly, the claims that I want to examine are as follows:

1. That the *PhG* takes what I shall be calling a "literary turn" at a notoriously crucial juncture – the transition from the chapter on "Reason" to that on "Spirit." Among the most striking facts about the
   PhG's use of literature, in fact, is its sudden eruption in the middle
   of the work: despite many allusions to philosophical and religious
   works, the shapes of consciousness in the first half of the book (from

16. *PhG* scholars who have addressed the literary imagery of the work include Harris, *Hegel's
    Ladder;* Donald Phillip Verene, *Hegel's Recollection* (Albany: State University of New York
    Press, 1985); John H. Smith, *The Spirit and Its Letter: Traces of Rhetoric in Hegel's Philoso-
    phy of "Bildung"* (Ithaca: Cornell University Press, 1988); and Koen Boey, "De literatur
    en haar betekenis in Hegels 'Phänomenologie,'" in *Om de waarheid te zeggen. Opstellen over
    filosofie en literatuur aangeboden aan Ad Peperzak*, ed. K. Boey et. al., (Nijmegen: Kampen,
    1992), 67–78.

"Sense Certainty" to the middle of the "Reason" section) are presented in a way that relies on virtually no resources from explicitly
literary texts.[17] By contrast, the last half of the book, beginning with
Hegel's apparently out-of-the-blue quotation from *Faust* in the middle
of the "Reason" section, is both structured by explicitly literary works
and genres and becomes concerned itself in the course of its development to provide something of an explanation of Hegel's turn to
the literary.

2. That the central point of focus determining both the suddenness
and the sustainedness of this "eruption" of the literary in the last half
of Hegel's text is the consideration of *agency* – a consideration that
is shaped by three moments that stem from the corrigibilist and social character of Hegel's epistemological approach. These three
moments – what I call retrospectivity, theatricality, and forgiveness –
are shaped in the most important respect by the literary genres of
tragedy, comedy, and the romantic novel.

3. Finally, that this triad of tragic retrospectivity, comic theatricality,
and novelistic forgiveness is visible in the structure of the *PhG* in
three quite different ways. Most noticeably and centrally, of course,
the triad can be seen as structuring the three parts of Spirit's development into the Ethical World, Culture, and Morality. The question
of how and why these literary moments provide this structure for
Spirit is then taken up explicitly in the consideration of the role (and
limitations) of the literary genres themselves, which Hegel turns to
in the immediately following chapter on "Religion." The most con-
fusing of the three appeals to literary genres is, however, the very first
one – that moment of literary "eruption" in the middle of the "Reason" chapter – and it is that appeal that we must consider more carefully in the remaining sections of this chapter.[18]

---

17. There is at least one very important exception: Hegel's apparent – although not undis-
puted – reference to Tieck's *Verkehrte Welt* at the end of "Force and the Understanding."
(Pinkard does not think that the play is at all at issue in the section itself; I tend to agree
with him, although Tieck will play a crucial role later in another moment of *Verkehrung*.)

18. Although I am claiming that this triad "underlies" the motion in each section, it is important to note that the actual progression in each case is quite differently structured,
given the tasks of each section. The *basic* pattern at issue is one of a "tragic" opening
up of action, a "comic" reflection on how appearance is involved in action, and a move
toward resolution. In the "Spirit" chapter this progression is determined by reference
respectively to a tragedy, a comedy, and a novel of forgiveness. But it will turn out that,
in the "Reason" section, Hegel in fact uses an underlying novelistic source at the same
time that he introduces tragic and comic views of action. Also, when there is an explicit

What has appeared to some to be a contingent and philosophically unimportant sort of "play" with literary images is, I will argue, actually quite carefully carried out, and the *PhG* that emerges is not only one that must be read as being in serious philosophical contention with Kant, Fichte, and Schelling, but also one that involves a sort of *agon* with Schlegel, Hölderlin, Goethe, and Schiller – the *literary* figures who compose the literary world of *appearance* within which the "Science of the Phenomenology of Spirit" must make its appearance.

I shall begin a consideration of the *PhG*'s literary side with a reading of the transition point that I am calling the "literary turn" of the *PhG*. Before looking to that "turn" itself, however, it is worth briefly stating a caveat applicable to the rest of this book's argument. Hegel's borrowings, literary and otherwise, are famously oblique. A mere glance at the commentary tradition on any of the shapes of consciousness I will take up in what follows will reveal a much wider possible resonance of literary reference than I will discuss. By suggesting the rather specific literary shapes that I do, my intention is not to rule out the *possibility* of other resonances – since it is clearly part of Hegel's project to present shapes that are not to be read, unequivocally, as determined by single authors or texts, but rather to present a more general account of the shapes of experience that makes use of the fecundity of certain literary works. My focus in what follows is rather to see if, among the varieties of possible reference in the various shapes from "Active Reason" onward, there is something that we might lift out as an operative narrative shape – or plot, if you will – in each case and in the larger narrative structure as a whole.

1. The *PhG*'s Literary Turn

It may surprise some readers of the *Phenomenology of Spirit* to hear the work described as taking a "literary turn" at all. Hegel's use of literary sources in the *PhG* has been widely taken to be, however brilliant, a somewhat random business, and one (consequently) involving varying degrees of effectiveness.

As I hope to show in what follows, Hegel in fact uses his literary

---

turn toward literary theory in the "Religion" section, the focus is on the Greek experience of genres, and includes as well epic and lyric forms, but does not push toward the novel but instead toward "revealed religion." I give an account of these differences later in this chapter.

sources with great care and a self-conscious awareness of how and why literature is required for the philosophical project(s) undertaken by the *PhG*. What may confirm for some the impression of randomness, however, is that the literary turn of which I am speaking is both an apparently unannounced affair and one that may not seem to open out into a sustained consideration of the literary at all.

The distinctive literary turn of the *PhG* comes, I claim, in the course of the "Reason" chapter – more precisely, in the transition from "Observing Reason" to "The Actualization of Rational Self-Consciousness through Its Own Activity." While previous sections of the *PhG* have their share of (clear and less clear) allusions to various other works (in almost every case, these references are to other philosophical texts), there is an unmistakable appropriation of specifically literary sources that begins toward the end of the subsection entitled "Observing Reason" and that sets up a specific concern with literature that will continue into and beyond the "Spirit" chapter. In order to examine this development, I shall begin with a brief discussion of what is at issue at this transition point and then turn to its literary character and why that is important.

The Crux. The moment in question is a central, one might say *the* central, crux of the book as a whole. Although the *Phenomenology of Spirit* is full of curious turns and seemingly unmotivated transitions, perhaps no single part of the book has been as much a center of dispute as this transition. The underlying question for scholars interested in the work's textual and philosophical unity has been why Hegel, in general, starts to motivate a transition to the category of "Spirit" within the chapter devoted to "Reason," and, more specifically, why it is the shapes of Active Reason (or "The Actualization of Rational Self-Consciousness through Its Own Activity") and "Individuality Real in and for Itself" that are the way to effect that transition.

It was precisely this transition point, for example, that a palimpsest reader like Haering claimed to be evidence for his argument that there was a fundamental shift in Hegel's plan while writing the *PhG* and hence that there is a fundamental incoherence to the work as a whole.[19] And contemporary readers – both those who stress the palimpsest view and those who stress the work's textual unity – have been concerned

---

19. T. Haering, "Die Entstehungsgeschichte der Phänomenologie des Geistes," in *Verhandlungen des dritten Hegelkongresses*, ed. B. Wigersma (Tübingen: Mohr, 1934).

particularly to account for this transition.[20] The central question of
recent discussion seems to be about how this move may be required by
Hegel's *philosophical* project. As Robert Pippin has observed, in an essay
appropriately entitled "You Can't Get There from Here: Transition Problems in Hegel's *Phenomenology of Spirit*, " the important question posed
by this crucial transition in the *PhG* is one of why an explicitly social and
historical category like Spirit must be seen to be explanatorily required
because of the failure of the impersonal account of "reason" that the
preceding chapter has explored.[21]

However, to accept the challenge of giving a philosophical account
of this transition will require also noticing something that has not been
remarked upon sufficiently (although it is no doubt part of what a reading such as Haering's is particularly at pains to notice about the "shift"
to the directly historical that the *PhG* takes at this point). What needs
to be added to the philosophical discussion of this crux is the extraordinary *literary* "jump" the narrative takes at precisely this point. From
this point on, in a way that marks the last half of the work as essentially
different from its first half, the narrative energy of the *Phenomenology of
Spirit* is determined by specific literary works and genres to such an
extent that the book must eventually, in the "Religion" chapter, turn its
attention explicitly to the role that literature is playing within it. In other
words, the transition in question is, I want to claim, crucial not only in
terms of *what* the project of the *PhG* is, but also in terms of *how* that project must proceed.

It is, of course, no surprise to commentators on the *PhG* that literature

20. To cite two quite different readings: Michael Forster, who thinks Haering is wrong
about precisely where the palimpsest break can be observed as well as about the ultimate incoherence of the book that emerges as a result, nonetheless agrees with him
that what must be explained is essentially a split between the chapters "Consciousness"
through "Reason" and the chapters "Spirit" through "Absolute Knowing." The issue, as
he sees it, is why Hegel attempted a "revision" of the "Reason" chapter while writing the
PhG (Forster, *Hegel's Idea of a Phenomenology of Spirit*, 502–3). One does not have to be
an advocate of the palimpsest theory, however, to read the *PhG* as a whole with a caesura
at the transition from Reason to Spirit: an advocate of the book's unity like Henry Harris, for example, rather boldly organizes his recent commentary on the *PhG* around
what he calls the "fulcrum" of this split (which he correctly places, more along Haering's
lines than along Forster's, within the "Observing Reason" section of the "Reason" chapter itself rather than at the chapter's very end).

21. Robert Pippin, "'You Can't Get There From Here': Transition Problems in Hegel's *Phenomenology of Spirit*," in *The Cambridge Companion to Hegel*, ed. Frederick C. Beiser (Cambridge: Cambridge University Press, 1993), 52–85. See also Terry Pinkard's account of
the move in *Hegel's "Phenomenology,"* 135–37.

is *involved* at this transition point. In fact, one of the famous oddities of the text is that Hegel here, without offering particular comment or guidance to his reader, simply opens "Pleasure and Necessity," the first subsection of "The Actualization of the Rational Self-Consciousness," with a four-line quotation that is unmistakably derived from Goethe's *Faust*. And, to push the matter further, the subsections that follow ("The Law of the Heart and the Frenzy of Self-Conceit" and "Virtue and the Way of the World") involve figures, as well, that have seemed to many readers – Josiah Royce and Jean Hyppolite, to name two – to have literary parallels: Hegel seems to connect the figure of the "heart" in a series of allusions to the figure of Karl Moor in Schiller's *Robbers,* and he sketches a comic "knight of virtue" who, although the resonance is looser, has reminded some readers (rightly, I shall argue in a moment) of Don Quixote.

But what is behind Hegel's selection here, if it is anything more than a colorful appropriation of certain figures for the description of the shapes of consciousness under consideration? Is there a connection among the three figures – the Faustian agent, the sentimental Karl Moor, and the comic knight of virtue? And what significance do they have for the ultimate transition at issue – the move toward Spirit?

Hegel's appropriation of sources in this section is among the most complicated of all of his literary borrowings in the *PhG*, since he not only makes use of the three individual figures mentioned but also places them within an overall plot scheme borrowed from a source that has frequently been overlooked in scholarly accounts. Let us examine the literary moves of this section in somewhat more detail.

The Skull of Yorick, the "Deed" of Faust, and the Opening of Immediate Agency into Tragedy. The first signal of the concern with literature that will mark the *PhG*'s second half comes in the section entitled "Observing Reason," where Hegel's account of claims of theoretical rationality is famous for its consideration of those curiosities in the history of science, phrenology and physiognomy. In his effort to show why a "science" such as phrenology is insufficient to account for the sort of individuality that it means to observe, Hegel contrasts phrenology's interest in the mere "*being*" of a skull with a vivid recollective account of the sort that Hamlet gives in his graveside remembrance of the *deeds* that characterized Yorick:

> A variety of ideas may well occur to us in connection with a skull, like those of Hamlet over Yorick's skull; but the skull-bone just by itself is such an indifferent, natural thing that nothing else is to be directly seen in it,

or fancied about it, than simply the bone itself. It does indeed remind us
of the brain and its specific nature, and of skulls of a different formation,
but not of a conscious movement, since there is impressed on it neither
a look nor a gesture, nor anything that proclaims itself to have come from
a conscious action . . . (§333)

With the image of Hamlet facing Yorick's skull still in his reader's
mind, Hegel represents the shift to "Active Reason" – or, in the *PhG*'s
awkward phrase, "The Actualization of Rational Self-Consciousness
through Its Own Activity"[22] – as a sort of breaking out of the rational
agent from its static observational concerns. And, without any preparation, there is suddenly inserted into the text a four-line quotation that
comes unmistakably – despite Hegel's perhaps sly alteration[23] – from
Goethe's 1790 *Faust-Fragment:*

> "It despises intellect and science
> The supreme gifts of man
> It has given itself to the devil
> And must perish . . ."

Whether or not Hegel knew while writing the *PhG* that Goethe had (apparently by 1806) added to his play a Faustian encounter with an un-
communicative skull similar to Hamlet's,[24] the animus behind Hegel's
quotation here seems clear. The world of reason as contained in dead
"observable" things – Yorick's skull, the world as science observes it – is
not the "living" world that the agent of "Active Reason" wishes to attain
and that can only be known through deeds.

As the first figure of "active reason," the Faustian agent seeks an apparently immediate end: pleasure. Its action is thus, as Hegel says, not
so much one of *making* its happiness by what it does, as it is one of *tak-*

---

22. Hegel used the simpler title to describe this section in the *Anzeige* for the *PhG*'s publi-
    cation; I will use it interchangeably with the longer title that appears in the text of
    the *PhG*.
23. As Harris notes (*Hegel's Ladder*, II, 67, n. 30), Hegel quotes the first and last couplets of
    Mephistopheles' famous soliloquy (lines 1851–2 and 1866–7 of *Faust*), but whereas
    Goethe wrote, "And even if it had not given itself over to the devil . . .", Hegel makes
    this surrender a fact. It is also worth noting that while Goethe's lines speak of despis-
    ing *Vernunft und Wissenschaft*, Hegel substitutes *Verstand und Wissenschaft*.
24. The encounter occurs in lines 664–667 of *Faust, Part I*, which was not published until
    1808. The editors of the Norton Critical Edition suggest that these lines were probably
    written as part of a section of the play Goethe composed in 1799–1800 (Goethe, *Faust*,
    trans. Walter Arndt, ed. Cyrus Hamlin [New York: W. W. Norton, 1976], 349). See the
    following note.

ing what is there, or given: "It takes hold of life much as a ripe fruit is plucked, which readily offers itself to the hand that takes it" (§361).

The "taking" involved in this action is precisely what renders it, however, an example of "active reason" and hence far from a simple and unproblematic deed. As with the Desire sought by Self-consciousness in the *PhG*'s fourth chapter, the grasping of what is there may seem to the agent a straightforward and immediate deed, but in fact the agent's own articulation of what he is doing belies such a claim of immediacy. For the agent of pleasure does not simply *accept* the way things are as a given, but takes himself to be acting in such a way as to make what is there his own. It is the agent's own stress on the importance of acting in a way that the agent himself identifies as his own that makes "pleasure"-seeking here a form of active *reason* – that is to say, a form of acting in which the standard is one that is not simply inherited or given.[25]

But the agent who acts on such an intention discovers, when he acts, that his deed involved something that he had not included in his intention. The *necessity* that the agent encounters in his action is experienced by him as something entirely alien: "Consciousness, therefore, through its experience . . . has really become a riddle (*Rätsel*) to itself, the consequences of its deeds are for it not the deeds themselves" (§365).

The narrative shape of this first form of active reason – from a deed that breaks open the world of action to an awareness on the agent's part that his deed cannot simply be understood in terms of what he intended – is clearly a tragic one. For an agent who explicitly understood himself in terms of "the deed" – as opposed to what is observed in nature – a glance at what his deeds were can only be alienating, since,

---

25. This reading of Hegel's appropriation of Faust has an echo in the language of the *PhG*'s prefatory discussion of the relation between culture and the individual: the cultural development of the world is, Hegel says there,

> the already acquired property of universal Spirit which constitutes the Substance of the individual, and hence appears externally to him as his inorganic nature. In this respect formative education, regarded from the side of the individual, consists in his acquiring what thus lies at hand, devouring his inorganic nature, and taking possession of it for himself. (§28)

Walter Kaufmann, a translator of both Goethe's *Faust* and Hegel's *PhG* preface, has pointed out Hegel's "strikingly similar" choice of words when compared to Goethe's lines: "What from your fathers you received as heir, / Acquire if you would possess it" (682–3). Kaufmann points out that Goethe's lines did not appear in the 1790 *Fragment* but were only published (post-*PhG*) in 1808 as part of *Faust, Part I;* nonetheless, he says that "the lines were written much earlier, and it is possible that Hegel had heard them somehow" (Kaufmann, *Hegel: Texts and Commentary* [Garden City, NY: Doubleday, 1965], 47, n. 6).

given the terms in which he understands his own action, such an agent does not yet have the resources to peel away his specific intention.

As many readers of the *PhG* have noticed, this tragic side of Hegel's Faust portrait bears no particular resemblance to Goethe's. It does, however, even in specific phrases, have a similarity to an account of Faust that Hegel read (and from which he jotted down in his notebook verbatim passages) while he was writing the *PhG:* a review, published anonymously in the *Allgemeine Literatur-Zeitung,* of a novel about Faust by the *Sturm und Drang* author F. M. Klinger.[26]

Central to the newspaper reviewer's reading of Klinger's novel, *Fausts Leben, Taten und Höllenfahrt,* is the sense not simply of Faust as tragic – something Goethe famously disclaimed – but of tragedy as concerned with an agent's experience of deeds that are difficult to construe as one's own: Faust encounters precisely the "chains of necessity," says the reviewer, since what he sees is that "no man is the master of his deeds." Like Hegel's Faust, Klinger's comes to the conclusion that human fate is a riddling one – as the novel's epilogue puts it, in a passage that the reviewer stresses and that Hegel copied down: "Everything is dark for the spirit of man; he is to himself a riddle (*Dem Geist des Menschen ist alles dunkel, er ist sich selbst ein Rätsel*)."[27]

26. The review was published in the *Allgemeine Literatur-Zeitung* of April 23, 1805, as part of a series on contemporary "*Romanen-Literatur.*" It is excerpted, frequently word for word, in one of Hegel's Jena "wastebook" entries (*Dokumente zu Hegels Entwicklung,* ed. Johannes Hoffmeister [Stuttgart: Frommann, 1936], 367–8). The two texts are compared side by side in Manfred Baum and Kurt Meist, "Hegel's 'Prometheische Confession': Quellen fuer vier Jenaer Aphorismen Hegels," *Hegel-Studien* 7 (1972): 79–90. Their comparison leaves little doubt about the error of Karl Rosenkranz's earlier claim that the wastebook entry represented some "confessional" statement of Hegel's own, since the two texts so clearly cohere, and there is evidence (Baum and Meist cite the Klinger scholar Max Rieger) concerning the authorship of the anonymous review (it was apparently written by one Johann Gottfried Gruber, whom Hegel knew). The importance of the review and wastebook entry for the *PhG* has been made clear in Gustav Falke's *Begriffne Geschichte* (Berlin: Lukas, 1996), 216–223.

27. F. M. Klinger, *Fausts Leben, Taten und Höllenfahrt* (Frankfurt: Insel, 1964), 197. Is the influence of Klinger's novel(s) on Hegel limited primarily to the review or part of a wider reading of the novelist? Meist and Baum stress in their account the wastebook excerpt's strong dependence on the review. It is also true that the details of the specific adventures of Klinger's Faust do not seem to emerge in the *PhG* section, although there are certainly passages from the novel that have a resonance with Hegel's own thought: following the passage quoted here, Klinger cites the German proverb "What the hand throws belongs to the devil" – a saying that makes its way into Hegel's thoughts on tragedy, as can be seen in a comment from his later lectures on the philosophy of right (*Elements of the Philosophy of Right,* ed. Allen W. Wood, trans. H. B. Nisbet [Cambridge: Cambridge University Press, 1991], §119A).

The influence of the Klinger review on the *PhG*, however, reaches somewhat more widely than just the section on Faust. The review examined two further characters in later novels by Klinger that bear remarkable similarity to Hegel's next two figures of Active Reason – the agent who pursues the "law of the heart" to the point of "frenzy" (*Wahnsinn*) and the "knight of virtue" who is engaged in a contest with the "way of the world" (*der Weltlauf*).[28] The review, in fact, reads much like an *Ur*-plot of Hegel's entire "Active Reason" section – one that provides an underlay for Hegel's later adoption of three additional literary figures. What seems to have particularly impressed Hegel about the review is the notion of a *series* of *novels* exploring the experience of a succession of figures devoted to different practical ideals: Klinger's expressed goal was the writing of *philosophical* novels in this sense. This wider influence raises some further questions concerning the status of literature in the *PhG*: while it is a novel – or, more correctly, a novelistic series – that seems to provide Hegel's initial inspiration for the movement of "Active Reason" as a whole, the *PhG*'s concrete portrayal of the figures in that series nevertheless involves, as we have seen in the case of the "tragic" Faust, distinct shapes from other literary genres. I will return to this question about Hegel's use of genre after a brief examination of the two remaining shapes of Active Reason.

The Self-Aware Tragic Agent Who Knows That His Intention Is a "Law." Like the Faustian agent of "pleasure and necessity," the agent who looks to the "law of the heart" is one concerned to bring about something in *action*. "My spirit thirsts for deeds (*Thaten*), my lungs for freedom" exclaims Karl Moor, the central figure of Schiller's *Robbers*, which has been taken by many readers as the inspiration for Hegel's treatment of the "heart."[29]

Unlike Faust, the agent of the "heart" does not experience necessity only in the unforeseen complications of his deed, but rather is conscious of the necessity of his own intention: "it knows that it has the universal

28. The three figures in the Klinger series represent, says the reviewer, the attempts of metaphysics, theology, and history, respectively, to come to terms with the moral self-consciousness's horror at the "dark way of world events (*den dunkeln Lauf der Weltbegebenheiten*)." The second figure, concerned about the frenzy (*Wahnsinn*) of religious persecution, claims to fulfill the "laws of humankind according to the capacity of my heart," and the third figure directly contrasts the purity of his heart with the "way of the world."
29. Friedrich Schiller, *The Robbers and Wallenstein*, trans. F. J. Lamport (New York: Penguin, 1979), 49.

of law immediately within itself" (§367). This "necessary" unity of individual and universal is very much *only* a matter of the heart, however: on the agent's own self-conception, what his heart tells him he should do is something that is in opposition to the "universal" in the world of existing institutions – and, it will turn out, the transindividual picture of the "hearts" of others, as well.

The agent of the heart is, then, a knowingly *transgressive* agent who is expecting in his action an experience of tragic conflict – even if he does not yet understand entirely the one-sidedness of his claim.[30] (With an eye on the development of the "Spirit" chapter, we might already notice how similar the tragedy of the Karl Moor character is in this regard to that of Antigone, whereas Faust's encounter with a necessity that he does not expect resembles more the sort of tragedy that Oedipus experiences.)

Tragedy in the case of Karl Moor (or Antigone) is, then, not something that emerges like the fate implicit in an immediate action, but is rather due to a structure of conflicts that are implicit in the world in action, and that therefore determine a side of the action, despite the agent's insistence on the purity of his intention or "heart." Both Hegel's Faust and his Karl Moor, however, experience in the end of their tragedies a (corrigibilist) moment of tragic recognition about what their actions actually involved: "[i]n giving expression to . . . its self-conscious downfall as the result of its experience, it reveals itself to be this inner perversion of itself, to be a deranged consciousness which finds that its essential being is immediately non-essential" (§376).

The Comic "Knight of Virtue." If the experiences of both Faust and Karl Moor have a tragic shape, the third section of "Active Reason" suggests a comic moment. Instead of a tragic recognition, the section turns on the awareness of an agent that the "in itself" of virtue that he thinks he defends is really not separate from the "way of the world" that he opposes: the knight means in his virtue to sacrifice the private (his talents, desires, etc.), but those elements of the private are precisely what the "way of the world" includes. In the end, aware that his fight is not *serious*, that his apparent action is only in *appearance* an opposition, the knight

---

30. Faust, of course, is *also* a "transgressive" agent in the sense that he expresses the wish to go beyond the confines of tradition. But the action he intends does not, like Karl Moor's action, articulate itself *as* a claim of a universal law that is necessarily opposed to a specific universal law or institution.

of virtue will "drop like a discarded cloak its idea of a good that exists [only] in principle" (§391).

The contrast here between a figure who defends a sacrificial notion of virtue and a less high-minded "way of the world" has suggested many possible readings of the section.[31] Is there a literary background to this figure, as well? Some commentators have heard in the knight of virtue the sound of Don Quixote, and some of Hegel's language is clearly meant to point in that direction: the "knight" is explicitly said to be a figure devoted to a "faith" (§383) in the implicit essence that is in the world, despite the world's perverted character; like Don Quixote, the knight of virtue faces a modern world where the values that characterized the past are no longer present (§390). Hegel's term for the comic "mirror-fight" (*Spiegelfechterei*), in which the knight finds himself essentially making use of precisely the weapons of individual gifts and abilities that are the content of the "way of the world," also brings to mind Don Quixote's fight with the disguised "knight of mirrors" early in the second part of Cervantes's novel.[32]

But, if Goethe's early portrait of Faust and Schiller's *Robbers* are the subjects of the two preceding sections – thus placing the account of "Active Reason" as a whole in the period of early Romanticism – what could possibly explain such an apparently anachronistic transition to a figure like Cervantes's hero?[33] The difficulty is resolved, however, when

31. Pinkard (*Hegel's "Phenomenology,"* 108) suggests a duel here between the views of someone like Shaftesbury and the views of someone like Mandeville in his *Fable of the Bees*. Forster and Harris both see a battle between Frederick the Great and Machiavelli, yet Harris is certainly more accurate when he complains that, if this were Hegel's intention, one might with good reason expect more evidence. Falke (*Begriffne Geschichte*, 227) suggests that the literary work behind the "knight of virtue" might be Schiller's *Wallenstein*, which has a scene reminiscent of the "dropping of the cloak" at the end of the *PhG* section, and which, moreover, is the third item behind *Faust* and *The Robbers* in a list in Hegel's discussion in the *Aesthetics* of dramatic figures who pursue ends that are "extensive, universal and comprehensive in scope" (*Aesthetics*, 1224). The *Wallenstein* comparison is suggestive, although, as I will suggest later, Schiller's figure has more similarity to the *initial* (tragic) figure in the "Knight of Virtue" section than to the ultimate comic one.

32. Miller's translation of *Spiegelfechterei* as "sham-fight" loses the important sense of the "mirror" (*Spiegel*) facing the knight in the *Weltlauf* before him; the comic character of the knight is something acknowledged even by those like Harris, who see the problems with associating the passage with the comic knight of La Mancha.

33. The difficulty here is one that Royce makes quite evident: on the one hand, he says, "Hegel is dealing with that type whose dialectic Cervantes had long since rendered classic"; on the other hand, "the hero of knightly virtues here depicted is no longer a medieval figure, and the portrait is not directly that of Don Quixote" (Royce, *Lectures on Modern Idealism*, 195).

we consider the knight from the perspective not of Cervantes's *Don Quixote* but of the *Don Quixote* that had become of passionate interest to the Romantic age – the *Don Quixote* that, as one literary critic has suggested, was related to "practically every aspect and phase of German life between 1750 and 1800."[34] The work was of particular interest to the Schlegel circle, which encouraged Tieck's famous 1799 translation of the entire work (novellas and poetry included); *Don Quixote* was in some sense "the novel" for the genre theory of the Romantics, just as Shakespeare was "the dramatist."[35]

More strikingly for our immediate purposes, however, is the interior connection that Schiller drew directly between Karl Moor, the protagonist of his *Robbers,* and *Don Quixote.*[36] Schiller's own connection between the Moor and Don Quixote suggests a reading of Hegel's "Knight of Virtue" section as capturing a move from a Romantic reading of Quixote as *tragic* (and thus in many ways resembling the Moor in his confidence in an internal "law" that puts him at odds with the world) to one of Quixote as *comic*. Hegel's presentation thus moves us from a consideration of the action of a hero who has found himself tragically at odds with the world to one who becomes oddly comic, finding himself (as does the hero of Cervantes's *Don Quixote,* Part II) in a world where everyone seems to know him as the famous character from the famous novel.[37] If the tragic agent, as on Hegel's portrayal of Faust, was con-

---

34. Lienhard Bergel, "Cervantes in Germany," in *Cervantes Across the Centuries,* ed. Angel Flores and M. J. Benardete (New York: Dryden Press, 1948), 319. I am grateful to my colleague Alan Smith for pointing out this source.

35. Schelling, for example, in the lectures on aesthetics he was giving while Hegel was at Jena, says that "it is not too much to assert that until now there have been only two novels" – *Don Quixote* and *Wilhelm Meister* (Schelling, *The Philosophy of Art,* trans. Douglas W. Stott [Minneapolis: University of Minnesota Press, 1989], 234).

36. Schiller's reference to Karl Moor in the preface to "The Robbers" as a "Don Quixote" (in *Friedrich Schiller: Werke und Briefe,* ed. Klaus Harro Hilzinger et. al. [Frankfurt: Deutscher Klassiker Verlag, 1988], II, 16–17).

37. One interesting parallel between Hegel's reading here and that of the Romantics is that he, like both Schelling and Schlegel, stresses the two-part structure of *Don Quixote.* Schelling sees in the first part of the novel a fight between ideal and real, but in the second part a more "mysticized" fight; Hegel's character, likewise, can be said to move somewhat from a "tragic" fighter with the world to a "comic" fighter who is part of a mere battle of mirrors: the first moment of *Zucht* or discipline connected with the knight, Hegel says, is the self-sacrifice of devotion to *law* (something that in fact has already been achieved by the final moment of the previous figure, in Karl Moor's willingness to give himself up to the authorities); the second moment is a discipline that the "heart" *cannot* achieve, since it means recognizing that one's activities are, in fact, mirrored in the "antagonist" of the world.

cerned with facing a dark world that has the shape of a riddle, the comic agent somehow knows its riddle in advance: it was, after all, Sancho, as Hegel puts it in another Jena notebook remark, who held that it was better to know the solution of the riddle beforehand.[38]

In moving from a figure like Faust to a figure like Quixote, what we have, in other words, is a connection that has been pointed up (independent of Hegel) by a contemporary literary critic who has suggested that *Don Quixote*, in sketching another great anti-intellectual hero of the *deed*, could in fact be profitably read as a critique of exactly the sort of action-oriented agent that Faust is.[39] It is a comic figure, then, that brings to a close the Romantic versions of individualist agency that characterize the "Active Reason" section, and opens up the possibility of a world of agents who are aware that no *sacrifice* of individuality is required and who can view their actions within such a world as some adequate form of self-*expression*.

The "Thing-in-Itself" and the Literary Reflectivity of Individual Agency. Having made such direct appeals in the "Active Reason" section to literary figures, Hegel now seems to move beyond a concern with the literary in the section entitled "Individuality Which Takes Itself to Be Real in and for Itself." What I should like to show, however, is that the narrative in this crucial section – which is both the culmination of "Reason" as a whole and the transition to "Spirit" – is structured first of all as an important reflection *on* the literary character of what has been experienced in "Active Reason," and second as a preparation for the (similar yet different) literary character of the development of Spirit as it comes on the scene.

What emerges now in the section "Individuality in and for Itself" does not make the same direct appeal to specific literary texts, but initially – in the first subsection, entitled "The Spiritual Animal Kingdom and Deceit, or the Thing-in-Itself" – is an examination of the kind of self-

---

38. Hegel's point in the remark is concerned with what *philosophy* begins or ends with: "As we read the last scene of a play, or the last page of a novel, or Sancho holds it better to say the solution of the riddle beforehand, so is the beginning of a philosophy also its result" (*Dokumente zu Hegels Entwicklung*, 363).

39. "Had *Don Quixote* appeared after *Faust*, the literally crazy exploits of the knight of La Mancha would have been interpreted as a superb send-up of Faust's carryings-on with Gretchen and later with legendary figures from all history" (Roger Shattuck, *Forbidden Knowledge: From Prometheus to Pornography* [New York: St. Martin's Press, 1996], 96). Shattuck's discussion ties the opening concern of Cervantes's novel with representing the *hechos* (deeds) of Quixote to Faust's own concern with *Taten*.

expression available in a "world" inhabited by "individuals" who are no longer Faustian or (tragically) Quixotic. The "individual" of this world will thus express himself in language that involves no tragic "exaltation, or lamentation or repentance" (§404), but instead lives within a realm that seems based on the "comic" premise that self-expression itself – and not the contrast between (inner) good and (outer) bad or universal and individual – is key: action here "simply translates an initially implicit being into a being that is made explicit" (§401). The issue of the relation between the "authors" of such "actions" and their "works" leads to a discussion of what Hegel calls "*die Sache selbst*" (the "thing-in-itself" or the "matter in hand"):

> A consciousness that opens up a subject-matter soon learns that others hurry along like flies to freshly poured-out milk, and want to busy themselves with it; and they learn about that individual that he, too, is concerned with the subject-matter not as an *object*, but as his *own* affair. On the other hand, if what is supposed to be essential is merely the doing of it, the employment of powers and capacities, or the expression of this particular individuality, then equally it is learned by all parties that they all regard themselves as affected and invited to participate, and instead of a mere 'doing,' or separate action, peculiar to the individual who opened up the subject-matter, something has been opened up that is for others as well, or is a subject-matter on its own account. (§418)

As others have suggested, such a world of concern with expression and the curious interaction of universal "subject-matter" and individual "interest" has features remarkably suggestive of the world of modern literary criticism.[40] The realm of *die Sache selbst* has, in fact, a similarity to the realm that Hegel will ultimately call *Bildung* in the "Spirit" chapter. At this stage of the narrative, however, the agents of the world of *die Sache selbst* still construe what they express in terms of their own individuality; there is as yet no figure like the highly imitative Rameau who can self-consciously express "himself" in a language equivalent to the language of the *entire* realm of *Bildung* itself.[41]

The literary concern of this section points up in yet another way Hegel's crucial concern here with the transition from claims of rational individuality in action to the perspective of Spirit. Even though the re-

---

40. Such was the suggestion of Hyppolite; Harris says it's more broadly the realm of "civil society," without a particular concern with economics (Harris, *Hegel's Ladder*, II, 108).
41. See Harris's rather suggestive notion of the Knight of Virtue and Rameau as the two figures marking the beginning and end of concern with *Bildung* in the *PhG* (II, 58).

maining two subsections of the section on "Individuality" – "Reason as Lawgiver" and "Reason as Testing Laws" – present a view of modern rationalist ethics that culminates in a notion that clearly resonates with Kantian moral philosophy, many readers have noticed that Hegel's own presentation of the figures in these last sections already seems to be setting up parallels with the characters who will come on the scene at the beginning of "Spirit" in Hegel's reading of Sophocles' *Antigone*. [42] We will return momentarily to Hegel's reasons for effecting this transition, but for the moment it is worthwhile to summarize the narrative structure of agency within "Reason" that we have seen up to now.

Summarizing the Narrative Shape of "Active Reason." To recap the movement we have seen within "Active Reason": reason becomes "active" in an initial "breaking out" of action on an apparently immediate plane that ends in a discovery of a larger web of necessity which the agent has not previously been consciously considering and which, while it "sticks" to the agent, is in another important respect distinguishable from the agent's

---

42. Readers of the *Phenomenology* who have been concerned to explicate Antigone's role in the text have heard – rightly for the most part, I think – deliberate echoes of the central conflict of that play in Hegel's description of all three of these forms of individualist agency. (I draw here particularly on the suggestions of George Steiner, *Antigones* [Oxford: Clarendon Press, 1984], 29–31, and Michael Schulte, *Die 'Tragödie im Sittlichen': Zur Dramentheorie Hegels*, 83–96.) If the three forms of agency associated with the "Actualization of Rational Self-Consciousness" are sketched with the aid of specific dramatic figures, the three forms of agency in "Individuality in and for Itself" do not so much refer each to specific works as they together show the extent to which the ethical substance that underlies the world of the *Antigone* is at this point already presupposed by these forms of Reason. (This presupposition of Spirit is first clear when Hegel shows that the universal and individual considerations involved in "The Matter in Hand" are really only two sides of "spiritual essence" [§418].) Because these final stages of Reason are thus presented from the perspective of the notion of Spirit that they presuppose, the progress from the "Matter in Hand" through "Reason as Lawgiver" and "Reason as Testing Laws" pre-enacts, as it were, the similar development that will be seen in the initial stages of "true Spirit": the presentation first of the harmonious equilibrium in "The Ethical World" and then of the conflicts that arise within it in "Ethical Action." At the start of both movements, action must be regarded as nothing more than a translation of the "night of possibility" into the "day of the present" (§396, §404; cf. §463, §464). The "laws" of which an agent is conscious are "immediately acknowledged": their "origin" or "justification" cannot be asked (§421, §423; cf. §437, §441). Yet from this immediacy of law's presence there emerges a challenge in which the two "essences" or "masses" of that law are seen to be pitted against one another in outrage and insolence (compare the distinction in §434 between *der tyrannische Frevel* and *der Frevel des Wissens*, associated with the moments of law-giving and law-testing reason, to the description in §466 of Creon's appearance to Antigone as *menschliche zufällige Gewalttätigkeit* and her appearance to him as *der Frevel*).

own *deed;* this action is followed by a more self-conscious but nonetheless also tragic agent who recognizes the universality *in* his intention or "heart" and whose discovery in experience is that the purity he thought to be in his "heart" is likewise not a necessarily justifying criterion for his action; finally, we encounter an agent who begins from a point of view that – unlike the "heart" – knows that his action is very much in a world constrained by rational laws of various sorts and knows what is to be expected from that world, to the extent that his "action" loses the sort of self-seriousness we could attribute to the "heart."

What we have seen, then, is the emergence from action's apparent immediacy of a necessary concern with *tragic* categories like necessity and fate; the *self-consciously transgressive tragic agent* who attempts to "take on" the determining necessity of his action; but the final *"comic"* awareness that no action can be entirely self-determined by an agent who attempts to abstract from the individual interest involved in the action. Each of these agents has so far been presented as a separate figure, one who does not realize his narrative debt to the preceding form of consciousness: their coherence in a pattern of immediate *action-tragedy-comedy* is so far something visible only to "us," the "phenomenological observers" who have the privileged position of watching the shapes of consciousness go by as part of the structured narrative of the *PhG*.

This same structure – from a tragic "breaking out" of action to a comic self-reflection about action as an appearance – will be visible again in the first two phases of "Spirit." What will be different, however, is the role that the novel will play in the development of "Spirit." As we saw, it was a review of a series of philosophical novels by the Romantic writer F. M. Klinger that somehow provided the inspiration for Hegel's development of the shapes of "Active Reason." But what does it say about Hegel's sense of literary genres and their relation to one another that he placed on top of that novelistic palimpsest a series of figures that, as we have argued, have a clear tragic or comic character?

One answer, which we will explore more carefully in Chapter 4, has to do with the Romantic cast of Hegel's consideration of the novel: as we will see there, it was the claim of Romantics like Friedrich Schlegel that the novel in fact rose above traditional genre categories. The novel's ability to appropriate other forms – that for the *tragic* side of Faust Hegel looks to Klinger's *novel* instead of to Goethe, or that for the *comic* side of agency he looks to Cervantes and not to a comic playwright – would thus seem to be at the heart of Hegel's reflection on its importance to the Romantic movement.

In Hegel's own first appropriation of literary forms in the *PhG*, however – in the immediate Romantic *Bildung* of Hegel's own time that is the context for the explorations of "Active Reason" – the questions of genre are not yet delineated, since Reason cannot yet give an historical account of itself. Before Hegel can present a theory of artistic genres (a task for the "Religion" chapter) the historical narrative of "Spirit" is first required. On that narrative, as we will see, tragedy and comedy arise for distinctive reasons from the *ancient* world, and the recollective, self-conscious activity of the novelist can only come on the scene after them. For this reason, it is only in the explicitly historical account in "Spirit" that Hegel takes up reconciliation or forgiveness as a peculiarly novelistic possibility.[43] We must now turn our attention to what Spirit is and why it comes on the scene as the successor to these shapes of Active Reason and Individuality.

Tragedy and Comedy in the "Spirit" Chapter. Among the stranger elements of the transition we are considering is the evidently unexplained appearance of Antigone at the end of the "Reason" section. As we noticed, Hegel sketches the final section of "Reason," "Testing Laws," not just with the internal difficulties of Kantian moral philosophy in mind; he also already seems to have an eye for how Antigone – and, with her, Spirit – is to be brought on stage. Why this apparent anachronism? Is she Sophocles' Antigone or has Hegel used her to represent some odd conclusion of the Kantian moment detailed in "Testing Laws"?

This is an issue for which the new reading of the *PhG* has given a particularly helpful answer. As Pinkard has suggested, what Hegel represents here is the shape of a certain reconsideration of the claims of Greek ethical life that now seems to press upon the immediate post-Kantian world. This interest in the Greek "alternative" to the claims of rationalist modernity that we have been exploring up to now in the "Reason" section reflects a move from an "impersonal" view of reason to a conception of rationality as a reflective social practice – a move that

---

43. The literary feel of the two sections of the *PhG* that Hegel turns over to the Romantic novel – the "Active Reason" section that we have just explored and the "Conscience" section at the end of the "Spirit" chapter – is reallly quite different: the former is quite muscularly focused on deeds, and the latter is quite evanescently concerned with reconciling them. It is interesting to note that the newspaper review of Klinger's novels that so influenced Hegel distinguishes in a similar way between the activist figures in Klinger's novels (so important for the "Active Reason" section) and the more philosophical characters in Jacobi's (which underlie the "Conscience" section).

Hegel's narrative presents as required or presupposed by the preceding shapes.[44]

The literary character involved in the action we will see in "Spirit" will likewise be shaped by the tragic and comic moments we have seen; but this time there is a completion of the triad in a way that "Individuality in and for Itself" did not permit. There will again be an initial "breaking out" of action in the first section of "Spirit," the "Ethical Order." This tragic moment of action can be represented in the first instance by an agent like Oedipus, who – like Faust in the "Reason" section – does not know at all what his deeds involve, and will experience a necessity that is alien to him in his action. But "more purely" tragic, as Hegel puts it, is the figure of Antigone – like Karl Moor, a self-consciously transgressive hero – who knows that she opposes a law, but acts from her consciousness of what is right. As with both Faust and Karl Moor, the conclusion of tragic action in "Spirit" involves a recognition on the part of the tragic agent who is now aware of how her action was also wrong.

The (Greek-inspired) "Ethical Order" gives way to (Roman) "Legal Status" and to the world of *Bildung*, which will feature as representative of its "perversion" a peculiar mimetic creature named after his uncle Rameau. As with Don Quixote's recognition of the impossibility of a "sacrifice" of individual considerations in agency, so this comic figure also will give a window onto an "unserious" view of action: like Quixote, who acknowledges this comic insight into action when he drops the

---

44. Hegel points out at some length how the initial moment of "Spirit" has been presupposed by *each* of the preceding shapes of Active Reason and thus gives us some sense about why the final section of "Reason" has been made to contain so many resonances with the looming conflict in the *Antigone*:

> What observation knew as a *given* object in which the self had no part, is here a given custom, but a reality which is at the same time the deed and the work of the subject finding it. The individual who seeks the pleasure of *enjoying his individuality*, finds it in the family, and the necessity in which that pleasure passes away is his own self-consciousness as a citizen of his nation. Or, again, it is in knowing that the law of his own heart is the law of all hearts, in knowing the consciousness of the self as the acknowledged universal order; it is virtue, which enjoys the fruits of its sacrifice, that brings about what it sets out to do, viz., to bring forth the essence into the light of day, and its enjoyment is this universal life. Finally, consciousness of the 'matter in hand' itself finds satisfaction in the real substance that contains and preserves in a positive manner the abstract moments of that empty category. That substance has, in the ethical powers, a genuine content that takes the place of the insubstantial commandments that sound Reason wanted to give and to know; and thus it gets an intrinsically determinate standard for testing, not the laws, but what is done (§461).

"cloak" or costume that he wore in a more tragic pose, so Rameau will be concerned with *unmasking* claims about givenness in action.

The literary action of "Reason" ended with the world of *die Sache selbst* – a world of criticism in which the specific literary genres seemed to have been put by, but which seemed to open out into infinite comedy: a nontemporal perspective, not particularly concerned with the *Bildung* that lies *behind* the inhabitants of the world itself, as Harris says. On their own terms the agents of "Individuality Real-in-and-for-Itself" cannot account for how their form of expressivity came to be, in particular how what it takes to be individual is connected to broader social claims.

Another way of stating the issue: an advance beyond the "comic" moment of action – to a notion of agency in which the self is somehow adequately "reconciled" to the impersonal forms that his self-expression requires – is not possible within the terms of Reason alone, but requires Spirit. The third moment of the triad – the moment associated with the novel – will thus appear only at the end of the "Spirit" chapter.

Hegel's literary reference in the final chapter of "Spirit" will also be different from the direct allusions we have seen to *Antigone* and *Rameau*. In this case, rather than a single literary work that is representative of the downfall of beautiful Greek *Sittlichkeit* or of the world of *Bildung*, we have instead a figure defined by several romantic novels concerned with the "beautiful soul," concluding with the possibility of a "forgiveness" that can acknowledge the retrospective and theatrical moments of the preceding narrative.

2. Accounting for the "Literary Turn": Narrative and the Project of the *Phenomenology*

The reader may at this point justly ask how one should make sense of the literary encounters he has seen, from Hamlet's musing over the skull of Yorick, through the end of the "Reason" section to the end of "Spirit." Why these two progressions – each beginning with a tragic moment of action and moving to a comic notion of action?

This is in fact the question that Hegel thinks the *PhG* narrative must take up next: since not only Spirit's arrival but also its development in its own sphere have been shaped by forms of the literary art, what is the status of art itself and the self-consciousness of forms of Spirit that it allows? For the *PhG*, this question about *art* is framed in terms of *Religion*, since art comes on the scene there as the religious mode specific to the

Greek experience of the divine – "Religion in the Form of Art," as Hegel puts it.[45]

The general move from Spirit to Religion involves a move to a form of self-reflection *about* the authoritativeness of the reasons for belief and action that have mattered in the forms of life visible in Spirit up to now and that can allow the identity of agents in each case to be put to the test. In Pinkard's view, it is only from the perspective of Religion that the *teleological* character of action can be explicitly taken into account – so it is only at the end of "Spirit" that a narrative self-consciousness or *story* about what has happened in action is genuinely possible.[46] We have seen something of the importance of this teleological self-consciousness in the claim about forgiveness as a form of recognition of what has been involved in reaching the achievement of the narrative process up to that point. In Hegel's terms, as we will see, the forgiveness of the beautiful soul just *is* the transition to the self-reflectivity of Religion.

The transition to Religion and the transition to Spirit both require Hegel to begin a narrative over, as it were, from a point that the phenomenological observer may first take as anachronistic: the consideration of Kantian law-testing from the perspective of Reason, we saw, required an explanatory account that had to begin again with a consideration of Greek ethical life; in this case, the "beautiful soul" figure of the Romantic era requires first an explanatory account that must start back at what Hegel takes to be the very origins of human experience with religion.[47]

It is a striking fact about the "starting over" in this case that it does not account for religion as a reflective practice by merely returning to the Greek experience; Hegel thinks that the account of how religion came into its self-reflective Greek status requires a look back to less reflective practices in earlier societies. And, within Hegel's account of the Greek art-religion, and the literary genres that are part of the "spiritual work of art," it is also the case that Hegel cannot simply begin with the

---

45. This is, of course, different from Hegel's later system, where Art, Religion, and Philosophy are distinguished as the three modes of Absolute Spirit. Despite the formal difference, however, there are significant ties between the account here and the later place of the *Aesthetics* in Hegel's system: most importantly, the locating of the primary experience of art or the beautiful in the Greek world, and looking at the transition to the post-Greek world in terms of a new religious view in which art is no longer the absolute.

46. Pinkard, Hegel's *"Phenomenology"*, 221.

47. On the Lukács and Forster reading, this makes for the third great cycle of the *PhG*; whether that is right or not, we see again, as with Spirit, that to account for something, a move back to another historical origin must take place.

genre of tragedy; the historically prior forms of epic and lyric are now brought explicitly into the discussion, as well.[48] But the account does give us something of a key to the specific literary works we have seen the *PhG* take up so far: from out of the realm of epic narration, there emerges a tragic action; that action implies a connection to a "given" or a mask that comedy must then take off in the self-consciousness of its own *Bildung;* what follows is then (famous Hegelian thesis) the "death of art," accompanied by the emergence of a religious perspective in which art is not the highest form of self-conscious reflection about divinity. The works of ancient tragedy and comedy are, from the perspective of developed Spirit, "fruit from a maiden":

> The works of the Muse now lack the power of the Spirit, for the Spirit has gained its certainty of itself from the crushing of gods and men. They have become what they are for us now – beautiful fruit already picked from the tree, which a friendly Fate has offered us, as a girl might set the fruit before us. It cannot give us the actual life in which they existed, not the tree that bore them, not the earth and the elements which constituted their substance, not the climate which gave them their peculiar charac-ter, nor the cycle of the changing seasons that governed the process of their growth. So Fate does not restore their world to us along with the works of antique Art, it gives not the spring and summer of the ethical life in which they blossomed and ripened, but only the veiled recollection (*eingehüllte Erinnerung*) of that actual world. (§753)

The literary forms that were the works of the Muse remain, of course, in the post-Greek world, but Hegel's point is that as forms of art, they now have a different function. Art is no longer the chief mode of access to the divine, as it was for the Greeks – and, much like his contempo-rary Friedrich Schlegel, Hegel understood that the problem of art in modernity was precisely one of coming to terms with the issue of the "pastness" of its traditional forms. By the time of his *Aesthetics,* Hegel ar-ticulated this issue in terms of a shift from the *Darstellung* associated with art to the *Vorstellung* of religious discourse, which, in turn, sheds its char-acter as a representation and becomes philosophy. In the *Phenomenology*

---

48. When Hegel discusses the role of epic in his *Aesthetics,* he distinguishes sharply between epic and tragic types of plot: epic is concerned with a notion of Nemesis as "simply the ancient justice which degrades what has risen too high only to restore by misfortune the mere equilibrium of good and ill fortune, and it touches and affects the realm of finitude without any further *moral* judgment." Epic is thus concerned with the field of *events* (as opposed to tragic *actions*), and in some sense establishes a "background" for the actions of the tragic heroes (*Aesthetics,* 1217).

of Spirit, as we consider the transition from the "Art-Religion" of the Greeks to the "Manifest Religion" of Christianity to "Absolute Knowing," we see a movement, as well, to a form of *philosophical* narrative that transcends its explicitly literary predecessors.

From the perspective of this penultimate chapter of the *PhG*, then, the *PhG*'s prior concern with literature from "Active Reason" to "Spirit" would appear not to be haphazard at all, but rather to follow something of a pattern. Both in "Active Reason" and in "Spirit," we have seen that a serious, tragic action (Faust and Karl Moor in "Reason," Antigone in "Spirit") first opens up a consideration of agency, and that this action is followed by a more self-reflective and comic consideration of agency (*Don Quixote, Rameau's Nephew*). We also have some way of accounting for the difference between how Reason and Spirit appropriate these literary moments: only within the context of Spirit is there the possibility of a *third* moment of reconciliatory "forgiveness."[49]

What the *PhG* presents, then, is an exploration of individual rationalist agency and agency within Spirit that is defined by and taken up as an exploration of the literary genres of tragedy, comedy, and the romantic novel. Harris has suggested a strong two-part reading of the *PhG* on which the second half of the work begins precisely at the literary "crux" we noticed: the move from phrenology's observational account of the skull to Hamlet's recollective account of Yorick's skull.[50]

Within that "recollective" second half of the *PhG*, one determined in

49. There is another large, interesting difference between the literary appropriations in the two chapters. Genre, which had its "classical" shape in Greece, seems to blur in the Romantic period. The "Romantic" character of the actions in these works is evident not only in the stress on the *individual* trying to bring forth something in the world, but also in the sense that the setting of each of these figures is importantly rooted in a *past* or context: this is most prominently true of Faust, a medieval figure resurrected by the Romantic age, and Don Quixote, whose actions self-consciously look back to a chivalric age that is difficult to recover in the present. Hegel says that individual agency need not have that character but is *vorgestellt* in this way because it is "more familiar" to the generation that initially was reading the *PhG*.

50. Suggestively, Harris reads this transition moment as the opening of a consideration that concludes only with the famous moment of the "place of the skull," or Golgotha, that figures in the transition from Religion to Absolute Knowing in the final chapter.

Literature isn't of course the only thing going on in this passage from "Observing Reason" to "Art-Religion" – there is also a concern with the category of religion itself, as Harris emphasizes well. But what I hope to have shown is how the fruit for which Faust appears to reach in the immediacy of his action is not something that is satisfactorily "grasped" until the *PhG* has embarked on an account of literature; what is handed back by the maiden is in fact an understanding of agency and the sort of account-giving required for it.

large part by the kind of "recollection" of Spirit that Religion is, I have argued that, on Hegel's own terms – his central notion being that of an "art-religion" reflective of Greek ethical life – a significant part of that development is explicitly determined by and concerned with the literary.[51] The "fruit" that the Faustian agent rushes toward with immediacy is, among other things, the fruit of *literature*. It is a fruit that cannot, as the *PhG* argues, be understood in its immediacy, but requires the hand of another narrative, a self-conscious maiden, for its enjoyment.

The claims that I have made here about the connection between *agency* and *literature* – and about the importance of the literary aspect of Spirit as the realm of acting on norms – need to be fleshed out in more detail. In the following three chapters, I will turn to a consideration of the narrative moments of agency in retrospectivity, theatricality, and forgiveness primarily by giving a close reading of Hegel's analysis of them in the "Spirit" chapter appropriations of *Antigone, Rameau's Nephew,* and the beautiful soul novel. But I will occasionally look forward to the analysis of art-religion in "Religion," and what I say about tragedy, comedy, and the novel will reflect back onto Hegel's use of it in "Reason," as well.

51. It is in this light that I understand Hegel's famous final appeal to literature in the *PhG:* the last lines of the book, in which he adapts a quotation from Schiller's *Die Freundschaft* in order to remind the reader particularly of the recollective character of the *PhG*'s journey.

2

TRAGEDY AND RETROSPECTIVITY:
HEGEL'S *ANTIGONE*

Action (*Handlung*) in its original Greek sense is a stepping-forth
(*Heraustreten*) from an undivided consciousness.

Hegel, *Aesthetics*

Tragedy is the first of the three moments of agency that Hegel considers,
because it is the moment from which the other moments "step forth"
or break open into view. As we shall see, understanding what action is
and how it can be justified is, for Hegel, an inherently *retrospective* practice of a sort that bears a remarkable similarity to the task facing the
tragic agent and spectator.[1]

Like more recent interpreters of tragedy such as Walter Benjamin
and Franz Rosenzweig, Hegel was impressed by the *silence* of the ancient
tragic heroes – and was led to think about the agent or self involved in
Greek tragedy in terms of what comes to be visible in an agent's action
once it is done.[2] The account Hegel gives of the tragic character of ac-

1. The importance of Hegel's concern in general with tragedy – something that characterizes his thought from the very earliest period (particularly in his Frankfurt essay) to
his final *Lectures on Aesthetics* – has always been much discussed in the scholarly and philosophical literature. For an overview of Hegel's developing views on tragedy, see Otto
Pöggeler, "Hegel und die griechische Tragödie," *Heidelberger Hegel-Tage, Hegel-Studien*
Beiheft 1 (1964): 285–305.

   More recently, the importance of tragedy for those interested in Hegel's philosophy
of action has come to the forefront: see, for example, the (rather different) recent ac-
counts of the Hegelian view of "tragic action" in Christoph Menke-Eggers, *Tragödie im
Sittlichen: Gerechtigkeit und Freiheit nach Hegel* (Frankfurt: Suhrkamp, 1996); Michael
Schulte, *Die 'Tragödie im Sittlichen': Zur Dramentheorie Hegels* (Munich: Fink, 1992); Martha
C. Nussbaum, *The Fragility of Goodness* (Cambridge: Cambridge University Press, 1986); and
Paul Ricoeur, *Oneself as Another,* trans. Kathleen Blamey (Chicago: University of Chicago
Press, 1992), 241–249.

2. "Franz Rosenzweig has demonstrated that the inarticulacy of the tragic hero, which dis-

tion takes on its more distinctive (and distinctly Hegelian) coloration in the concern it has for the ultimate *articulation* of what emerges from that initially inarticulate silence: for Hegel, what is at issue in ancient tragedy is some notion of an *implicit* reflectiveness in action that is not yet explicitly articulated. Action is thus seen as beginning from a prereflective sense of a whole that can be articulated only in the action itself.

Hegel's interest in the character of action in ancient tragedy was not an antiquarian one, but stemmed in fact from a consideration of distinctly modern difficulties in giving an account of agency. In the first chapter, we saw that the epistemological task of the *PhG* as a whole is concerned with avoiding what McDowell calls the "familiar predicament" of modern philosophy's concern with the "given." The *PhG* begins with no assumption about the role that a necessary "given" (an "immediate," unrevisable, or "incorrigible" datum) must play in experience, but pursues a skeptical program – unlike the Cartesian one – that Hegel calls a "highway of despair": the examination of what certain claims involve just on their own terms and of whether, in the light of experience, such claims would necessarily need to be revised in order to be justifiable.

What will be determinative for Hegel about *agency* thus cannot be any set of "leading assumptions" (since the book is to *test* anything that might count as such) nor any set of "ethical intuitions" that must be ratified within ethical theory as a whole (since no "given" or "immediate" intuition can count until it is articulated and tested in experience). The link between the retrospectivity inherent in what we have called a "tragic" notion of action and elements of what the *PhG* pursues in terms of a "corrigibilist" notion of agency – where there are no assumptions at the start to ratify, and claims are examined precisely in the light of experience with them – is at the moment a merely suggestive one. It may gain more depth, however, if we carefully examine how Hegel is able, by means of such a corrigibilist philosophical approach, to open up a way of reconsidering some familiar leading assumptions within recent (particularly Anglo-American) philosophy of agency.

tinguishes the main figure in Greek tragedy from all his successors, is one of the foundation stones of the theory of tragedy. 'For this is the mark of the self, the seal of its greatness and the token of its weakness alike: it is silent. The tragic hero has only one language that is completely proper to him: silence. It has been so from the very beginning. The tragic devised itself the artistic form of the drama precisely so as to be able to present silence. . . .'" Walter Benjamin, *The Origin of German Tragic Drama* (Frankfurt: Suhrkamp, 1977), 108; quotation from Franz Rosenzweig, *Der Stern der Erlösung* (Frankfurt: 1921), 98–9.

The first of the assumptions his approach will question is one common to intentionalist or voluntarist accounts of action: the assumption that a coherent account of agency depends on the isolation of a prior mental state, to which an agent has unrevisable access, and which can be said to "cause" a given action. As in the case of the "tragic" figures with which we began, action must be seen from a perspective that does not simply assume a distinction between an intention and the action it supposedly "causes." Indeed, as Charles Taylor has described it, Hegel's philosophy of agency in general can be characterized as having a "qualitative" or "teleological," as opposed to a "causal," concern with action: Hegel's view of action, like Aristotle's, does not look on intention and action as necessarily separate elements of agency. Instead of pursuing a search for an isolatable mental state that is causative, the Hegelian attempt to understand what an action involves and how it can be mine is something that is realized only in action itself.[3] In other words, what an agent does cannot be decided by the privileging of an agent's (presumably unrevisable) prior intention but must be come to, in an important sense, retrospectively.

The second assumption can be found in philosophies of agency that, like Frankfurt's well-known account of the relation between first-order and second-order desires, understand an agent's freedom in terms of an "internal" account of the desires on which an agent wants to act.[4] Such accounts, from Hegel's perspective, overlook an important feature of desire-based agency: the question of how I as an agent came to have my desires at all. Without such an account of desire formation, I am left with the possibility that my action may not be free (or really "mine") at all, since many of the desires on which I may want to act may be due to the influence of a particularly unfree social realm.[5] My desires, in other words, cannot "count" for me just by occurring in me. Thus, we have a second kind of concern with retrospectivity: on the one hand, the ac-

---

3. Charles Taylor, "Hegel and the Philosophy of Action," in *Hegel's Philosophy of Action*, ed. Lawrence Stepelevich and David Lamb (Atlantic Highlands, NJ: Humanities Press, 1983), 1–18; a later version of this paper appears as "Hegel's Philosophy of Mind," in Taylor, *Human Agency and Language: Philosophical Papers I* (Cambridge: Cambridge University Press, 1985), 77–96.

4. Harry Frankfurt, "Freedom of the Will and the Concept of a Person," *The Journal of Philosophy* 68:1 (January 1971): 5–20.

5. See the helpful formulation of this criticism of Frankfurt and other relevant theories in Michael Quante, "Personal Autonomy and the Structure of the Will," in *Right, Morality, Ethical Life: Studies in G. W. F. Hegel's Philosophy of Right*, ed. Jussi Kotkavirta (Jyvaskyla: University of Jyvaskyla, 1997), 75–92.

count we can give of *what* an agent does must look backward at what the deed involves in order to accurately see how the agent is "in" that deed; on the other hand, the account an agent may give of *why* he acted as he did also requires retrospectivity, since an important element of the deed's being mine is bound up with the account of how I have come to have the desires I do.

But having distinguished the ultimate concern of Hegel's philosophy of agency from causalist or voluntarist theories, on the one hand, and theories that make internalist assumptions about desires on the other, what implications follow for a coherent account of action? Causalist and voluntarist theories, after all, are thought to give an account of a number of phenomena of action usually regarded as important for preserving the agent's perspective on his action, such as responsibility, regret for wrong action, and agentive identity. Can a theory that eschews causalist assumptions really account for such phenomena? As for the assumptions concerning desire formation, it might be thought that in this case, too, Hegel's intention to avoid those assumptions may brush too quickly over certain elements that any account of agency that includes the agent's perspective would want to involve: don't I experience my desires in a more immediate way than the retrospective account of desire formation will allow? What sort of social or historical conditions are relevant for my being able to take my desires as "really" mine?

Addressing these questions will depend in part on the answer that we give to a third question that is central to the retrospectivity of Hegel's account: an agent's *identity*, over and beyond the question of what an agent understands himself to do and his motivation for doing it. It is this question that will lead us into the expressive dimension of Hegel's account of the retrospectivity of the three issues of what an agent does, why he does it, and how he is "in" the action in a way that he can identify.[6]

In what follows, we will begin with a consideration of an issue where Hegel's concern with the "corrigibilist" view of action in tragedy would seem to have its most obvious correlate in recent philosophy of action: the notion of moral luck. We will then look at Hegel's now-famous reading of Sophocles' *Antigone* in the *Phenomenology* to see how he unpacks from that interpretation elements of his answer to the questions we have raised concerning action's retrospectivity.

6. As I make clear later, I owe this tripartite formulation to Terry Pinkard, *Hegel's "Phenomenology,"* 188.

1. From Moral Luck to Expressive Agency:
The Origins of an Hegelian "Poetics" of Action

One way of pondering these questions is to consider how the perspective on agency that Hegel opens up here touches the sorts of concerns that have animated recent discussions in ethical philosophy of the issue of moral luck. Consider, for example, what draws a philosopher like Bernard Williams to Vernant's description of the tragic side of action:

> In the tragic perspective, acting, being an agent, has a double character. On the one side, it consists in taking council with oneself, weighing the for and against and doing the best one can to foresee the order of means and ends. On the other hand, it is to make a bet on the unknown and the incomprehensible and to take a risk on a terrain that remains impenetrable to you.[7]

The tragic oscillation between an agent's deliberation and the necessary risk or wagering inherent in action is one element of what led Hegel to look to the Greek tragedians for a way of getting some purchase on the importance of retrospectivity for an account of agency. The inherent contingency in action that any adequate discussion of justification and responsibility must acknowledge plays, of course, an important role in Hegel's view of action: "a stone thrown is the devil's," as one of his favorite German proverbs has it.[8] Hegel's concerns, however, are broader than those that might be construed simply in terms of the retrospectivity at issue in cases of moral luck. At the deepest level, retrospectivity is of concern for Hegel because of what he sees as the inherent *expressivity* of agency. And it is *Greek* tragedy that interests him, because he, like Aristotle, understood that the notion of *character* for the ancient tragedians was derived from a larger construal of what is involved and expressed in an *action*, taken as a whole.

The linking of Aristotle's poetics with Hegel's view of agency may seem strange; it is, after all, well known that for Aristotle tragedy turned on the notion of a *hamartia*, a mistake such as Oedipus', rather than on the sort of larger, presumably unavoidable social conflict that we associate with Hegel's reading of *Antigone*. While this view of a difference

---

7. Bernard Williams, *Shame and Necessity* (Berkeley: University of California Press, 1993), 19.
8. Hegel, *Elements of the Philosophy of Right*, §119A. For a discussion of how the issue of moral luck enters the treatment of agency in the PR, see Allen Wood, *Hegel's Ethical Thought* (Cambridge: Cambridge University Press, 1990), 142–4, 191–2.

between a tragedy of *hamartia* and a tragedy of conflict in the ethical realm is essentially right, it misses an important and underlying point of agreement between Aristotle and Hegel: the notion that tragedy, at root, is *about action*. To the general comparison that Taylor suggests between Aristotelian and Hegelian orientations about agency, I shall argue, it is important to add how for both the consideration of action leads to the development of a poetics that takes tragedy as revealing something essential about action as a whole.

That tragedy so strongly influenced Hegel's philosophy of action has not really been argued before, although some recent works concerned more explicitly with literary theory have argued persuasively for the reverse: that a notion of action is fundamental to Hegel's philosophy of tragedy. Michelle Gellrich, for example, has underscored in her study of conflict and tragedy in Hegelian and Aristotelian poetics the extent to which "Hegel's aesthetic system is predisposed from the beginning . . . to favor action."[9] Vittorio Hösle, in his work on Hegel and Greek tragedy, points to the hierarchical structure of the art forms within Hegel's *Aesthetics:* if poetry for Hegel is higher than architecture and sculpture because it is capable of "unfolding the totality of an *event* (*Begebenheit*)," so the ascending order of poetic forms – epic, lyric, and tragic – also progressively better represent an action. Drama is thus the highest art form for Hegel in the sense that "in the end it is determined through the interaction of *agents* (*handelnden*) and therefore of subjects objectifying themselves in a mutual relation."[10]

As both Gellrich and Hösle see, Aristotle's *Poetics* is of crucial formal importance to Hegel's own thought about tragedy.[11] For Aristotle, who points to the etymological root of drama in the word *dran*, "action,"

---

9. Michelle Gellrich, *Tragedy and Theory: The Problem of Conflict since Aristotle* (Princeton: Princeton University Press, 1988), 93.

10. Hösle, *Die Vollendung der Tragödie* (Stuttgart and Bad Cannstatt: Frommann, 1984), 21.

11. Hösle, following von Fritz (*Antike und moderne Tragödie* [Berlin: de Gruyter, 1962]), notes the similarity of interest between Aristotelian and Hegelian theories of tragedy and the way in which Hegel attempted to treat those concerns in a more complete philosophical way: "In many things, Hegel completes Aristotle thematically, but beyond that also seeks to ground phenomena which Aristotle merely perceives" (*Die Vollendung der Tragödie*, 25, n. 22). Gellrich, while at pains to show how Hegel's notion of tragic conflict differentiates his theory of tragedy from Aristotle's, nevertheless acknowledges the extent to which Hegel appears to have taken it as his task to fit the explication of his ideas at least formally under a framework of concepts derived from Aristotle: "even when Hegel directly takes up and interprets Aristotelian concepts in terms of *Kollision* . . . he says nothing of the fact that he is making over conventional ideas to fit an essentially new formulation of tragic action and character" (Gellrich, *Tragedy and Theory*, 15).

tragedy is essentially defined as the imitation of *action* – rather than, for example, the sketch of a character. Tragedy, because it tells a story about the fortune and thus the happiness of a person, is therefore "about action and life," not about character.[12]

It is true that the relation of influence between poetics and ethics appears to run in different directions for Aristotle and Hegel. While Aristotle applies terms from his evidently earlier *Nicomachean Ethics* to the study of tragic action, it was Hegel's reading of the ancient tragedies that seems to have influenced his theory of action. Nevertheless, Hegel follows the fundamental Aristotelian insight into action as the center of tragedy in his insistence, for example, in a comment he scribbled in his notes on the lectures on the *Philosophy of Right,* that "the dramatic interest is an interest of action," that drama is "essentially actions (*Drama. Handlungen wesentlich*)."[13] The context of these remarks shows Hegel's insistence that there is nothing tragic in events that are merely natural – things that can be said to happen to one "from outside." Tragedies capture our interest because they begin in some willed action that nevertheless has unforeseen or unforeseeable consequences. "When something happens to me from outside, that is no relation of dignity, no dramatic interest, no interest of art. . . . [Dramatic interest] is a higher thing than that which only has natural consequences [and is] a result of external conditions."[14]

Hegel's stress on the *will* as opposed to what is *outside* in this interpretation is, of course, not Aristotelian,[15] but it is important again to notice where Hegel and Aristotle agree. Hegel's notion of tragedy – like Aristotle's – is broader than the particular plot structure associated with instances of contingent (what Hegel would call "external") factors that,

12. See the excellent treatment of the importance of the notion of action to Aristotle's *Poetics* in John Jones, *On Aristotle and Greek Tragedy* (New York: Oxford University Press, 1962), as well as the discussion in James Redfield, *Nature and Culture in the Iliad: The Tragedy of Hector* (Chicago: University of Chicago Press, 1975).

13. "Randbemerkungen," in *Grundlinien der Philosophie des Rechts,* ed. J. Hoffmeister (Hamburg: Meiner, 1955), 382.

14. This passage comes from the especially rich Hegelian appeal to tragedy in the 1824–5 lectures on the philosophy of right as recorded by his student von Griesheim (*Vorlesungen über Rechtsphilosophie,* ed. Karl-Heinz Ilting [Stuttgart and Bad Cannstatt: Frommann-Holzboog, 1974], 4, 319). I discuss further in Chapter 5 Hegel's appropriation of tragic situations and imagery for his treatment of topics such as legal and moral responsibility in the course on the philosophy of right.

15. As J. M. Bernstein puts it ("Conscience and Transgression: The Persistence of Misrecognition"), it is precisely this "apperceptive" character of action that makes Hegel's reading of tragedy different from Aristotle's.

as it were, stick to action in moral luck.[16] For Aristotle, the (moral luck) plot that shows a good man encountering undeserved misfortune is one that does not arouse pity or fear; the reverse plot, which shows a bad man passing into undeserved fortune, is likewise untragic. What makes the "Oedipus" plot interesting for him, by contrast, is precisely that it is a sort of "mean" – involving an action whose results stem not directly from what is deserved or undeserved, but rather in some sense from the tragically fertile middle ground of a *mistake.* [17]

Hegel's reading, too, seems to involve this middle ground, although his interpretation of that middle ground now involves the un-Aristotelian category of the will. From his Frankfurt years, Hegel had developed a strange (and quite un-Greek) notion of fate as "self-caused": at Frankfurt, this notion lay beneath his portrait of a "beautiful soul" figure who, in an act of *amor fati,* could tragically take on all consequences.[18] Echoes of this earlier reading of Hegel's can be seen in the "recognition"

16. Martha C. Nussbaum, in *The Fragility of Goodness,* has linked more tightly the issue of moral luck with Aristotle's interest in tragedy; but see the criticism of this by Jonathan Lear ("Katharsis," *Phronesis* 33:3 (1988): 297–326), who points out that while Aristotle admits that a virtuous man can be destroyed for no reason at all, such an event is, while unfortunate, not tragic in Aristotle's sense. (Lear cites in this context the important passage at *Poetics* 13, 1452b30–36.)

17. For Aristotle, as James Redfield has suggested, the *Poetics* may represent an opportunity for something of an ethical experiment: the virtues as they are presented in the *Ethics* are mere potentialities, *dunameis,* but in tragedy the spectator can witness their actualization. For Hegel, the more general applicability of tragic categories is similarly tied up with a relation between ethical ideal and actualization. For Hegel, as for Alasdair MacIntyre in our time, the ethical questions of the modern world arise in a realm of discourse that exists essentially "after virtue"; the relation between tragedy and ethics for him may more properly be said to concern in a concrete way how reason is to be practical. This difference – between the actualization of virtues and the making of reason to be concretely practical – is perhaps the most telling one between the Aristotelian and Hegelian uses of tragedy. Hegel's employment of tragedy for the task of interpreting the world of action or *Handlung,* while clearly having roots in the Aristotelian attempt to understand drama as praxis, nevertheless has a particularly post-Kantian ring.

18. Hegel's striking portrait of this figure is part of a dense but rich set of fragments that he wrote at Frankfurt in the years before coming to Jena. These fragments were published posthumously by Herman Nohl under the title "The Spirit of Christianity and Its Fate" (*Hegels Theologische Jugendschriften,* ed. Herman Nohl [Tübingen: Mohr, 1907], 243–342; English translation in Hegel, *Early Theological Writings,* trans. T. M. Knox [Chicago: University of Chicago Press, 1948], 182–301). Hegel's religious-cum-political speculations there on the possible grounds for forms of unity that go beyond the divisions of Kantian morality have been read in part in terms of Hegel's extraordinary friendship at the time with Hölderlin (see Christoph Jamme, *Ein ungelehrtes Buch: die philosophische Gemeinschaft zwischen Hölderlin und Hegel in Frankfurt,* 1797–1800 [Bonn: Bouvier, 1983]).

scene of Hegel's *Antigone* interpretation in the *PhG*, but in some sense Antigone in the first section of "Spirit" will set up the need for a reconciliation that will not arrive until the final section of "Spirit," where the beautiful soul appears. The *PhG* is thus a splitting apart by historical/ teleological motion of two things the Frankfurt essay had brought together: the (Greek) tragic hero(ine) and the (modern and conscientious) beautiful soul.

Because Hegel places so much stress on the way in which Antigone's deed "breaks open" the set of concerns that we will have with justification, motivation, and identity in action, we will first turn to his construal of the Sophoclean play – or, it might be better to say, to the Hegelian *version* of *Antigone*, since the *Phenomenology* offers the initiation of a distinctive Hegelian dramatic *ergon*. Given the stress we have placed on the *non* immediate character of agency in Hegel, it might be thought strange to look to a character such as Antigone, whose action would seem to be the very picture of immediacy. As I hope to show in what follows, however, such an appearance is only part of the received view of "Hegel's Antigone" that needs to be questioned.[19]

2. The Hegelian Antigone

Sophocles' Antigone is perhaps the most vivid example of the sort of "silence" we have mentioned as characterizing the heroes and heroines of ancient tragedy: her conversation with her sister in the dark outside the city walls is striking in part because it involves no apparent deliberation or even hesitation about what her purpose must be. She comes before the spectator already as a determined and very decided agent.

The Antigone so central to the opening pages of Hegel's "Spirit" chap-

19. Hegel's account of the conflict of the Antigone is perhaps best known from his *Lectures on Aesthetics* (Hegel, *Werke: Theorie Werkausgabe*, 20 vols., ed. Eva Moldenhauer and Karl Markus Michel [Frankfurt: Suhrkamp, 1970], 15,549–50; translation in Hegel, *Aesthetics: Lectures on Fine Art*, trans. T. M. Knox [Oxford: Clarendon Press, 1975], 2, 1217–18) and what George Steiner in his book *Antigones* (Oxford: Clarendon, 1984, 37) has called the "canonical text" equating Creon's right and Antigone's in the *Lectures on the Philosophy of Religion*. In the English-speaking world, Hegel's thesis has been much discussed since A. C. Bradley's influential 1909 essay on "Hegel's Theory of Tragedy" (republished, along with translations of the relevant Hegelian texts in *Hegel on Tragedy*, ed. Anne and Henry Paolucci [New York: Harper and Row, 1975; reprint ed., Westport, CT: Greenwood Press, 1978]), most recently in studies by Michelle Gellrich, *Tragedy and Theory: The Problem of Conflict since Aristotle* (Princeton: Princeton University Press, 1988), and Martha Nussbaum, *The Fragility of Goodness: Luck and Ethics in Greek Tragedy and Philosophy* (Cambridge: Cambridge University Press, 1986), Chapter 3.

ter in the *PhG* arrives in a similarly silent fashion. Hegel gives the phenomenological spectator no prior account of why her deed in burying her brother will count so importantly for the initial explication of Spirit. Nor, for that matter, is there an explanation of how she "got" to the beginning of the "Spirit" chapter at all – for, as we discussed in the previous chapter, she comes on the scene at one of the most notoriously difficult transition points of the whole book, that from the chapter on "Reason" (which culminates in the clearly Kantian moment of "law-testing reason") to the "Spirit" chapter (which requires a chronological move back to the world of ancient Greece).

The philosophical reasons underlying the larger transition from Reason to Spirit I have discussed in the foregoing chapter, but let us focus for the moment on Antigone's striking appearance within that transition. What are we to make of the fact that Hegel uses her famous lines about the eternity of the "laws" according to which she has acted ("they are not of yesterday or today, but everlasting") as a sort of bridge from a clearly Kantian moment to the concerns that will make their appearance in "Spirit"? To ask the question most naively: are we to read the Hegelian Antigone, looking forward to her role in the "Spirit" chapter, as a Sophoclean figure revealing the structures of Greek ethical life? Or, looking back to the chapter her words have just concluded, are we to see her rather as a figure whose deed is to be unpacked in terms of the explicit concerns with conscience and beauty so important to the moral world opened up by Kant?

In some sense, as we shall see in the following, she is both – at once the breaking open of action in its Greek immediacy and a figure whose role in the *PhG* will be determined by the concerns of (particularly Romantic) readers of the generation to which Hegel belonged, a generation that construed itself in the wake of Kant's "critical" revolution. As we discussed in Chapter 1, this is a famously difficult transition; we showed there that Spirit introduced a new explanatory consideration for agency; and that Hegel seems to take up a post-Kantian, Romantic set of claims about something that was implicit in the Greek ideal and hence a "new alternative" for the self-consideration of modernity. This dual-sidedness – Antigone's role as opening up the question of action in "Spirit" and, as will be shown in Chapter 4, her role in its recapitulatory "reconciliation" – is part of what makes her "Hegel's Antigone." At the same time, it will allow Hegel's reading to have a singular advantage over some other reigning interpretations of the play that, often despite their best efforts to distinguish the Greek context of her action,

nonetheless cannot avoid reading Antigone as a modern heroine of conscience: Hegel's account, I will claim, notices the important differences
in a construal of Greek agency – the priority of action over character,
for example – while at the same time showing how her action initiates a
consideration of claims about agency that will in fact lead on to modern
considerations of conscience.

In setting up this account of Hegel's Antigone in the *PhG*, it is important first to distinguish the reading that will follow from a certain received view of Hegel's reading of *Antigone* – a view that is almost always
traceable to Hegel's later (and, I claim, less philosophically fecund)
readings of the play in his Berlin lecture series on aesthetics and on religion. Among the most frequently made criticisms of Hegel's interpretation of the *Antigone*, for example, are that (1) in justifying the
"right" of Creon against Antigone, it ignores the greater sense of no-
bility many readers have attached to Antigone and thereby reduces the
drama of Sophocles' play to a struggle between two equally justified an-
tagonists,[20] and that (2) it seeks in an untragic way for Sophoclean hints
at an ultimate resolution of their conflict – that Hegel's reading finds
more "closure" than the tragedy allows.[21] Only recently has it been
shown by George Steiner (and, following him, Michael Schulte)[22] the
extent to which this version of Hegel's reading of the *Antigone* has been
based almost exclusively – "canonically," in Steiner's assertion – on passages from Hegel's *Aesthetics* and *Philosophy of Religion*. A concentration
on these later works has thus ignored Hegel's earlier reading of the play
in the *Phenomenology of Spirit*. In this section, I will attempt to show how
rich this earlier Hegelian treatment of the *Antigone* is for his philosophy
of action, while at the same time presenting a reading that neither ignores the "tragic" fact of collision nor merely equalizes the strength of
Antigone's claim vis-à-vis Creon's.

The fundamental claim behind this reading for Hegel's philosophy
of action is that the ethical action associated with Antigone's deed –
while being an essentially *failed* instance of action – nevertheless is for

---

20. Recent attention to the inequalities in Hegel's treatment of Antigone has been given
by Martha Nussbaum (*The Fragility of Goodness*, 66–7), who maintains Hegel's intention
to describe equally justified sides but who suggests nevertheless possible Hegelian
grounds for why one may regard Antigone as nobler than Creon.

21. Cf., for example, Gellrich, *Tragedy and Theory*, 23–93, and Nussbaum, *The Fragility of
Goodness*, 52.

22. Steiner, *Antigones*, 37; Michael Schulte, *Die "Tragödie im Sittlichen": Zur Dramentheorie
Hegels*, 11.

Hegel a privileged instance of action in general, a sort of "ideal type" of action from which important elements of Hegel's account of modern ethical agency can be seen in relief.[23] Thus, it is a question for Hegel how Antigone's deed, like any action of modern ethical life, is to be regarded as the "agent's own" deed – an intentional action, which can be understood in some sense to be "free."

As Terry Pinkard has suggested, this tie between the Antigone of the world of Sophocles and the Antigone of the world after Kant can be articulated precisely in terms of the freedom Hegel claimed for the agent of Greek ethical life: both Antigone and modern agents can be said to be free – or genuinely "in" their actions – insofar as they (1) know what they do, (2) know why they do it, and (3) identify with their actions.[24] I shall use this three-part claim about agency to structure the discussion of Hegel's account of Antigone's deed. In each case, as we shall see, the inherent retrospectivity of agency on the Hegelian view will come to light: first, how an action can be understood as intentional without assuming some incorrigible access of the agent to his own prior intention; second, how desires and reasons are not understood in terms of a given, prior "motivational set," but are themselves "come to" in the light of what actually occurs in the action; and finally, how the agent's identification with an action arises in an expressive way from the deed itself.

Oedipus, Antigone, and Agent's Regret: The Retrospectivity of "Agent's Knowledge." Hegel makes what would appear to be two incompatible claims about the agent's knowledge in the tragedy-inspired section of the *PhG* he entitled "The Ethical Order." On the one hand, "the absolute right of the ethical consciousness is that the deed, the *shape* in which it *actualizes*

---

23. It is for this reason, I maintain, that Hegel's account of Antigone in the *Phenomenology* – where, as opposed to the *Aesthetics*, the concern is more explicitly with the notion of action – reveals less the familiar equivalencies of right usually associated with Hegel's reading of the play than a more sympathetic account of Antigone's character and role.

A similar claim about tragedy as a sort of "ideal type of action" may be found in the discussion of Schulte, *Die 'Tragoedie im Sittlichen,'* 185: "ethical action is at once an extreme case of action generally and, precisely because it is an extreme case of action, is a model of what action generally is which can be described more sharply than in the experience of other structures of action." Schulte appears to mean, however, something quite different about what of action is revealed in the case of Antigone than will be maintained here: his understanding of Hegel's account of action links action too closely with *Sollen* and does not take into account the explicit discussion of action in Hegel's later *Rechtsphilosophie.*

24. Pinkard, *Hegel's "Phenomenology,"* 188.

itself, shall be nothing else but what it *knows*" (§467); on the other hand, ethical self-consciousness can only "[learn] from its deed the developed nature of what it *actually* did" (§469).

These two quotations suggest that, for Hegel, whatever it can mean for a deed to be the agent's "own" is something that cannot simply be understood in terms of an agent's awareness of her prior intention. Something of what the deed *is* – and hence who the agent is to be taken to be – can only emerge for the agent's knowledge *in* the action itself.

The famous Greek concern with this question – how, for example, guilt for an action whose particulars an agent has not fully known can, on the view of responsibility considered in the first *Oedipus* play, nonetheless "stick" to an agent – is part of Hegel's concern here.[25] ("[T]he son does not recognize his father in the man who has wronged him and whom he slays, nor his mother in the queen whom he makes his wife. In this way, a power which shuns the light of day ensnares the ethical self-consciousness, a power which breaks forth only after the deed is done, and seizes the doer in the act." [§469])

But the more *interesting* case of retrospective reconsideration of action, on his view, is that of an agent whose actions are, on her own descrip-

---

25. As with his take on the *Antigone,* Hegel's account of the Oedipus plays requires understanding that there is at work in the plays both a standard of responsibility and intentionality that is no longer valid in modern morality, and an heroic figure whose active willing pushes toward the changing of that existing standard. Hegel's discussion of Oedipus in the *Philosophy of Right*'s account of "morality" reflects both of these sides. It was Oedipus' act of taking responsibility for his deeds that, Hegel thought, first pointed away from the Greek tendency to look to external objects (oracles and divine signs) as grounds for action and toward the modern notion of agency, under which there is a "right of the action to evince itself as known and willed by the subject as thinker" (PR #120). The "right of the thinker" or "right of intention," as Hegel calls it, means that the modern agent must be considered as cognizant of certain facts about the world: only those persons to whom we do not accord full mental capacity (children and the insane) can be allowed to claim that they did not know, for example, that striking a match in a refinery would lead to a conflagration.

As a hero of ancient drama, Oedipus of course takes on a wider responsibility for his deed than a modern would, because the distinction between the subjective and objective sides of a deed (or, as Hegel puts it, between the mere deed, or *Tat,* and what I would agree to call my action, *Handlung*) had not yet come into being. But because Oedipus' action nevertheless involves a step toward that taking of responsibility characteristic of what we call moral action, Hegel sees in Oedipus a notion of honor or dignity that bears some resemblance to the "honor of being a thinking individual and will" (§120R) that the modern will accords itself (*Die Philosophie des Rechts: Die Mitschriften Wannenmann [Heidelberg 1817/18] und Homeyer [Berlin 1818/19],* ed. Karl-Heinz Ilting [Stuttgart: Klett-Cotta, 1983], 78).

tion, quite knowing:[26] in Antigone's case, the "ethical consciousness is more complete," the guilt "more inexcusable" because she "knows *beforehand* the law and the power which it opposes" and yet "knowingly commits the crime" (§470).

Hegel's focus on Antigone rather than Oedipus here suggests that we will have to explore more fully the retrospective character of intentionality and motivation involved in Antigone's deed. But, for the moment, it is worth looking at what may be the central piece of the distinctively Hegelian interpretation of Sophocles' play: Hegel's (somewhat un-Sophoclean) reading of the *regret* he hears expressed in Antigone's lines as she is about to be led off to the burial chamber:

> Should the gods think that this is righteousness,
> in suffering I'll see my error clear.
> But if it is the others who are wrong
> I wish them no greater punishment than mine.
>
> (lines 925–8)[27]

That second line Hegel translates as "Because we suffer, we acknowledge that we err" (§470). As many have pointed out, such a reading is a mistranslation of Sophocles' lines; but Hegel's intention is clearly less that of textual fidelity than that of interpretive reconstruction of Antigone's deed in terms of a wider notion of tragic agency and regret.[28]

We must return to the question asked at the chapter's start about how Hegel's nonvoluntarist view of action will account for notions like regret and responsibility. On the voluntarist notion of agency, regret is a matter of acknowledging that one could have acted in a different way: that the intention taken to be causative of one's deed could have been a different intention. Hegel's understanding of Antigone's lines suggests a different notion of the relation between action and regret – a regret that, as in cases of moral luck, does not express a wish that the agent might have acted differently, since the agent is in fact aware that she

---

26. At Frankfurt, it had been the *Oedipus at Colonus* that made the more interesting case, in Hegel's view. Despite all that the account of the "Ethical Order" in the *PhG* owes to Antigone, the effect of the second Oedipus play on Hegel in the *PhG* should not be discounted.

27. Here and elsewhere in this chapter, I have used Elizabeth Wyckoff's translation of Sophocles' Antigone in David Grene and Richmond Lattimore, ed., *Sophocles I* (Chicago: University of Chicago Press, 1954), 157–204.

28. It has been speculated, of course, that these lines might represent part of Hegel's own earlier (and now lost) translation of *Antigone*.

could *not* have acted differently. Rather, regret must be taken to open up a reconsideration of just how the agent *is* in her deed. We need to look more carefully at what a desire or intention is on this view and how it is that an agent understands her action as her own.

What kind of account of responsibility, then, is finally suggested by the retrospective considerations of action we have seen in Antigone's case? Or does assessing responsibility become just a matter of detailing a casuistry in which the *intentional* side of action is put aside?

The retrospective view of action that Hegel puts forward here *does* seem to require a casuistry, but that does not mean that Hegel is blocked from giving an account of intentional agency.[29] Hegel's account of agency will also incorporate an intentional or first-person element of action, but it will be one that is not determined by an incorrigible content to which the agent has exclusive access; rather, what can be taken as intentional is something shaped by a process of revision in which an agent's account of what he did and why he did it is necessarily part of an ongoing dialectic between impersonal and personal sides of agency – in Antigone's case, between her (personal and prereflective) commitment to "family" and the (impersonal and retrospectively understood) relation of those claims to the broader ethical world in which they can be articulated.

Retrospectivity is a factor not just in terms of an agent like Antigone's saying *what* it is that she has done, however. The motivation underlying such an action as hers is also something that is subject to retrospectivity, as we will see in the following section, which explores the nature of Antigone's prereflective commitments to her family.

Desire and Retrospectivity: Assessing the "Why" of an Agent's Action. Although we have seen from the first consideration that Antigone comes to recognize in her agent's regret that *what* she attempted to do proved in the end different than she thought, we still have to consider the way in which she comes to understand *why* she does what she does. Hegel's well-known claim about her deed – that she acts out of an underlying ethical connection to family, as opposed to Creon's claim on behalf of the city – suggests again a kind of immediacy or givenness. The story is, however,

29. The casuistical side of Hegel's account is evident in his discussion of agency in the "morality" section of the *Philosophy of Right*, where Hegel makes clear how intentionality comes to count within a scheme of modern agency.

more complicated: the apparent immediacy of motivation in Antigone's action will be shown to have a retrospective character as well.

Hegel is quite clear about the apparent immediacy:

> The ruin (*Untergang*) of the ethical Substance and its passage (*Übergang*) into another form is thus determined by the fact that the ethical consciousness is directed towards the law in a way that is essentially *immediate*. This determination of immediacy means that Nature as such enters into the ethical act, the reality of which simply reveals the contradiction and the germ of destruction inherent in the beautiful harmony and tranquil equilibrium of the ethical Spirit itself. (§476)

What does Hegel mean by this claim? In presenting the transition from the Kantian realm of "law-giving and law-testing reason," Hegel stresses that the "laws" of the sort Antigone cites "simply *are*, and nothing more" and stresses throughout the *Phenomenology* section on *Sittlichkeit* the "immediate" character of Spirit and consciousness at this stage.[30] An understanding of this immediacy is clearly crucial for the transition Hegel intends from agency on the model of the Kantian moral law to the notion of "Spirit." But what this immediacy consists of and how it is to be understood in connection with an analysis of Antigone's and Creon's actions and their motivation is a question that requires a closer look at Hegel's reading of the play.

What Hegel means by the "immediacy" of an ethical law can perhaps best be seen in the way in which Sophocles initially portrays Antigone. An edict has been passed whose meaning she sees clearly: she is not to be allowed to bury her brother. "Such orders they say the worthy Creon gives to you and me – yes, yes, I say *me* – " (line 31): Antigone seems to have realized in the very hearing of the edict what it means in terms of her own action. She will not be seen in Hamlet-like deliberations about what she should do, but has made up her mind to die in the face of the law regardless of any possibility of another penalty. It is Antigone's assumption, on hearing the law, that Creon had set his sights on her in particular; Creon of course was thinking of no such thing. "What *man* has dared to do it?" he asks (line 248) when told of the burial. Antigone

---

30. Cf., for example, §441: "Spirit is the ethical life of a people insofar as it is immediate truth"; and §450: the "moment which expresses the ethical sphere in this element of immediacy or [simple] being, or which is an immediate consciousness of itself, both as essence and this particular self, in an 'other,' i.e. as a natural ethical community – this is the Family."

herself tells Creon when the two first encounter each other, "I knew that I must die; how could I not? even without your warning" (lines 460–1).

Hegel's description of the immediate laws of the realm of Spirit suggest Antigone more than her antagonist: "they are . . . unalienated spirits transparent to themselves, stainless celestial figures that preserve in all their differences the undefiled innocence and harmony of their essential nature" (*PhG* §437). Yet Hegel's plural reference to the laws of immediate spirit seems to include Creon, and a look at the play shows that Creon is presented as being as unhesitating and decisive as Antigone (lines 162–210). The army has just left the night before, and already in the night he has made the decision about burial. The Creon who appears in public immediately announces his ascension to the throne, denounces all who do not take the state as their first friend, so to speak, and states the edict: Eteocles will have the city's honor, Polyneices will not be buried.

Both Antigone and Creon are, then, presented as acting without hesitancy or prior deliberation, but it must be noted – and this will become a key point of Hegel's reading – that Antigone reacts with a much keener sense of what else her action must involve. Hegel's sense of Antigone's greater self-awareness can be further glimpsed in the relative length and sensitivity of his accounts of the two "laws." The "human law" that Creon represents is described in a single paragraph (§455) in which it is difficult to find any distinctive aspect of Creon's character as revealed in the play; instead, Hegel discusses there rather generally the power of the state to demand citizens' service in war. The description of Antigone's "divine law," on the other hand, is not only some three times longer (§456–459), but every significant detail seems to be drawn on the character and plight of Antigone.

Most significant for Hegel's account of the law that Antigone represents is not, as we might have expected, her initial speech before Creon with its famous claim about the "eternal law":

> For me it was not Zeus who made that order.
> Nor did that Justice who lives with the gods below
> mark out such laws to hold among mankind.
> Nor did I think your orders were so strong
> that you, a mortal man, could over-run
> the gods' unwritten and unfailing laws.
> Not now, nor yesterday's, they always live,
> and no one knows their origin in time.
>
> (lines 450–6)

Hegel does indeed quote from these lines in the transition from the "Reason" chapter to the "Spirit" chapter, but when he comes to analyze Antigone in the "Spirit" chapter itself, he turns rather to the peculiar "law" that she articulates in an often-disputed speech later in the play:

> Had I had children or their father dead,
> I'd let them moulder. I should not have chosen
> in such a case to cross the state's decree.
> What is the law that lies behind these words?
> One husband gone, I might have found another,
> or a child from a new man in first child's place,
> but with my parents hid away in death,
> no brother, ever, could spring up for me.
> Such was the law by which I honored you.
>
> (lines 906–14)

How are these lines of apparently contingent and prudential reasoning – which Antigone only retrospectively articulates *as* relevant to her reasons for acting – to be understood to express Antigone's motivation when compared to the absolute sound of her initial speech about the "eternal law"? And how is the appeal to such a piece of reasoning consistent with the "immediacy" associated with Antigone's action?

Hegel will argue that the deepest sense of her motivation is, in fact, what is articulated retrospectively. I will turn momentarily to Hegel's reading of the lines themselves and what he thinks they reveal about the practical identity visible in Antigone's action as that of a *sister* on behalf of a brother in the specific ethical context of ancient Greece. Before looking at the content of the speech, however, it is worth considering what Hegel wants to make of the fact of the retrospectivity involved in intention and motivation here.

We have said that Hegel's analysis of tragic action in Antigone's case seems to claim something like the following: that the desire or intention relevant for understanding her deed is not to be found in prior deliberation, but is rather *embodied* in the deed itself and read off of it retrospectively. If this is right, one might ask how far an example like Antigone's may go toward illuminating elements of an account of agency more generally.

Perhaps the strongest point in favor of Hegel's argument is that *if* a consideration of retrospectivity in certain cases is crucial to understanding an action, then a voluntarist account, by its own assumptions, will not be able to take into account such elements. But perhaps retrospectivity is not so important a feature of our agency. Aren't there many ordinary actions in everyday life that would seem to require no particular retrospective consideration on our part? I am thirsty and take a drink of water, for example, or I wish to see a friend and walk next door to speak to him: where is retrospectivity involved in these cases?

As Michael Quante has argued, a retrospectivity about the content of actions can be present even in such ordinary cases.[31] Thus, I may have been self-deceived about the content of my purpose (on his example, I really wanted beer but thought I wanted ice cream), or I may come in my action to see that the content of my purpose has in fact altered (I did want ice cream when I ordered it, but now I want beer). Revisability may concern not only the wider ramifications of seeing how my purpose is objectified in the world ("didn't this marriage really have a prudential aspect in that it forged a business alliance?") but also my own self-understanding of the "inner" side of my purpose at the time ("could I really have been acting out of love if I treated her that way?").

Quante sees such examples as arguing for the revisability of the *content* of my intention (that X, not Y was my purpose) but not of the *form* of my action (my sense that *I* was performing *some* action X or Y): "a subject cannot be wrong *that* a purpose is *his,* that it is *his* mental state."[32] Knowledge of the content, then, is revisable, but knowledge that I was doing something – "agent's knowledge," or what Quante calls the *Wissen um das Mein* in an action – would sound like the sort of immediacy that Hegel describes as at first displayed in Antigone's action.

Yet, if the content side of my intention is so inherently corrigible, we might ask, what is left of *das Wissen um das Mein* except the merely formal claim that it is indeed "me" in whatever action it is that I am supposed to have done? If agent's knowledge is to have any thickness, it must consider the relation of the corrigible elements of the deed to the "I" of the agent supposedly in them. Coming to know oneself as an agent, then, would involve a move from the personal and immediate sense that one is "in" the action one intends to the impersonal and corrigible consideration of what exactly that action was and how it might be "mine," given the motivations or intentions I can retrospectively read off of it. In this process of correlating personal and impersonal aspects of my action, my experience is one of coming to make more articulate

---

31. Michael Quante, *Hegels Begriff der Handlung* (Stuttgart and Bad Cannstatt: Frommann-Holzboog, 1993), 104–108.

32. Quante, *Hegels Begriff der Handlung,* 107.

the elements that are implicit in my action. This side of action – what Hegel scholars have spoken of in terms of the "praxical presuppositions" of agency or the "prereflective whole" that is not yet explicit for an agent[33] – is precisely what must now be taken into consideration in terms of the most fundamental issue of agent retrospectivity: the inherently *expressive* practical identity of the tragic agent.

Identity of the Tragic Agent: Nature, Sexual Difference, and the "Mask" of Givenness. In order to look at how the identity of a tragic agent is connected to her action, I will turn back to the *content* of Antigone's retrospective speech about the obligation to bury her brother, as opposed to other family members. One of the striking things about Hegel's account is that it looks to this speech as a crucial window onto Antigone's identity. It is sometimes argued, for instance, that perhaps Antigone is confused and intent on the action that caused her death and does not really know what she is saying at all but is merely trying to express her unqualified affection for Polynices.[34] Hegel, however, takes what she says seriously as an articulation of Antigone's reasons for acting. For him, this speech does not qualify her sense of family obligation but rather shows her to be the one person in her whole world who understands what the family (and thus the ethical order as a whole) ultimately means. The sister, he says, "has the highest intuition (*Ahnung*) of ethical essence (*Wesen*)" (§457).

What does Hegel mean by this "intuition" of the ethical captured in Antigone's speech? First of all, Hegel's stress on the ethical character of the relation between Antigone and Polynices seems to point up the fact that the motivation for Antigone's "immediate" action is not a matter of desire or feeling for Polynices as a distinct person. Antigone describes not a feeling for *Polynices,* but a sense of obligation for her brother – or, it almost seems, for Brother.[35] She does not recall his personal traits, she does not notice *what* her brother has done. She does not distinguish

---

33. The first expression is that of Joseph Flay (*Hegel's Quest for Certainty* [Albany: State University of New York Press, 1984]); the second is that of Terry Pinkard, "Virtues, Morality and Sittlichkeit: From Maxims to Practice," *European Journal of Philosophy* 7:2 (August 1999): 217–239.

34. Many readers of the play over the centuries have, of course, simply obelized her lines here as being an interpolation into Sophocles' original text. Yet if the lines are an addition, they are a very early one, indeed, since one of our ancient sources for them is Aristotle's *Rhetoric.*

35. Cf. Nussbaum, *The Fragility of Goodness,* 63–67, in arguing against the view that Antigone's attachment to Polynices is motivated by eros.

him, in fact, from her other brother, Eteocles, except to notice that one has been buried and thus does not require her services, whereas the other lies there unburied. When Ismene asks her, for instance, if she will break the law to do this deed, Antigone reminds her of the important fact: "He is my brother, and yours, though you may wish he were not" (line 45). Antigone can only imagine what it will be like to lie next to her dead brother when she herself has died in burying him: "Friend shall I lie with him, yes friend with friend, when I have dared the crime of piety" (lines 73–4).

Hegel sees that Antigone's devotion to Brother, not to Polynices, means in effect a duty not to her living brother, but to her brother as dead. Her two brothers died fighting each other, but she cannot distinguish them to see their enmity, nor that one's action made him a patriot while the other's action made him a traitor. Her brother is not what he has *done,* but rather what he *is.*

> [Antigone's] deed no longer concerns the living but the dead, the individual who, after a long succession of separate disconnected experiences, concentrates himself into a single completed shape, and has raised himself out of the unrest of the accidents of life into the calm of simple universality. (§451)

Thus we see the objective quality of Antigone's relation to her brother: to love someone for what he *is,* for his being, is to love him in his inaction, is to love a corpse. We have also thereby some insight into Antigone's "hot mind over chilly things," for her attachment to the realm of the dead.

The obligation that Antigone as a member of her family feels toward her dead brother has two important consequences for the relation between the two fundamental "laws" of ethical life: in the first instance, Hegel presents the family's duty of burial as the only possible avenue of legitimation for the political regime within immediate ethical life and for the reconciliation of individuals to it;[36] second, Antigone's sense

---

36. As Hegel presents it, the legitimacy of the political order in ethical life – most importantly, the authority of the city to demand the service of individuals in war – depends on the family's services of burial. Even when death is asked for as the greatest sacrifice an individual can make for his fellow citizens – a willed act of courage in battle – it does not appear so to the individual members of families within the city themselves, as individuals. The city's power to declare war can thus appear as a coercive one that upsets the "established order" of citizens and "violates their right to independence" (§455):

> This movement [death in battle] falls, it is true, within the ethical community, and has this for its End; death is the fulfillment and supreme 'work' which the

that the general family obligation to perform the funerary observances devolves on her particularly as his sister is crucial to the possibility of her recognition of herself as a woman and thus also of reconciliation with the ethical order.

The notion that Antigone's deed has a purpose and shape that is specific to a particular sex is something which Hegel takes up through a consideration of how the pain of the loss of a family member in war is especially acute when a sister loses a brother. A sister cannot really recognize herself in any of her other relationships, Hegel holds, because they all involve by their nature the contingency of loss, the impure element of desire or an inequality of relation (§456–7). Her union with her husband is unequal, based on desire, and produces a child, who grows up and goes away. Her relation to her parents, which is rooted in inequality, also ceases to be the same as it was when the daughter reaches maturity. But in her brother she recognizes her own blood, and a relationship without

> individual as such undertakes on its behalf. But in so far as he is essentially a particular individual, it is an accident that his death was directly connected with his 'work' for the universal and was the result of it. (*PhG* §452)

Antigone sees Polynices' death still as something natural and accidental – an event "without consolation and reconciliation" (§452). It is the task of the family to effect some reconciliation between individual experience and ethical universal by claiming back the memory of the dead individual family member from the ravages of nature with a service – a ritual burial – that preserves his memory as someone who is an individual.

> The dead individual, by having liberated his being from his action or his negative unity, is an empty singular, merely a passive being-for-another, at the mercy of every lower irrational individuality and the forces of abstract material elements, all of which are now more powerful than himself: the former on account of the life they possess, the latter on account of their negative nature. The Family keeps away from the dead this dishonoring of him by unconscious appetites and abstract entities, and puts its own action in their place, and weds the blood-relation to the bosom of the earth, to the elemental imperishable individuality. The Family thereby makes him a member of a community which prevails over and holds under control the forces of particular material elements and the lower forms of life . . . (§452)

The act of burial, as an intentional and ethical action, thus renders the death of an individual in war as something that other family members can experience not as a contingent or coerced event, but as part of an ethical order.

Cf. the helpful discussion in Schulte (*Die 'Tragödie im Sittlichen'*), where Hegel's *Phenomenology* account of the action that justifies the ethical realm and "purifies" it from a merely natural state of coercion is compared to his account of the same moment in the *Natural Law* essay: in the latter, it is only the sacrificial act of the aristocrat soldier that constitutes the ethical order, whereas in the *Phenomenology* account, the role of the justifying ethical action is given primarily to the female members of the family. The difference in these two accounts reveals as well Hegel's new understanding in the *PhG* of the role of the family and the private realm.

any contingency, desire, or relation of domination. The brother–sister relation is thus for Hegel the purest ethical relation:

> [Brother and sister] are the same blood which has, however, in them reached a state of rest and equilibrium. Therefore, they do not desire one another, nor have they given to, or received from, one another this independent being-for-self; on the contrary, they are free individualities in regard to each other. (§457)

This equilibrium opens the possibility that the relation between sister and brother, unlike every other relation in the ethical realm, involves recognition of individuality: "the moment of the individual self, recognizing and being recognized, can here assert its right, because it is linked to the equilibrium of the blood and is a relation devoid of desire" (§457). Yet, despite Hegel's insistence that "the individual self, recognizing and being recognized, can here assert its right," the character of that recognition, as we have seen in Hegel's description of Antigone's regard for her brother, also cannot yield ethical individuality: she does indeed recognize him as Polynices, an individual distinct from others, but, because of her neglect of the law of the masculine realm in which her brother participated, does not see him as an individual *agent*, a particular family member who also toils for the universal.

The unavailability of a sufficient recognition of individuality within the Greek ethical realm will point up a central facet of Hegel's account of practical identity. As Terry Pinkard has put it, agency within the Greek context is, on Hegel's view, *free* agency in the sense that agents know what they are doing, why they are doing it, and can find their identity within their actions. Yet, in comparison to *modern* agency, the construal of individuality within the Greek context rests on certain given social roles – the "natural" determinations of sexual difference, for example, in the laws of male and female agents.[37]

Hegel's narrative within the "Spirit" chapter portrays this givenness of Greek agency – that what Antigone represents is necessarily a feminine "law" and what Creon represents is necessarily a masculine "law" – in terms of the *masks* of tragic characters. Masks reflect a certain determination of action implicit in tragic characters before they even act – and are hence one part of the tragic spectator's experience of the decidedness or "silence" of heroes that we have mentioned.

---

37. Despite the crucial importance of sexual difference to agency in the first section of "Spirit," there has been surprisingly little attempt to spell out Hegel's intentions here. For a helpful reading, see Daniel Dahlstrom, "Die Quelle der Sittlichkeit in Hegels Phänomenologie des Geistes," *Hegel-Jahrbuch* 1987: 256–261.

This implicit givenness behind Greek agency is something that does not allow agents to be completely reconciled to their actions. Hegel's stress on Antigone's words "*Because* we suffer, we acknowledge that we erred" suggests that it is only by a sort of tragic acceptance of the necessary partitiveness (or maskedness) of the action – an *amor fati* – that tragic agents can come to terms with their identities in the actions they have performed.[38]

A consideration of the maskedness of agency in tragedy gives us grounds, then, for seeing how Antigone will figure twice in Hegel's account of practical identity. Considered as a character within the Greek context, her action can be "reconciled" only in an *amor fati*. But if her mask can somehow be dropped, and the givenness of social roles in Greek agency replaced by a notion of practical identity that looks to the individual's freedom of choice, there is a possibility that the Antigone more familiar to our modern age – Antigone construed as a heroine of conscience – may emerge. We will see the appearance of this different Antigone in the shape of the beautiful soul, once agency has come to terms with its own maskedness or "theatricality."

3. From Tragic Action to Comic Theatricality

What, then, has emerged from a concern with the tragic moment of action? We have seen a retrospectivity and expressivity of agency from a reflection on the "result"-oriented character of tragic action, as well as

---

38. One thing this reading underscores is that those who label Hegel as a nontragic "reconciliationist" in his reading of Sophocles misunderstand what he means by reconciliation. That Hegel does not intend Antigone's moment of recognition to be a moment of resolution in the sense of a "closure" that suppresses conflict may be seen in his remark in the second *Phenomenology* discussion of tragedy that there are two possible "resolutions" of the conflictual elements of tragedy: the resolution of "death" (as in the *Antigone*), where both parties are destroyed, and the resolution of the "upper world" in some sort of reconciliation that allows a deed to be pardoned (§740). Thus, Hegel does not view Antigone's recognition as reconciliatory. As a mere recognition of error, it portends a redemptive possibility neither for Antigone (who is about to die) nor for the ethical world (whose loss she may also be mourning in acknowledging her "error"). In stressing Antigone's incomplete, unreconciling moment of recognition, rather than the later and genuinely reconciling model of a play like the *Oedipus at Colonus,* Hegel thereby leaves his second model for a role in shaping what I have called the second appropriation of tragedy in the *Phenomenology:* the reconciliation effected at the end of the treatment of Spirit's action. As we will see in that case, however, it will not be the Greek reconciliation play but the modern romantic novel of the beautiful soul's forgiveness that is the most determinative model for understanding the possibility of reconciliation in modern agency.

a concept of an agent's practical identity in the unreconciled terms of a tragic hero's acceptance of the fatedness of a *mask*.

But the possibility of *dropping* that mask is one that Hegel raises at the very end of his account of the tragic art. This awareness of the mask's presence suggests that another attitude of an agent toward her action might be possible, given the new importance of *interpreting* action as it takes place before a set of spectators: that is, for the agent to adopt a notion of self-consciousness that is conscious of itself precisely *as* appearing before spectators. Such a notion is implicit already in Hegel's strange claim that the tragic heroes themselves, by their very language, are "the artists themselves." This is Hegel's account of what is involved in tragedy's emergence as a genre from the epic form of narrative, where the bard was the (self-conscious) "artist" making his various heroes articulate. In Hegel's view of tragedy, we have instead, first of all, heroes who "step forth" to speak their lines before an audience. Unlike Aristotle, who thought the gist of a tragedy could be gained simply by reading it, Hegel held that it was crucial that drama involves a presentation in front of an audience. Moreover, what those tragic heroes *say* when they step forth reveals them as self-conscious artists, Hegel thinks:

> They [the tragic characters] are artists, who do not express with unconscious naturalness and naivety the *external* aspect of their resolves and enterprises, as happens in the language accompanying ordinary actions in actual life; on the contrary, they give utterance to the inner essence, they prove the rightness of their action, and the 'pathos' which moves them is soberly asserted and definitely expressed in its universal individuality, free from the accidents of circumstance and personal idiosyncrasies. (§733)

Hegel is particularly struck by the ability of tragic characters to speak about their situation in *impersonal* terms – by metaphor or by analogy, as in Antigone's description of her own situation as she prepares to be buried alive in the rock chamber as like that of Tantalus' daughter Niobe:

> Pitiful was the death that stranger died,
> our queen once, Tantalus' daughter. The rock
> it covered her over, like stubborn ivy it grew.
> Still, as she wastes, the rain
> and snow companion her.
> Pouring down from her mourning eyes comes the water that soaks the stone.
> My own putting to sleep a god has planned like hers.
>
> (lines 824–31)

When we consider such a speech not from the perspective of an acceptance of fate on the part of a *character*, but rather from the perspective of a self-consciously *artistic* ability involved in *playing the role* of a character, we have what a reader of the *PhG* might imagine as a sort of "skeptical" response, as opposed to the "stoic" moment of *amor fati*. This move (from a "stoic" to a "skeptical" attitude) gives rise to the next moment of action: what I have called the "theatricality" of agency, which Hegel seems to link most closely to the self-consciousness of the *comic* actor who has dropped the mask of tragic agency. I will turn to this moment of action in the next chapter.

3

COMEDY AND THEATRICALITY: DESIRE, *BILDUNG*, AND THE SOCIALITY OF AGENTS' SELF-KNOWLEDGE

> Hegel remarks somewhere that all the great events and characters of world history occur, so to speak, twice. He forgot to add: the first time as tragedy, the second as farce.
>
> Marx, *The Eighteenth Brumaire of Louis Bonaparte*

> [H]is talent depends not, as you think, upon feeling, but upon rendering so exactly the outward signs of feeling, that you fall into the trap. He has rehearsed to himself every note of his passion. He has learnt before a mirror every particle of his despair.
>
> Diderot, *Paradoxe sur le comédien*

Both in the *Phenomenology of Spirit* and in his later official theory of dramatic genres, Hegel sees comedy as a sort of end or completion of tragedy.[1] In the *Aesthetics*, Hegel speaks of tragedy and comedy as "opposed ways of looking at human action": "comedy has for its basis and

---

1. This is *not* to claim that comedy is the "highest form of art" for Hegel. Rather, it is just to notice that certain elements of comedy represent a reflectiveness about the dramatic art that Hegel sees as coming out of the experience of tragedy. Gary Shapiro ("An Ancient Quarrel in Hegel's *Phenomenology*," *The Owl of Minerva* 17:2 [Spring 1986]: 177) has understood the dialectical move from tragedy to comedy in the *PhG* as part of a shift on Hegel's part from an "Aristotelian" to a "Platonic" consideration of drama: if in the "Spirit" chapter Hegel stresses the legitimate philosophical insight into *action* that Aristotle thought tragedy provided, the "Religion" chapter would then offer in the transition to the self-certainty of comedy the philosophical overcoming or expulsion of the substantiality of tragic conflict. In his commentary on the *PhG*, Henry Harris gives a persuasive argument about why Hegel did not understand comedy as the highest form of art, but rather as a culminating and most "philosophical" form of literature (*Hegel's Ladder*, II, 647–8). See also the recent discussion in Mark Roche, *Tragedy and Comedy: A Systematic Study and a Critique of Hegel* (Albany: State University of New York Press, 1998).

starting-point what tragedy may end with, namely an absolutely reconciled and cheerful heart."[2]

Many of Hegel's readers have discerned what they take to be a similar
move within the larger narrative framework of his view of human action –
a move that is not infrequently attributed to the perceived Hegelian tendency toward reconciliation. As Judith Butler puts it, for example:

> [F]or Hegel, tragic events are never decisive. There is little time for grief
> in the *Phenomenology* because renewal is always so close at hand. What seems
> like tragic blindness turns out to be more like the comic myopia of Mr.
> Magoo whose automobile careening through the neighbor's chicken coop
> always seems to land on all four wheels.[3]

The notion of the comic perspective in the *PhG* as an essential *resolution,* a brighter and higher result that is forever putting tragedy in
some sense behind it, is one that we must reconsider. At the moment,
it is worth stressing some evidence to the contrary: that while Hegel was
quite aware of the "comic" potential of his book, he was nevertheless in-
sistent that the *PhG*'s ultimate dramatic tone was not one that was meant
to get beyond the tragic, since that would leave out "the seriousness, the
suffering, the patience and the labor of the negative" that are essential
to its movement (*PhG* §19). But the farcicality suggested by Butler's picture of myopia and in the "quotation" that Marx attributes to Hegel may
take us somewhat further into the problem of why a comic moment of
agency is also necessary.[4] For comedy considered simply by itself is, on
the Hegelian view, far from being a bright and easy place of reconciliation. Hegel looks, rather, to the comic moment to raise a crucial further
set of questions about how a corrigibilist view of agency such as his can
wrestle with the conditions for judging actions and how an agent comes
to self-knowledge. Most sharply stated, the question that will concern
us here is what the corrigibilist view that has been discussed in the first

---

2. *Aesthetics,* 1208, 1220.

3. Judith Butler, *Subjects of Desire: Hegelian Reflections in Twentieth-Century France* (New York:
Columbia University Press, 1987), 21.

4. The editors of the Marx Library think that "it is doubtful whether Hegel ever wrote these
words" and seek Marx's Hegelian "source" for this observation rather in some suggestive
comments of Engels (Karl Marx, *Surveys from Exile: Political Writings,* vol. II, ed. David
Fernbach [New York: Vintage, 1974], 146, n. 7). As will be suggested in what follows, the
remark is not at all far from Hegel's approach to the stages of action in the *PhG,* where
comedy in fact opens up a crucially different second moment of agency after tragic retrospectivity, one involving a greater awareness on the agent's part of the inherent theatricality (or possible farcicality) of action.

two chapters implies about an agent's access to his own desires and motivations: if such an agent has no exclusive epistemic access to desires
or motivations in the sense of a "given" or incorrigible datum, but comes
to them "retrospectively" in the way that we have discussed, then what
sort of self or self-knowledge is possible for him? If desire and motivation,
on the corrigibilist view, have instead a socially mediated or "theatrical"
character, is there a notion of self that can escape the alternation between
hypocritical imitation or role playing on the one hand and reflection
about it on the other?

The move from a tragic consideration of action to a comic one involves, thus, a new stage in the self-awareness of the agent. On the view
of the ancient tragedians, agency involves a set of conditions for action
and character – whether in the prior commitments to her family that
Antigone has as a female member, or in the determining fate that Oedipus will only come to discover – that might be understood to coalesce
in the fixedness of a *mask*. It is the task of the *comic* actor, as Hegel puts
it, to *tear that mask off*:

> [The subject] drops the mask just because it wants to be something gen-
> uine. The self, appearing here in its significance as something actual,
> plays with the mask which it once put on in order to act its part; but it as
> quickly breaks down again from this illusory character and stands forth
> in its own nakedness and ordinariness, which it shows to be not distinct
> from the genuine self, the actor, or from the spectator. (§744)

Hegel's description of this comic mask-dropping scene is revealing
in more than just the obvious sense suggested by the act of tearing away.
The "subject" at first appears to be interested in a move that will reveal
something hypocritical about the tragic agent. Comedy, on such a view,
involves the familiar role of *baring* a pretense and showing what is genuinely "behind" it. And yet this passage makes clear that the activity of
the comedian is more complicated. The comic actor both *plays* with the
mask and wishes to be seen as a self on his own; he has a self that is at
once both *actor* (*Schauspieler*) and *spectator* (*Zuschauer*).

What the agent in this mask-dropping scene recognizes about himself
and the mask with which he plays is something about an inherent theatricality involved in self-knowledge and action. No action or motivation of his is *directly* his own, but must be assessed in the light of others'
reactions to it; he understands himself by constantly looking at his
actions in the light of the mask that he wears in them.

The issue of agency that comes to the fore here – that of giving an account of desire formation – is, as we saw in the chapter on tragedy, not

one that is taken to be important in all philosophies of action.[5] We are concerned from this perspective not only with how the agent is "in" the action in terms of whether it can be imputed to him or whether he can reasonably regret it, but also with what sort of *motivating* content the agent can take as his own in his deed. And that account requires, since notions of incorrigibility or exclusive epistemic access to desires have been put by, an examination of the various social conditions for the formation of an agent's motivations. As with the account of retrospectivity, this issue will also require a consideration of the expressivity of action, in this case one that will particularly raise issues of self-reflectiveness and the authenticity available within such an experience of theatricality.

One of the primary experiences of this theatricality, according to Hegel, comes within the realm of "culture" (the most usual translation of the German word *Bildung* so central to Hegel's *PhG*), a realm in which the self finds itself alienated by being at once spectator and spectacle, observer and "mask." Hegel's insight through comedy into the inherent "theatricality" of agency and the "cultured" world is, of course, far from original. Just as he drew on the ancient tragedians for an account of the action's retrospectivity, so Hegel here takes up previous cultural reflections on the phenomenon of action's sociality – those in the (quite different) views of theatricality of Rousseau and Adam Smith. Both Smith and Rousseau are, not coincidentally, philosophers of the concerns of civil society – a realm where the "artificiality" of social exchange and correlate issues such as property and poverty (and the possibility of freedom associated with either) come to be important. As we will see, Smithian and Rousseauian views of the artificiality of action lie behind Hegel's treatment of the issue of agency's "comic" character.

In what follows, I will begin with Hegel's account of how the self-reflectiveness associated with the dropping of the mask arises within comedy as a genre, and then turn to how such a "comic" concern with action's theatricality is present in life in the world of *Bildung*, which Hegel sketches by making use of one of the strangest characters in one of the most theatrical of all social milieus, that of Diderot's *Rameau's Nephew*.[6] The chapter will conclude by looking at Hegel's account of

---

5. See the discussion of Quante's article in Chapter 2 of this volume.

6. On the issue of *audience* for Diderot and the arts of his time, see Michael Fried, *Absorption and Theatricality: Painting and Beholder in the Age of Diderot* (Berkeley: University of California Press, 1980); and David Marshall, *The Figure of Theater: Shaftesbury, Defoe, Adam Smith and George Eliot* (New York: Columbia University Press, 1986), and *The Surprising Effects of Sympathy: Marivaux, Diderot, Rousseau, and Mary Shelley* (Chicago: University of Chicago Press, 1988).

how philosophy is drawn to the attempt to wrestle with these comic issues of agency.

1. The Comic Agent

Although a tragic agent like Antigone acts from a prereflective sense of the whole, she is nonetheless, as we saw in the previous chapter, a self-conscious agent. Antigone's self-consciousness about her action is not characterized, however, by her identification of a prior intention that "caused" the action, but is rather made clear only *in doing* the action itself and in her *retrospective* recognition of the tragic meaning of what resulted from it.

Something of what is involved in the tragic agent's retrospective recognition of her deed – and of herself as an agent expressed in that deed – makes already for a transition to the sort of self-consciousness about action that will be inherent in the "comic" view of agency. Antigone's retrospective consciousness of her deed, for example, involves both a new articulation of her prereflective attachment to "family" and a reconsideration of the significance of her deed in comparison to Creon's. A new account emerges, in other words, of both (1) what was before taken to be the "givenness" of the action – Antigone's commitment as a woman to upholding the values of the family, and (2) who the agent is in her action, since the agent can now regard her deed as a "spectacle" viewed by other spectators in addition to herself.

Both of these facets of the tragic hero's retrospective self-consciousness – the awareness of the "givenness" of action, and the consciousness of oneself from one's deed as both spectacle and spectator – are involved in the "comic" view of agency, as well. But there is a further intensification of the notion of "self" that comedy offers. To get at it, we must return briefly to the theory of artistic genres that lies behind Hegel's account. As we saw in the previous chapter, Hegel understands the tragic hero's self-consciousness as a sort of "stepping forward" from out of the narrative form of epic. (Within the drama, the tragic heroes, as opposed to the heroes of epic, do not have to rely on a bard who will speak for them; they themselves "are artists," as Hegel puts it: they "give utterance to the inner essence, they prove the rightness of their action and the 'pathos' which moves them is soberly asserted and definitely expressed in its universal individuality" [*PhG* §733].)

In comedy, Hegel claims, the notion of the self as a sort of "artist" of its own deeds becomes not just something that emerges retrospectively in a final recognition scene, but something that is a matter of playful exploration right from the start. The comic medium itself, in other words, allows for the emergence of a self that, as we have seen, can come out from behind a mask and, with a wink at the audience, play ironically with the dramatic illusion. The "self" that is artist/hero in comedy is not simply the character, as in tragedy, but what Hegel calls the "*actual* self" (*PhG* §742) of the actor playing – or rather, playing *with* – a given character on stage.

What is implied in this new notion of self and agency to emerge from comedy? First of all, as in tragedy, there is a reflection on action that *puts aside a view that there is an inherent given involved* (an agent's incorrigible access to a prior intention or desire; a gender-based attachment to acting on behalf of a particular value). The comic agent now makes the issue of givenness an explicit one by asserting her power over the "mask" that was presumed to express the fixed givenness of her character's action. The "artist" in comedy is free to play with the strictures of drama that the tragic character could only "recognize," but could not give up.

Second, the comic artist is not just an actor who must appear before spectators – the explicit *theatricality* of the new dramatic situation – but, as Hegel's quotation acknowledges, the comic agent cannot simply "put off" her mask and be free of it. She now finds herself to be an agent in a drama where the difference between "masked" and "unmasked" selves – or the potential *hypocrisy* of action – has become an explicit issue.

Finally, comedy heralds more generally a change in the realm of value. A tragic agent like Antigone could express her initial "reason" for acting in terms of laws "not of yesterday or today, but everlasting / Though where they came from, none of us can tell" (*PhG* §437). With the explicitness of its concern with theatricality, comedy raises the possibility that such laws are perhaps only a set of imitations and hypocrisies. It is with this question that the comic playwright may even bring philosophy and its practitioners on stage to raise the question of whether "the good" or "the true" is something that has any content at all.

Each of these moments of "comic" agency is part of Hegel's explicit treatment of the dramatic genres in the section on the "art-religion" of ancient Greece (the second part of the "Religion" chapter of the *PhG*). Hegel claims there (*PhG* §742–747) that the comic moment of theatrical action that he describes emerges in some sense from out of the practice of the ancient Greek tragedians. His notion of the "dropping of the mask" in comedy is best interpreted not as the (historically dubious) claim that Greek comic actors no longer wore masks in the tradition of Greek tragic actors, but rather as an interpretive claim about the sort of "self" and self-consciousness visible in comedy. On this reading, Hegel is concerned with the emergence within the dramatic art itself of a self-critical reflection on the conditions of action as presented in tragedy: that is, that it requires actors to wear masks, uses a certain stylistic language in speeches and choruses, and draws on a stock of dramatic characters and situations that are defined by certain stories involving certain gods and the values embodied by them.

In this sense, one can discern in the comedy of Aristophanes – and even, already, in the work of a tragedian like Euripides – the moments of self-reflective agency we have described:

1. Even in a tragic work like Euripides' *Electra*, there are examples of characters "playing" with their roles – for instance, the spoofing of the seriousness of the recognition scene in Aeschylus' *Libation Bearers*.[7] But Aristophanes, most directly in the *Frogs*, may be said to make the task of self-reflection about the conditions of drama the essential *aim* of his work, as he allows Aeschylus and Euripides themselves to be on stage justifying their respective artistic decisions.

2. Not only Aeschylus and Euripides but Aristophanes himself – in a famous chorus meant for the second production of the *Clouds* – "steps forward" as a speaking character in his own work. Further, Aristophanes allows the entire audience of spectators to be represented by a character on stage, as the ever-deceived *Demos*. Thus the "actual" self revealed on the comic stage may be at once playwright, actor, and spectator.

3. A large part of Hegel's description of the language of ancient comedy is clearly drawn from the Aristophanic play that most touches the concerns of philosophy and value – the *Clouds*. Comedy is thus seen as itself the place where there is recognition of the work that rational thinking does in "depopulating Heaven" and showing the evanescence of ideas like the beautiful and the good.[8]

---

7. Henry Harris well characterizes Euripides' Electra as an uncomic but rather "consciously *hypocritical* tragedy" (Harris, *Hegel's Ladder*, II, 633).

8. "With the vanishing of the contingent character and superficial individuality which imagination lent to the divine Beings, all that is left to them as regards their *natural* aspect is the bareness of their immediate existence; they are clouds, an evanescent mist, like those imaginative representations. The essence of these having been given the form of *thought*, they have become the *simple* thoughts of the Beautiful and the Good, which tolerate being filled with any kind of content. . . . The pure thoughts of the Beautiful and the Good thus display a comic spectacle: through their liberation from the opinion which contains both their specific determinateness as content and also their absolute determinateness, liberation, that is, from the firm hold of consciousness on these determinatenesses, they

What Hegel says in the "Religion" chapter of the *PhG* about the specific dramatic art that allows for a consideration of the comic "moment" of action turns heavily, then, on his reading of Aristophanes and ancient comedy. We saw in the previous chapter that there was a direct correlation between the "Religion" chapter's account of the "language" of tragedy and the sort of tragic conflict that had been experienced in the "Spirit" chapter. It is true that the discussion of tragedy in "Religion" broadens beyond a mere consideration of ancient works such as *Antigone* and *Oedipus*[9] and that – one might say – the "place" of tragedy in the *Phenomenology's* scheme as a whole is now treated differently because it's been revealed in a more explicit way; but the later chapter may still be understood as concerned with *how* Hegel got to something like a reading of *Antigone* (with the importance of a conflict between two divine forces, etc.) in the "Spirit" chapter at all.

When we look within the "Spirit" chapter for its "comic moment," however, a different structure seems to emerge. What follows the *Antigone* section is the emergence of the "condition of right" in the Roman world, where indeed one may understand the outlines of social interaction to be comic in the sense that all "personality" is now mediated by an experience of social arbitrariness. But it is only in the realm of Spirit's self-alienation – what Hegel calls *Bildung* ("culture," in Miller's translation) – that anything like a literary appeal to the "comic" moments of action discussed earlier can be discerned. What will be at issue there is a figure embodying a very different culture from that of the Greeks – one for whom the important issue is not so much how the "actual" world of society, as in Aristophanes' plays, may come to appear on stage, but rather how the actor's art – with all its potential for theatricality and hypocrisy – may emerge into the world of society. To understand Hegel's treatment of this issue we must first explore briefly his concept of *Bildung* and then the sort of "comic" figure from literature who Hegel thought most fully embodied that concept.[10]

---

become empty, and just for that reason the sport of mere opinion and the caprice of any chance individuality." (*PhG* §746)

9. Hegel includes in this discussion (*PhG* §737) apparent references to Macbeth and Hamlet, as well as to Oedipus and Orestes: it would appear that Hegel thinks the treatment of the "art-religion" must account not only for the Greek experience with tragedy, but also for the emergence of tragedy as an art form present in the modern world (but no longer that world's most authoritative representation of the divine).

10. *Rameau's Nephew* is, of course, not entirely easy to classify according to genre, and there are good reasons for *not* considering it as "comic" at all, since part of what's at issue there is a move to something that's not really in a genre, but comprehensive of the

2. The Notion of *Bildung* and Its Importance to "Spirit"

In employing the concept of *Bildung* in the *PhG*, Hegel takes over a rich tradition of meaning associated with the thought both of the Pietists (for whom the notion of a cultivation, or *Bildung*, of one's talents looked to the presence of God's image, *Bild*, in human beings) and of Enlightenment figures such as Mendelssohn and Herder.[11]

Hegel's use of *Bildung* in the *PhG* shows, as Harris has noted, both a general and a specific sense.[12] The *PhG* itself, as concerned with the *coming-to-be* or the *appearance* of Science, is shaped as a certain project of *Bildung*. Science is first of all not something that – in Hegel's famous image – is "shot from a pistol" (*PhG* §27), but rather something that comes on the scene as the result of a process of formation. And that *Bildung* of Science is something that must be recapitulated at the level of the individual: Hegel takes part of the *PhG*'s task to be the "pedagogical" one of "leading the individual from his uneducated (*ungebildeten*) standpoint to knowledge" (*PhG* §28).

The notion of *Bildung* is crucial to the *PhG*'s philosophical project in a way that grows out of the issues of corrigibility and givenness discussed in the previous chapter. If there is no epistemological "given," if the claims of the "space of reasons" are normative ones that cannot merely be derived from natural facts about the world, how are we to understand our capacity for such normativity? What kind of account can we give of how we come by our status as inhabitants in such a "space of reasons"?

McDowell's suggestion is that it is Hegel's notion of *Bildung* that offers the sort of account we need: "although the structure of the space of reasons cannot be reconstructed out of facts about our involvement in the realm of law, it can be the framework within which meaning comes

general culture of wit in the age of Enlightenment. I follow Henry Harris's reading, however, that "Rameau expresses the rational *comedy* of the Enlightenment" (*Hegel's Ladder*, II, 303; his stress): for our purposes, the central issue in *Rameau* is still – as in Aristophanes' *Clouds* – the wearing of masks and the possibility of their "removal." (See also the following discussion of comedy versus satire.)

11. Rudolf Vierhaus, "*Bildung*," in *Geschichtliche Grundbegriffe: historisches Lexikon zur politisch-sozialen Sprache in Deutschland*, ed. Otto Brunner, Werner Conze, and Reinhart Koselleck (Stuttgart: Klett, 1972), 508–551, especially 508–510. See also the discussion of *Bildung* in its relation to Hegel in James Schmidt, "The Fool's Truth: Diderot, Goethe and Hegel," *Journal of the History of Ideas* 57:4 (1996): 630–1; John H. Smith, *The Spirit and Its Letter: Traces of Rhetoric in Hegel's Philosophy of "Bildung"* (Ithaca: Cornell University Press, 1988), 45–54; and Terry Pinkard, *Hegel: A Biography* (Cambridge: Cambridge University Press, 2000), 49–51.

12. Harris, *Hegel's Ladder*, II, 306, n. 3.

into view only because our eyes can be opened to it by *Bildung,* which is an element in the normal coming to maturity of the kind of animals we are."[13] McDowell compares such a notion of *Bildung* to an Aristotelian conception of "second nature," but how closely these two notions can be taken together is not clear, especially in light of the account of alienation and the self that seems to be part of the more specific notion of *Bildung* that is operative in the *PhG.* Within the space of the larger project of accounting for the normative coming into nature, this more specific moment of *Bildung* is one that in fact has seemed to many commentators to twist the Enlightenment and Pietistic notions of "culture": "*Bildung*" is in fact the subheading of the second section of "Spirit," a section whose main title – "Self-Alienated Spirit" (*sich entfremdeter Geist*) makes clear the shift of meaning Hegel is suggesting. The middle realm of Spirit is one that is concerned precisely with a realm where the self that is at issue is a self only by alienation – an alienation that is self-caused, rather than imposed upon it.[14]

Since the stress in Hegel's specific account of *Bildung* is upon a self's awareness of its own self-making through the process of alienation, the concern with agency in this case is with the particular side of desire. Subjectively, this means an exploration of how an agent can regard any particular desire *as* motivating, if no desire can *count* as simply being given. Objectively, it means a concern with the particular content of those particular motivations – for example, with the role of individuals' desire for wealth and its relation to the universal good.

What Hegel's account would seem to need here for such an examination of the particular side of agency is a figure who can render the alienation, rupture, and falsehood of the world of appearances that *Bildung* is. The presentation of such a figure will touch on the issues of masks and their revelation that we have seen were part of Greek comedy, but it will do so in an inverted way: in ancient comedy, it was the recognition of real life coming onto the stage that was at issue in the comic actor's dropping of his mask, whereas here we will be concerned with how the theatrical comes into life. The three issues important for Hegel's reading of Aristophanes will thus appear again, except this time in an analysis of roles and imitation in social life itself.

13. McDowell, *Mind and World,* 88.

14. As Robert Pippin puts it ("Hegel on Historical Meaning: For Example, The Enlightenment," *Bulletin of the Hegel Society of Great Britain* 35 [Spring–Summer 1997]: 1–17), the "game" being played here "is a self-dissolving game, played with itself; it is not fated or necessitated or caused; it is self-initiated and self-sustained."

3. Hegel's Rameau

The second of Hegel's three great literary appropriations in the "Spirit" chapter of the *PhG* is the one that critics have usually regarded as his most contingent. Hegel had translated Sophocles' *Antigone* at Tübingen (1788–93), and had written about the notion of the "beautiful soul" during his Frankfurt years (1797–1800); as the Berlin lecture series shows, both figures were also to remain quite central to Hegel's mature thinking about issues of aesthetics and ethics. Diderot's *Rameau's Nephew,* on the other hand, essentially fell into Hegel's lap while he was in the midst of writing the *PhG*[15] and – despite one interesting later reference in a review – appears to be a work that Hegel essentially allowed to go back onto his shelf.[16]

---

15. The story of how Diderot's curious text, locked by its author in a desk drawer until his death, came to have its first publication in a translation by Goethe at the very time Hegel was writing the *PhG* is worth a study in itself. See the account in Schmidt, "The Fool's Truth: Diderot, Goethe and Hegel," particularly on the role that Goethe plays in this "translation" of Diderot's text to a German context; see also Roland Mortier, *Diderot en Allemagne (1750–1850)* (Paris, 1954), 254–263.

    Hegel's appropriation of Diderot's sketch has stirred a wide variety of commentary: see, among others, Lionel Trilling, *Sincerity and Authenticity* (Cambridge, MA: Harvard University Press, 1972): 26–52; David W. Price, "Hegel's Intertextual Dialectic: Diderot's *Le Neveu de Rameau* in the *Phenomenology of Spirit,*" *Clio* 20:3 (1991): 223–233; James Hulbert, "Diderot in the Text of Hegel: A Question of Intertextuality," *Studies in Romanticism* 22 (1983): 267–291; E. J. Hundert, "A Satire of Self-Disclosure: From Hegel through Rameau to the Augustans," *Journal of the History of Ideas* 47 (1986): 235–248; Hans Robert Jauss, "The Dialogical and the Dialectical *Neveu de Rameau;* or, The Reciprocity between Diderot and Socrates, Hegel and Diderot," in Jauss, *Question and Answer: Forms of Dialogic Understanding,* trans. Michael Hays (Minneapolis: University of Minnesota Press, 1989), 118–147; Marie-Jeanne Königson, "Hegel, Adam Smith et Diderot," *Hegel et le Siècle des Lumières,* ed. Jacques D'Hondt (Paris: Presses Universitaires de France, 1974): 51–70.

16. The one striking later reference to *Rameau* is in Hegel's review of his Berlin colleague Solger's collected writings. I will quote the full context, since the remark has some bearing on the way in which Hegel appears to understand the notion of "dialogue": "We have masterpieces of dialogical discourse in modern languages (one only has to refer to Galiani's dialogues, Diderot, Cousin, and Rameau). But here the form is at the same time subordinated to the matter, nothing idle. The matter is, however, not a speculative content, but rather a kind that, entirely according to its nature, can be the subject of conversation. In that plastic form of Plato, *one of the conversationalists keeps the thread of continuation in his hand,* so that all the content falls into the questions and only the formal agreement falls into the answers. The instructor remains master and does not give information about questions one addressed to him or answers to objections brought forward." English translation in G. W. F. Hegel, *Encyclopedia of the Philosophical Sciences in Outline and Critical Writings,* German Library, vol. 24., ed. Ernst Behler (New York: Continuum, 1990), 316 (stress mine).

The contingency underlying Hegel's *choice* of the work corresponds to something in its literary character. In comparison to *Antigone* and the classical sources Hegel used for his study of the tragic moment in action, *Rameau's Nephew* clearly had at the time (not to mention since) a rather uncanonical status.[17] It is also not entirely clear how it fits into any genre classification – or even whether it is meant to be of a certain genre at all. Diderot evidently considered it satire rather than comedy, but the tie that Hegel wishes to make between it and the (clearly comic) Aristophanic plays is that in both cases what "playing with a mask" means is that an actor is both "in" and "out" of a role within a play, both imitator and spectator.[18] To that end, Hegel's own quotation from Diderot stresses in particular that the most remarkable thing about the figure of Rameau is his "musical" ability to "mix together" themes "of every sort," tragic, comic, or whatever (*PhG* §522). The chief difference between Diderot's satirical figure and Aristophanes' comic one is that now the "acting" appears to be going on in the context of everyday life.

Diderot presents a conversation between two figures, "he" (*lui*), identified as the nephew and namesake of the French composer Rameau, and "myself" (*moi*), whom the nephew hails as "*Monsieur le philosophe*," but who may or may not be distinct from the narrative voice that introduces the dialogue.[19] The straightforward identification of the dialogue partners by first- and third-person pronouns already suggests that, as with the tragic action that interested Hegel, a dialectic between first- and third-person perspectives on agency will also be of great concern here.

17. On the non-necessity and uncanonicity of this borrowing, see Pippin ("Hegel on Historical Meaning," 5–6) and Harris (*Hegel's Ladder,* II, 275–6). Harris makes the further point that, since *Rameau* had become known *only* through Goethe's 1805 translation, it is "about the latest cultural phenomenon of his world that Hegel's 'recollection' comprehends" (*Hegel's Ladder,* II, 298) – a point that makes clear the extent to which Hegel views Rameau as embodying the spirit of "absolute culture" as pure self-making.

18. Cf. the remark of the First Interlocutor in the *Paradoxe sur le comédien:* "Satire deals with *a* tartufe; comedy with *the* Tartufe" (Diderot, *The Paradox of Acting,* trans. William Archer [New York: Hill and Wang, 1957], 39). Whether *Hegel* considered it as comic or satirical is something that can be looked at in light of his discussion in the *Aesthetics* concerning satire and comedy: "There is nothing comical about the vices of mankind. A proof of this is given us by satire, all the more tediously, the cruder are the colors in which it paints the contradiction between what actually exists in the world and what virtuous men ought to be" (*Aesthetics,* 1200). Comedy, by contrast, is defined by the "infinite light-heartedness and confidence felt by someone raised altogether above his own inner contradiction and not bitter or miserable in it at all" (*Aesthetics,* 1200) – a description that may not fit Rameau the character himself completely, but that does tally well with the *perspective* on the social world that Diderot's dialogue offers as a whole.

19. Schmidt, "The Fool's Truth," 642.

Another clue as to what will interest Hegel can be seen at the start in the narrator's explanation of the occasion for the dialogue: he has, he tells his readers, now and then a need to converse with "such eccentrics" as Rameau in order to break the "tedious uniformity which our education, our social conventions and customary good manners have brought about." A character like Rameau, the narrator says, "shakes and stirs us up, makes us praise or blame, smokes out the truth, discloses the worthy and *unmasks* the rascals."[20]

Although Diderot is careful to portray Rameau as having, like his uncle, some musical talent, it is the nephew's gift for noticing the social "masks" of an affected age and how they may successfully be worn that he seems to have developed the most. The dialogue portrays him not only as a particular artist of the pantomime ("he begins to smile, to ape a man admiring, a man imploring, a man complying." [82]) but also as an astute observer of how such pantomimes are used by agents to obtain what they desire. He knows "more than a hundred ways to begin seducing a young girl, next to her mother, without the latter's noticing it" (44); he revels in the most elaborate stories of courtiers' ingratiation of themselves with those in power. "Pay court, pay court, know the right people, flatter their tastes and fall in with their whims, serve their vices and second their misdeeds – there's the secret" (35).

Rameau is, then, an entertaining (yet insightful) social parasite. But what does such a character reveal about agency? One may first think of him as an agent who looks at himself and others in terms of the necessary self-interestedness of all motivation: "in a subject as variable as manners and morals nothing is absolutely, essentially, universally true or false – unless it be that one must be whatever self-interest requires, good or bad, wise or foolish, decent or ridiculous, honest or vicious" (50). And, to take this account further, Rameau at various points appears to characterize his own self-interest in terms of certain obvious and natural desires: "I want a good bed, good food, warm clothes in winter, cool in summer, plenty of rest, money, and other things that I would rather owe to kindness than earn by toil" (85); "The great thing is to have both [money and reputation] and that is precisely what I am after when I employ what you call my vile tricks" (33).

20. Diderot, *Rameau's Nephew and Other Works*, trans. Jacques Barzun and Ralph H. Bowen (Indianapolis: Library of Liberal Arts, 1956), 9–10; stress mine. Further quotations in this chapter from *Rameau's Nephew* are by page number to this translation.

But the centrality of pantomimes and masks to Rameau's account of himself and others suggests that the challenge he poses for understanding agency is more problematic. For Rameau is not – as Trilling puts it in Freudian terms – an id-dominated creature of desires, but rather an ego-centered agent focused on concerns with place and power in society. It is cutting a certain social figure – that of the "irreplaceable" wit – that concerns him most. In Hegelian terms, understanding a figure like Rameau is not about "unmasking" certain determinate natural satisfactions as "givens," but rather about getting at the inherently socially mediated character of desire formation itself.

What is most at issue, then, is what I have called the question of *theatricality* in action – the mediation of desire and feeling by the imagination or fiction inherent in the relation between actor and spectator. Diderot himself seems to have viewed *Rameau's Nephew* as a sort of companion piece to his *Paradox of Acting*,[21] which presents a dialogue in which one interlocutor claims that the actor must be a cold copyist who does not himself *feel* the emotions he portrays, but who is successful at arousing an audience's sympathies because he has learned how to *imitate* gestures and motions that have a certain effect.

> If the actor were full, really full, of feeling, how could he play the same part twice running with the same spirit and success? Full of fire at the first performance, he would be worn out and cold as marble at the third. But take it that he is an attentive mimic and thoughtful disciple of Nature . . .[22]

Against this view, a second interlocutor asks whether it is not the case that, in certain moments, an actor's "natural sensibility" allows him to "forget that he is on a stage":

> He is tormented, indignant, desperate; he presents to my eyes the real image, and conveys to my ears and heart the true accents of the passion which shakes him, so that he carries me away and I forget myself, and it is no longer Brizart or Le Kain, but Agamemnon or Nero that I hear.[23]

When we compare Diderot's dialogue about acting to *Rameau's Nephew*, Rameau gives us perhaps most strongly the impression of a nimble but not personally affected imitator who could fit the first interlocutor's

---

21. Hegel could not have known this work at the time of writing the *PhG*, since it was published only in 1830.
22. *Paradox of Acting*, 14.   23. *Paradox of Acting*, 61.

description of the actor's art. "I am myself and I remain such, but I act and speak just as I ought to" (50), Rameau says: he can put on and take off particular masks, all depending on what the social situation seems to call for. The startling thing – at least as Diderot seems to present it – is how successfully Rameau makes use of the theatricality associated with the stage for pursuing relationships in real life.

This theatricality of everyday agency in the world of "absolute culture" means that no one *is* what he is except by being taken by others to play that role. Likewise, an agent cannot claim exclusive epistemic access to his own desires and feelings except through the "mirror" of the spectatorship implicit in the social situation.

One image of this theatricality can be seen in Hegel's appropriation of *Rameau's Nephew:* unlike the section on *Antigone*, where Antigone herself is actually *named* in Hegel's text, the quotations from *Rameau* are not identified.[24] Like the simple third- and first-person pronouns that characterize the interlocutors in Diderot's dialogue, Hegel's rendering of the "chatter" of agency in the world of culture is one of anonymous and self-constructed selves. Tragic heroes are characterized by fixed *masks;* the comic actor is characterized by a self that knows its own *power* over the masks it picks up. As Hegel puts it in describing the language of "base flattery" that is the starting point of Rameau's "disrupted" consciousness: the self does not here take anything about its agency as inherently given, "for what it pronounces to be an essence, it knows to be expendable, to be without any *intrinsic* being" (*PhG* §520). Rameau's emotional dexterity in "running up and down the entire scale of feelings from the profoundest contempt and dejection to the highest pitch of admiration and emotion" (*PhG* §522) is evinced – in particular, it seems to Hegel – by a tone of knowing derision that "takes their *nature* from them" (*PhG* §522).[25]

24. Commentators have also remarked on the problematic character *of* the *Rameau* quotations, since Hegel makes rather liberal use of Goethe's translation: most often, he is simply paraphrasing, rather than giving verbatim quotations, despite the fact that he puts what he paraphrases in quotation marks. Jauss ("The Dialogical and the Dialectical *Neveu de Rameau*") says that Hegel "supremely disregards the rules of the game of citation"; see Harris's response to this (*Hegel's Ladder*, II, 311–12).

What is problematic about the citation in this case is also, however, different from what is problematic about the lines of Hegel's *Antigone* "translation": in this case we have an approximation of (anonymous) *chatter;* there, we had a conscious retranslation of a line from a specific work of poetry.

25. I diverge here from Miller's translation; my stress on the removal of *nature* (Miller translates this simply as something that "spoils" the performance of these emotions) is jus-

The comic actor who can, like Rameau, take up any role is essentially, as we also saw in Hegel's account of Aristophanes, a split self: he is part *Schauspieler* (actor), performing the role of whatever mask he plays with at the moment, and part *Zuschauer* (spectator), keeping an eye on how that performance is coming off and what he should take up next. Such a duality would perhaps suggest that what is most at issue here is a kind of *hypocrisy*. But Diderot's presentation of Rameau goes out of its way to deny this:

> There was in all he said much that one thinks to oneself, and acts on, but that one never says. This was in fact the chief difference between my man and the rest of us. He admitted his vices, which are also ours: he was no hypocrite. Neither more nor less detestable than other men, he was franker than they, more logical, and thus often profound in his depravity. (74)

As Harris has argued, it is this "frankness" of Rameau – the clarity with which he both sees and admits his own greed and ambition – that makes him, on Hegel's reading, the perfect embodiment of or spokesman for the whole world of culture, not just one player in it. "Mine's the opinion and common speech of society at large" (46), Diderot has him say. On Harris's interpretation, Rameau is "the self for whom things truly are as they are universally."[26]

But while Rameau escapes the charge of hypocrisy, the split character of his persona makes him a figure who – again on both Diderot's and Hegel's views – seems condemned to a necessary form of self-contempt. Rameau may mock the world in which he lives, but, as he claims all must do, he takes up his place within that world as a role player and handout seeker.

Rameau's position is one that sees the world, we might say, as a kind of *infinite comedy* from which there is no escape – a comic position whose dark side can be quickly imagined: as Hegel characterizes it a few paragraphs later, this "disrupted consciousness" has "the most painful feeling and truest insight about itself: the feeling that all its defenses have broken down, that every part of its being has been tortured on the rack and every bone broken" (*PhG* §539).[27]

---

tified, I believe, by Hegel's own mode of quotation. As Harris points out, this line about de-naturing is the closest Hegel comes in this citation to directly quoting Goethe's translation: the preceding description of the performance of emotions Hegel merely paraphrases (Harris, *Hegel's Ladder*, II, 312).

26. Harris, *Hegel's Ladder*, II, 304.

27. As Harris puts it, this isn't quite our experience of Rameau, who may be tortured and

Is there any way out of Rameau's self-contempt and the "infinite comedy" that he represents? Is there any possibility of *overcoming* the theatricality that such a comic world presupposes?

Such questions lie at the heart of several responses to theatricality in agency, all of which can be characterized as "philosophical." In the final section of this chapter, I will explore some important philosophical attempts to come to terms with the sort of theatricality that comedy, and particularly the figure of Rameau, have made agents conscious of. As we saw in the case of Aristophanes' *Clouds,* comedy – in a way quite unlike tragedy – establishes a relation with philosophy by actually appearing to bring the philosopher directly on stage, as part of its own critical examination of the self and action. Is such a move part of what Hegel thinks Diderot is up to philosophically, and is there a more comprehensive philosophical perspective on what Diderot takes his project to be? Considering such questions will show how Hegel's discussion of theatricality emerges from the context of a conversation about the philosophical claims made for and against the Enlightenment – claims that are particularly represented, as Hegel thought, by the philosophical approaches of Adam Smith and Rousseau.

4. Philosophy and the Task of Overcoming Theatricality

At the end of Diderot's dialogue, the Philosopher protests that Rameau's view of society as an infinite comedy of pantomime and mask is not entirely correct: "[T]here is one human being who is exempted from the pantomime. That is the philosopher who has nothing and asks for nothing." (84) The Philosopher takes as his example the Cynic Diogenes, who "made fun of his wants" and when he could not obtain what he wanted, "went back to his tub and did without." When Rameau claims that he could not himself give up the things that he wants, the Philosopher responds: "That is because you are a lazy, greedy lout, a coward and a rotting soul." Rameau's straightforward answer: "I believe I told you so myself" (85).

As a dialogue, Diderot's *Rameau* does not make clear that either Rameau or the Philosopher "wins" the verbal contest. The third voice of the narrator does not call the victory or give a final assessment of the conversation from the point of view of *moi;* the dialogue ends simply

extended, but like an india rubber man, "he stretches to fit the rack and his bones do not break" (*Hegel's Ladder,* II, 333).

with Rameau's final line ("he laughs best who laughs last"), leaving it to the reader to decide how or whether that standard might apply.

Commentators have noticed that Hegel's appropriation, by contrast, not only *narrates* the whole contest, but also appears to give the decisive win to Rameau rather than to his opponent.[28] The *PhG* narration makes clear that this opponent – not identified by Hegel, even as "*Mein Herr Philosoph,*" but alternately called the "tranquil" (*ruhig*) or "honest" (*ehr-lich*) consciousness and the "simple" (*einfach*) or "plain" (*gerade*) consciousness – has no toehold in direct verbal combat with his counterpart (again, not named as "Rameau" but only as the "disrupted" [*zerrissen*] or "perverted" [*verkehrt*] consciousness).[29]

On Hegel's account, the simple or plain consciousness gives either "monosyllabic" responses to the more loquacious disrupted consciousness or finds itself making points that the disrupted consciousness has already acknowledged ("I believe I told you so myself"). It may attempt to point to *individual examples* (either true or fictitious) to bolster its point, but in the end is outflanked by the universal language of the disrupted consciousness. To attempt something like the Philosopher's appeal to Diogenes will fail, because the individual – "even Diogenes in his tub" – is conditioned by the world of culture around him, "and to make this demand of the individual is just what is reckoned to be bad, viz., to care for *himself qua* individual" (*PhG* §524). Finally, the Philosopher's pointing to Diogenes cannot be meant to indicate the possibility of a return to *natural* simplicity as a way of overcoming theatricality:

> [I]t cannot mean that Reason should give up again the spiritually developed consciousness it has acquired, should submerge the widespread wealth of its moments again in the simplicity of the natural heart, and relapse into the wilderness of the nearly animal consciousness, which is also called Nature or innocence. On the contrary, the demand for this dissolution can only be directed to the *Spirit* of culture itself, in order that it return out of its confusion to itself as *Spirit*, and win for itself a still higher consciousness. (*PhG* §524)

---

28. See Schmidt, "The Fool's Truth," 641–2.

29. "Honest" and "tranquil" concern the *thought responses* of the opponent to the "disrupted" consciousness's performance; it is only the "simple" or "plain" consciousness that actually *formulates a response in speech*. The latter two terms thus seem to cohere around the *speech* of the dialogue partner, while the former consciousness may come closer to the narrating author. This is borne out by Hegel's later use (*PhG* §539–540) of *ruhig* to describe Diderot as the author.

What sort of philosophical attempt to overcome the theatricality of Rameau's world does Hegel attribute here to the "simple" consciousness? Hegel's description of the position of the simple consciousness is reminiscent, as is the appeal to Diogenes by the Philosopher in Diderot's dialogue, of a view that is often *attributed* to Rousseau. But whether or not Rousseau is intended as the representative of this position, it is clear from the quotation that Hegel thinks that the position itself is finally impossible as a move intended to get clear of the problems within the world of *Bildung*. (As I will argue later, Hegel in fact appears to have a reading of Rousseau that does not turn on a demand to go "back" to a "natural" simplicity, but rather moves "forward," to a universal notion that would be continuous with the notion here of a "still higher" perspective of Spirit.)

Many commentators have thought that Hegel means further to link the "simple" consciousness of this supposedly Rousseauian position to Diderot himself, yet Hegel seems to join Diderot in blocking that simple move as well. Hegel is attentive to the presence of the third, narrative voice in the dialogue and constructs around its presence another philosophical position that he *does* think represents Diderot's position concerning the possibility of overcoming theatricality.

This second philosophical stance toward overcoming theatricality is that of Diderot as the dialogue's *author*. *Rameau's Nephew* is, after all, a response to a theatrical account of the *philosophes* and their social role – Palissot's play *Les Philosophes*, which, much like Aristophanes' *Clouds*, presents the putatively philosophical life in a negative and comic light. Diderot, in turn, paints Rameau as part of a class of social parasites that includes Palissot. Hegel's claim is that to *present* such figures, Diderot must take a stance as narrator and author quite different from that of the angry defender of "natural simplicity."

It's at this point that a reconsideration of the apparent "win" of the "disrupted" consciousness in Hegel's account is needed. The account we've given so far is one that's often linked to Hegel's only later comment about Diderot: that he represented the ideal form of dialogue, where one interlocutor "holds all the strings of progress." This comment can be understood as a gloss on the disrupted consciousness's "win" only if it does not take into consideration Hegel's comments a few paragraphs later, at the beginning of the section of the *PhG* on "Enlightenment." There he makes clear that something of the *moi* is necessary to bring together the dialogue at all:

Since this language [the brilliant insight of a figure like Rameau] is that of a distracted mind, and the pronouncement only some twaddle uttered on the spur of the moment, which is again quickly forgotten, and exists as a whole only for a third consciousness, this latter can only be distinguished as *pure* insight if it brings these scattered traits into a general picture and then makes them into an insight for everyone. (§539)

Hegel makes clear that he means this third (narrative) consciousness as the "tranquil" consciousness – here, it seems, Hegel has reason to differentiate it from the "simple" consciousness and its objections. Why Hegel calls the narrative or authorial Diderot "tranquil" can be seen in the literary persona he seems to portray – that of a literate, bemused, almost disengaged observer of life who happens to encounter the very hot wire of our friend Rameau. It is a persona primarily concerned with *exhibiting* Rameau, not with criticizing him as does the Philosopher who *speaks* (the "simple" consciousness).

Hegel holds that this third and narrative persona is required for Diderot to be able to *capture* the significance of language like Rameau's. The latter is "disrupted" in part because it is constantly third-person: the *apprehending* or insightful appropriation of his language requires a first person, requires a *moi*. But this first-person figure cannot have a *particular* perspective (*besondere Einsicht*), as Hegel puts it. His "I" must be one whose private interest has been raised or "cultivated" to the universal. Hegel's language about what makes possible this persona of Diderot's narrator is harsh: by being the offerer of a "collection" of sayings, he is a persona in whom "the sole remaining *interest* [stress mine] is eradicated, and the individual judgment is resolved into the universal insight" (*PhG* §540). As Harris reads this: "By writing the dialogue Diderot turns the wit of the single critic into universal enlightenment."[30] The "philosophical" response to theatricality on Diderot's part is, then, this new, first-person yet *universal* voice.[31]

---

30. "Diderot, as the author who put the ravings of all the moments together in this pattern, recognizes that Rameau's insight is absolute (though inverted); if it is translated back into a *universal* insight it can become an engine for change. Diderot is tranquil precisely because his indignation as a participant is a pretense, while his indignation as author is the self-certainty of Reason." (Harris, *Hegel's Ladder*, II, 334)

31. This universal "I" may perhaps call to mind Hegel's interpretation of the first-person pronoun in the Cartesian *ego cogito:* "By the term 'I' I mean myself, a single and altogether determinate person. And yet I really utter nothing peculiar to myself, for everyone else is an 'I' or 'Ego,' and when I call myself 'I,' though I indubitably mean the

Hegel's claims here about what is required for Diderot's authorial voice as the overcoming of theatricality in the form of "pure insight" take us a long way toward his larger criticisms of the Enlightenment, which we cannot take up here.[32] The question that we must instead focus on, given the interest in agency we have taken up, is how or whether the essentially universal self that has come to be expressed in this Enlightenment project can help with the question of theatricality in *agency*. If it is philosophy that comes on the scene to challenge Rameau's claim about the infinite comedy of all persons performing pantomimes, then it must be explained how the stance that overcomes theatricality can be integrated into life and in particular into the lives of *individual* agents.

To consider this question, I will turn from the authorial self in Diderot's dialogue to two claims about a philosophical stance with respect to theatricality in agency that also emerge from the Enlightenment. I shall pose these two claims in the following way. On the one hand, the considerations about theatricality that we have explored might lead us to think that the philosopher, despite his capacity for spectatorial distance from what happens on stage, is nevertheless inescapably *in* the theater; his spectatorship is that of a good drama critic who occasionally needs to play some sort of role himself. On the other hand, a figure like Rameau, who captures with devastating wit the essential falsehood and deceptiveness involved in acting, might lead us to think that drama criticism as such is an insufficient form of reflection about the theatricality inherent in agency, if our concern is to assure ourselves of a sense of selfhood that could in any way be taken as *authentic;* on this line of thinking, it is not just the drama that must be understood as false, but also those criticisms of it that do not acknowledge the essential chasm in life created by such falsity.

The two stances I have outlined – that of the drama critic within the theater of life and that of the seeker for an authentic self that does not countenance society's falsehoods – correspond to those of two philosophers whose views are deeply important to Hegel's account of *Bildung*

---

single person myself, I express a thorough universal. 'I,' therefore, is mere being-for-self, in which everything peculiar or marked is renounced and buried out of sight; it is as it were the ultimate and unanalyzable point of consciousness. We may say 'I' and thought are the same, or more definitely, 'I' is thought as a thinker." (*Hegel's Logic*, trans. William Wallace [Oxford: Clarendon Press, 1975], 38)

32. For a general discussion of Hegel's account of the Enlightenment, see Lewis Hinchman, *Hegel's Critique of the Enlightenment* (Gainesville: University Presses of Florida, 1984).

in the *PhG* – Adam Smith and Rousseau.[33] As we will see, the different analyses that Smith and Rousseau give of theatricality point toward different "resolutions" of its place in action.

Smith's account of theatricality in agency is staged, as it were, very much from within a reflection about ordinary life and the origin of moral sentiments such as sympathy.[34] Our experience of what others feel, as Smith's argument presents it, is not an immediate affair at all: we are required if we wish to consider others' situations to concern ourselves with what we should feel in the same situation. Our connection to others' sentiments thus requires that we be aware of the spectator within us – a spectator who is crucially dependent upon the faculty of *imagination* for forming an adequate conception of what others feel. ("Though our brother is upon the rack, as long as we ourselves are at ease, our senses will never inform us of what he suffers. They never did, and never can, carry us beyond our own person, and it is by the imagination only that we can form any conception of what are his sensations.")[35]

But it is not just in judging what *you* must feel that I must involve myself in the mediated processes of spectating and imagining; my access to my own emotions is no more immediate a business. If I do not know what you are feeling except by imagining what is involved in your situation, so, when I wish to express my own emotions, I can have no idea what others are feeling about them except by placing myself in the same act of spectation. Thus, if I want your sympathy, I will "cool" the representation of my emotions in order to place myself in the position of you

33. Although neither is mentioned by name, both Smith and Rousseau feature in Hegel's text here – Smith is certainly at issue in the background of Hegel's discussion of the general prosperity and happiness that comes from individual pursuit of wealth (*PhG* #497); Rousseau would appear to be on Hegel's mind in the demand of the "honest" consciousness for a dissolution of the world of perversion (*PhG* #524). Hegel's actual appropriation of Rousseau, in particular, is more complicated, as I will argue later.

34. I assume here a relation between Smith's discussion of sympathy (and the "impartial spectator") in his *Theory of Moral Sentiments* and the argument of his *Wealth of Nations*. Hegel's sense of theatricality in Smith may stem only from *WN*, however.

35. Adam Smith, *The Theory of Moral Sentiments*, ed. D. D. Raphael and A. L. Macfie (Oxford: Clarendon Press, 1976), 9. The questions that emerge from Smith's account here are, of course, notorious in the literature: am I limited in my sympathy in every case simply to what *I* would feel in the like circumstances? Both Knud Haakonssen (*The Science of a Legislator: The Natural Jurisprudence of David Hume and Adam Smith* [Cambridge: Cambridge University Press, 1981], 48) and Charles Griswold (*Adam Smith and the Virtues of Enlightenment* [Cambridge: Cambridge University Press, 1999], 102) speak of a necessary ambiguity in Smith's account here.

as a spectator. No agent, then, has, as Griswold puts it, "exclusive epistemic access" to his or her emotions.[36]

The consequences of Smith's view of theatricality for a view of agency
are difficult immediately to reconcile. What sort of identity does an agent
have, if it is always so socially mediated? What prevents the sympathy
among spectators from being anything more than that of a mutual flat-
terers' society?

Smith will look for a resolution of these issues to his notion of the
"impartial spectator";[37] but the philosophical worry behind them becomes sharper if we examine Rousseau's consideration of this issue. If
the importance of theatricality for Smith can be seen by beginning from
a point internal to the everyday experience of his reader, the importance of theatricality for Rousseau, by contrast, has to be seen in terms
of how he draws the reader's attention directly to the large difference
between the illusion of the theater and the possibility of authenticity.
Thus, while our Smithian account of theatricality began with an analysis of how imagination and spectatorship are involved in cases of ordinary action, a Rousseauian account of theatricality would perhaps best
begin with his critique of the theater itself and the artificiality of relations within it.

"People think they come together in the theater, and it is there that
they are isolated," says Rousseau in his famous *Letter to D'Alembert on the
Theater*.[38] A play like Molière's *Misanthrope*, for example, does not show
us how society might rub off the edges of one of its most expressly bitter critics, but rather is guilty of the same vices that are endemic to society itself – namely, the flattery and dishonesty that the misanthrope
rails against.

What Rousseau thinks is not possible within the theater or any "theatrical" relation of agency is, as Jean Starobinski has argued, the
achievement of a kind of *transparency* – a visibility to all others that is
the only thing that can allow genuine autonomy.[39] The "theatricality"
inherent in the sentiments experienced in society thus cannot be me-

---

36. As Griswold argues, Smith's point has important consequences for certain claims in
    contemporary interest-group politics – particularly claims about experience that can-
    not be shared (*Adam Smith and the Virtues of Enlightenment*, 96–99).
37. Griswold, *Adam Smith and the Virtues of Enlightenment*, 128.
38. Rousseau, *Politics and the Arts: Letter to M. D'Alembert on the Theatre*, trans. Allan Bloom
    (Ithaca: Cornell University Press, 1968), 16–17.
39. Jean Starobinski, *Jean-Jacques Rousseau: Transparency and Obstruction* (Chicago: University
    of Chicago Press, 1988).

diated simply by a critical attention to the role of the spectator and the imagination, but require, as Rousseau will argue in the *Social Contract*, an explicit move to the level of universal willing.

We might also see Rousseau's aspiration toward "transparency" in the novel that he published shortly after the *Letter to D'Alembert: Julie, ou La Nouvelle Héloïse,* which begins with the story of two lovers (Julie and her tutor, Saint-Preux) whose passionate love first rejects the falsity of existing conventions but who then – through their membership in a community formed by Julie's husband, Wolmar – undergo a second development in which they virtuously abstain from those passions themselves (they are not married to one another). The goal – albeit one not successfully achieved in the novel's own terms – has been termed a sort of "transparent" community.[40]

How does Hegel's approach to the issue of theatricality relate to those of Smith and Rousseau?[41] Like Rousseau, Hegel seems to focus his account not on examples of theatricality in ordinary agency, but rather on a consideration of explicitly theatrical experience that is *false*. Yet there is a crucial difference: Rousseau makes his point about the falseness of theatricality most sharply in a reading of the *Misanthrope* that argues for the impossibility of a continuity between the virtue of its central character and the falseness of the society around him: like Rousseau himself, writing the preface to the *Letter to D'Alembert* from a solitude "far from the vices which irritate us," Rousseau's reading of the "true" misanthrope is "a good man who detests the morals [manners] of his age and the viciousness of his contemporaries; who, precisely because he loves his fellow creatures, hates in them the evils they do to one another and the vices of which these evils are the product."[42] A similar conflict between a virtuous individual and the falseness of society is visible in the Philosopher's reaction to Rameau – and, as we saw,

---

40. The formulations in this paragraph – the double *Bildung* and its goal of "transparency" – are from Starobinski (*Jean-Jacques Rousseau: Transparency and Obstruction,* 86–87).

41. Despite the great importance that attaches to the relations among these three philosophers, there is relatively little in the literature on the topic. For a discussion of Hegel's appropriation of Adam Smith, see Norbert Waszek, *The Scottish Enlightenment and Hegel's Account of "Civil Society"* (Dordrecht: Kluwer, 1988). On the importance of Rousseau for Hegel, see particularly Robert Pippin, "Hegel, Ethical Reasons, Kantian Rejoinders," *Philosophical Topics* 19:2 (Fall 1991): 99–132. For a comparison of the views of Hegel, Smith, and Rousseau on the issue of civil society, see Paul Redding, *Hegel's Hermeneutics* (Ithaca: Cornell University Press, 1996). Redding does not make a complete case for Smith in this comparison, however.

42. Rousseau, *Politics and the Arts: Letter to M. D'Alembert on the Theatre,* 37.

there is something about the Philosopher's final complaint that *sounds* very much like Rousseau.

Such a view would, however, misconstrue both Rousseau on his own terms and Hegel's reading of him. We must remember how it is that Hegel reads *Rameau* as a comedy of theatricality differently than Rousseau reads Molière. In Hegel's comedy, there is not a move to a solitary critic of social vices of the sort we see on display in Rousseau's preface to the *Letter to D'Alembert*. Instead of the Philosopher, it is Rameau who appears to be the basis from which a "resolution" of things seems to be emerging.

Rousseau may appeal to the virtue of the ancient world and to the term "nature" as a critic of society's vices, but the ultimate project of a work like the *Social Contract* is not "back" toward some immediacy of nature, but "forward" – to a notion of the general will that can provide the only basis of autonomy to which moderns can have access. The aspiration toward the "transparency" that would come with such a move suggested, as we saw, a kind of two-stage negation or *Bildung* in *Julie* – the passionate rejection of false and conventional desires, followed by the virtuous or rational rejection of the unconventional passions themselves.

Such a reading of Rousseau – which stresses the move to the universal as essential to the notion of freedom for any individual – can be seen most clearly in the pattern of the *PhG*'s progress to the end of the *Bildung* section: from the move to the universal that Rameau represents, there is a straight line directly to the notion of the universal that lies behind the Revolution and its terror, and to the universalist and formalist consideration of morality in Kantianism.

Like Kant, Hegel seems to have viewed the Rousseauian concern with "nature" exactly in terms of how a "second nature" might emerge from the world of culture.[43] That is what Hegel means, I would argue, when he hears in the "dissolution" of Rameau's voice the "all-powerful note which restores Spirit to itself" (*PhG* §522). The essential Rousseauian motivation behind Hegel's concern with theatricality is how a notion of "one's own" agency can be attained, given the "theatrical" social conditions that are inherent to action. Like Rousseau and Kant, Hegel acknowledges that such an attempt to come to terms with one's own action requires – paradoxically – a move to universal, "transparent" considerations of agency. But as the immediate moves in the near distance of

---

43. As Starobinski quotes Eric Weil: "'It took Kant to *think Rousseau's thoughts.*'" (Starobinski, *Jean-Jacques Rousseau: Transparency and Obstruction,* 115.)

Hegel's "Spirit" chapter suggest, Hegel's concern will be precisely how that move to the universal can avoid the problems of formalism inherent politically in something like the Terror and morally in something like Kant's ethics.

To shape the question that will animate his concerns as the "Spirit" chapter looks for a possible resolution to the issues of retrospectivity and theatricality: how can the *particular* in action – the desires that would seem to be most "my own" and that are nonetheless subject to the theatrical set of relations we have noticed in society – be recognized within a universal scheme without being rooted out? The *Bildung* of desire implies a kind of "purification" that, much like Rousseau's notion of *Bildung* in *Julie*, requires overcoming an initial connection to the impulses, and that emerges with a new rational or virtuous form. But that form with which it emerges must have, on Hegel's view, a continuity between desire and reason that does not just remove the desires from the picture of agency.

The Rousseauian project, as Starobinski has suggested, has in its aspiration toward "transparency" a tendency toward a notion of a solitary sort of "beautiful soul" – a figure who, like Wolmar in *Julie,* can only achieve a transparency of judgment by removing himself from action.[44] It is just such a figure – embodied not in Rousseau's Wolmar, but in a version of the German Romantic concern with the beautiful soul that was clearly inspired by him – to which Hegel's narrative will now directly turn. The contradictions inherent in such a soul, and the possibilities of its being reconciled to the world of individual agency, will form the beginning point of Hegel's interest in forgiveness and the romantic novel.

44. Starobinski, *Jean-Jacques Rousseau: Transparency and Obstruction,* 261–267.

FORGIVENESS AND THE ROMANTIC NOVEL: CONTESTING THE BEAUTIFUL SOUL

> Novels are the Socratic dialogues of our time.
> F. Schlegel, *Critical Fragments* #26

In the previous two chapters, we have shown how two important elements of Hegel's concept of agency – what we have termed "retrospectivity" and "theatricality" – derive their particular force from a consideration, respectively, of tragedy and comedy. The *Phenomenology*'s task is to show how both of these two moments of agency require recognitive, interpretive structures capable of integrating first- and third-person perspectives of agency. In each case, the *PhG* is deeply guided by a reading of specific tragic and comic works, as in the appropriation of *Antigone* and *Rameau's Nephew* in the first two main sections of the "Spirit" chapter.

The explorations of both retrospectivity and theatricality have left further questions for our account of agency: Do unintended consequences just leave an agent – as the "tragic" experience of action suggests – with the need to accept a case-by-case determination of what must be regarded as "sticking" to the action for which he is responsible? Is the spectator/spectacle split between the agent who acts in the (external) world and the (internal) judge of that action always present, as the "comic" experience of action suggests? The historical situations of tragedy and comedy that Hegel has probed in the "Spirit" chapter – that of the tragic hero's relation to fate and the comic hero's awareness of the maskedness of all action – left little in the way of resolutions for viable modern agency: neither the tragic agent's *amor fati* nor the fractured sense of a divided self which afflicts the comic agent seems to hold possibilities for a genuinely free and rational agent who can in some sense "return" to himself from out of these tragic and comic moments of his agency. But on what grounds *could* an agent come to terms with or (to use Hegel's own language) be adequately *reconciled* to these moments of action?

This Hegelian question about the possibility of a reconciling moment of agency – one that acknowledges the inherent theatricality and retrospectivity of action but does not simply accept the tragic or comic "resolution" of the issues involved – will push our argument into new territory. The context for Hegel's discussion of this issue in the third main section of the "Spirit" chapter ("Spirit That Is Certain of Itself. Morality") is the endeavor of many philosophical contemporaries of Hegel to find a notion of the self that allows for getting *beyond* the problems of retrospectivity and theatricality. Both the "moral" self and "conscience" are sketched along these lines. The "moral view of the world" – a Kant- and Fichte-inspired picture of morality – is grounded in a notion of self that, on Hegel's view, is so formally construed as to be free, on the one hand, of the unintended consequences of its actions and, on the other hand, of seeing what it does as merely an "appearance" whose justification cannot be independent of the perspectives of various social observers. But the self that can flee both of these sides of action is in fact also too formal to be the self that is present in any actual action. Instead, the moral self finds that it is caught in an essentially dissembling or duplicitous pose between real agency and supposed freedom from retrospectivity and theatricality. The problem with "conscience" is somewhat different: unlike the moral consciousness, it no longer attempts to separate out a "pure" self from its entanglements in real actions, but it claims to be able to find in its own conviction an *authority* or authenticity for its deeds that has been missing in the retrospective and theatrical modes of agentive self-knowledge. But conscience's attempt to be the author of its own deeds will reencounter the very issues it has tried to avoid. At its most inward, conscience may simply be a withdrawn figure of pure and silent yearning unsullied by any action – the so-called "beautiful soul." But insofar as the beautiful soul is considered in its actuality, as an agent or even a judge in the world, it again has to face the issues we have singled out.

The possibility of a reconciliation here that does not simply avoid action and the issues of retrospectivity and theatricality that action implies will turn on the notion of *forgiveness* – a notion of crucial importance to Hegel's philosophy of agency and ethics. As with the moments of retrospectivity and theatricality, there is something in the ordinary experience of forgiveness that will open up larger questions for a philosophical account of agency. But part of our clear awareness of retrospectivity and theatricality came through an expressivity possible in the literary genres of tragedy and comedy. Does Hegel look to any literary experience for a similar appeal in the case of forgiveness?

Until this point, the discussion of Hegel's use of literature in his *PhG* account of agency has been (almost strictly) comparable to the structure of the official literary theory of his later *Lectures on Aesthetics*. As the *PhG* concerns itself with the move from tragedy to comedy, so the *Aesthetics* lectures undertake an examination of drama in terms of the same transition. But is there in either case a concern for a literary form that might go beyond tragedy and comedy?

There are suggestive elements in the *Aesthetics* about a "third" and reconciling form that is neither tragedy nor comedy. Hegel's eye there is particularly drawn to what he calls "reconciliation dramas" – plays such as the *Oedipus at Colonus* or *Philoctetes*, where the action has tragic seriousness but a resolution of a sort that one is more likely to expect in comedy. Such dramas, Hegel says, show that, "despite all differences and conflicts of characters and their interests and passions, human action can nevertheless produce a really fully harmonious situation."[1]

If we look back to the *PhG*, the context seems quite different indeed: the question of what gets beyond tragedy and comedy does not seem to be taken up in terms of literary genres at all. The explicit discussion of genres that Hegel undertakes in the "Art-Religion" section *ends* with comedy and is itself succeeded by a new and unartistic form of religious expression, the "Manifest Religion" of Christianity. In the "Spirit" chapter, the consideration of something beyond tragedy and comedy is taken up in connection with a discussion of *language:* among the recapitulatory moves that Hegel makes in the final section of that chapter is his com-

---

1. *Aesthetics*, 1 203. Hegel's respect for this third form of drama – examples of which include modern works such as Goethe's *Iphigeneia auf Tauris* and particularly such ancient works as the *Eumenides*, *Philoctetes*, and *Oedipus at Colonus*, which bore the name "tragedy" but did not conclude in a destructive conflict – has been taken by Vittorio Hösle as a suggestion that the third form, as synthetic of the substantial interest of tragedy and the subjective harmony of comedy, represents really the highest form of dramatic art (Vittorio Hösle, *Die Vollendung der Tragödie*, 26). It is worth noting that in his account in the *Aesthetics*, Hegel never says that reconciliation dramas are higher, but rather presents them as a median case: "in the center (*Mitte*) between tragedy and comedy" (*Aesthetics* 1202; Hegel, *Werke: Theorie Werkausgabe*, 20 vols., ed. Eva Moldenhauer and Karl Markus Michel [Frankfurt: Suhrkamp, 1970], 15, 531). Cf. also the reference to modern reconciliation dramas as *"diese Mitteldinge zwischen Tragödien und Komödien"* (Hegel, *Werke* 1 5, 568).

parison of the two languages that have been previously considered – the "comic" language of court culture in Rameau and the tragic language of Antigone – to the form of language that is now present in the realm of conscience.[2] "The content which language has here acquired is no longer the perverted, and perverting and distracted, self of the world of culture"; nor is it "the language of the ethical Spirit . . . [i.e.,] law and simple command, and complaint, which is more the shedding of a tear about necessity." The language of conscience is instead the language of

> the *self that knows itself as essential being.* This alone is what it declares, and this declaration is the true actuality of the act, and the validating of the action. Consciousness declares its *conviction;* it is in this conviction alone that the action is a duty . . . (§653)

Instead of the movement traced by the *Aesthetics* from tragedy and comedy to reconciliation drama, then, the *PhG* seems to be on a course that takes it beyond the literary: tragedy's language of "complaint" and comedy's language of "perversion" push forward in this case rather to the apparently more straightforwardly ethical (and religious) language of conviction. A literary model on the order of *Antigone* or *Rameau* does not seem so immediately apparent to a reader of the final section of the "Spirit" chapter.

What the section's scholarly readers *have* noticed, however – in a many-sided and passionate debate – are allusions of a somewhat more distant character to various works and figures of Hegel's own time, particularly those of the Romantic generation who pursued notions of conscientious conviction and the beautiful soul.[3] Hegel seems to allude

---

2. This recapitulatory move with respect to language may be compared, for example, to Hegel's discussion of the self of conscience as "the third self" within "Spirit" as a whole (§633).

3. Emanuel Hirsch, "Die Beisetzung der Romantiker in Hegels Phänomenologie: Ein Kommentar zu dem Abschnitte über die Moralität," in *Materialen zu Hegels "Phänomenologie des Geistes,"* ed. H.-F. Fulda and Dieter Henrich (Frankfurt: Suhrkamp, 1973), 245–275; Otto Pöggeler, *Hegels Kritik der Romantik* (Bonn: Bouvier, 1956); Moltke Gram, "Moral and Literary Ideals in Hegel's Critique of 'The Moral World-View,'" *Clio* 7:3 (1978): 375–402; Gustav Falke, "Hegel und Jacobi: Ein methodisches Beispiel zur Interpretation der Phänomenologie des Geistes," *Hegel-Studien* 22 (1987): 129–42, and *Begriffne Geschichte: Das historische Substrat and die systematische Anordnung des Bewusstseinsgestalten in Hegels Phänomenologie des Geistes* (Berlin: Lukas, 1996), 318–330; Daniel Dahlstrom, "Die 'schöne Seele' bei Schiller und Hegel," *Hegel-Jahrbuch* 1991, 147–156; Dietmar Köhler, "Hegels Gewissens-dialektik," *Hegel-Studien* 28 (1993): 127–141; H. S. Harris, *Hegel's Ladder. II: The Odyssey of Spirit* (Indianapolis: Hackett, 1997), 457–520.

at least twice, for example, to Jacobi's famous statement about the "majesty" of conscience.[4] The notion of a "beautiful soul" who dwindles away has suggested to many the writer Novalis, who died of consumption;[5] and the notion of the "hard heart" at the very end of the section has frequently been thought to refer to Hegel's friend Hölderlin.[6]

Underlying these scholarly claims about Hegel's allusions, however, is an issue that has not, to my knowledge, been seriously pursued. It is the distinctly *novelistic* shape of the treatments of the beautiful soul that influence Hegel's account. In fact, with one important exception, all of the Romantic sketches of the beautiful soul that are usually taken to lie behind Hegel's allusions here come within the pages of novels: Goethe's *Wilhelm Meister*, Novalis's *Heinrich von Ofterdingen*, Schlegel's *Lucinde*, Jacobi's *Allwill* and *Woldemar*, and Hölderlin's *Hyperion*. These writers, in turn, were influenced directly or indirectly by the famous "beautiful soul" novels of the earlier part of the century, such as Rousseau's *Julie, ou La Nouvelle Heloise* and Wieland's *Agathon*.[7]

In his sketch of the various eighteenth-century literary portraits of the beautiful soul, Robert Norton has suggested that "it may have been

---

4. PhG §646, §655.

5. PhG §658: "In this transparent purity of its moments, an unhappy, so-called 'beautiful soul,' its light dies away within it, and it vanishes like a shapeless vapor that dissolves (*schwindet*) into thin air." The German word for "consumption" is *Schwindsucht*.

6. PhG §668. See the connections drawn to Hölderlin's *Hyperion* and *Empedocles* in Gram, "Moral and Literary Ideals," 396; Hirsch, "Die Beisetzung der Romantiker," 261; and Harris, *Hegel's Ladder*, II, 497–498.

7. The one "exception" to the novelistic portraits of the beautiful soul is, of course, Schiller, whose essay "Über Anmut und Würde" (1794) takes up the concept. For a discussion of the differences between Hegel's portrait and Schiller's, see Dahlstrom, "Die 'schöne Seele' bei Schiller und Hegel."

There may be other, even more obscure works concerned with the "beautiful soul" that lie behind Hegel's account. In a letter to von Knebel that most likely dates from the Jena period, Hegel thanks his correspondent for allowing him to borrow a *Confessions of a Beautiful Soul* and says that the book has "made a very favorable impression on me" (Hegel, *Letters*, 375). Various works have been suggested in this context – for example, the anonymously published *Bekenntnisse einer schönen Seele von ihr selbst geschrieben* (Berlin: Unger, 1806), whose author was apparently Friederike Helene Unger – but, as far as I know, there has been no convincing scholarly case specifying which beautiful soul account Hegel is referring to (Unger's beautiful soul does not, for several reasons, precisely fit Hegel's description in the letter).

For a general discussion of the origin of the "beautiful soul" figure in earlier German literature, see Hans Schmeer, *Der Begriff der 'schönen Seele' besonders bei Wieland und in der deutschen Literatur des 18 Jahrhunderts* (Berlin: Ebering, 1926). Recently a case for the importance of the notion of the "beautiful soul" has been made within Anglo-American philosophy by Colin McGinn, *Ethics, Evil and Fiction* (Oxford: Clarendon Press, 1997), 92–122.

more than simply fortuitous that the beautiful soul entered the mainstream of literary culture just as the modern novel appeared in Europe." In many respects, he adds, "the beautiful soul and the novel seem to have been made for each other."[8]

Given the argument we have made in the preceding chapters about the importance of the genres of tragedy and comedy for Hegel's account of agency, we might ask whether this curious connection between the birth of the novel and the (re)emergence of the beautiful soul is something that Hegel considered in the writing of the final section of the "Spirit" chapter. There is much that seems to push against such a possibility. While we have noticed the importance of a dramatic genre such as the reconciliation play in Hegel's eventual aesthetic theory, for example, that theory does not seem to give much consideration to the novel as a form at all, much less to something that could serve as an Hegelian "theory of the novel."[9]

It will be argued here, however, that in this one great divergence from Hegel's later aesthetic theory, we can see something important with respect to the *PhG* project concerning agency. It will mean reading the last section in a somewhat different light – not so as to catch various allusions, but rather in order to see how Hegel may be conscious, in a more experimental way than in his previous two literary engagements, of the issues that come to the fore in the novelistic form. Thus I will be concerned with two issues: first, whether there is something that we might call the overall narrative structure or "plot" of the section; and second, if reflection on that "plot" can tell us something about Hegel's attitude toward the novel itself as a form.

With respect to plot, our interest is primarily in how *forgiveness* emerges as a way of dealing with the issues of theatricality and retrospectivity. In this regard, it will be shown that, among the several Romantic accounts of the beautiful soul, one novel figures most strongly in terms of the ultimate narrative shape of Hegel's own account of the beautiful soul: Jacobi's *Woldemar*.[10]

---

8. Robert Norton, *The Beautiful Soul: Aesthetic Morality in the Eighteenth Century* (Ithaca: Cornell University Press, 1995), 139.

9. There have been some notable attempts, of course, at a "theory of the novel" that begins from Hegelian roots – particularly that of Georg Lukács, *The Theory of the Novel: A Historico-Philosophical Essay on the Forms of Great Epic Literature*, trans. Anna Bostock (Cambridge: MIT Press, 1971). See J. M. Bernstein, *The Philosophy of the Novel: Lukács, Marxism and the Dialectics of Form* (Minneapolis: University of Minnesota Press, 1984).

10. The claim for the distinctive importance of the *Woldemar* to the entire section on

But Jacobi's influence on the plot is only part of the account we must give concerning the importance of the novelistic form to Hegel's sketch of the beautiful soul and the possibilities for its forgiveness. Among the Romantic generation, the beautiful soul became a central novelistic figure precisely at a time when the novel itself and the question of what sort of genre it was had become a literary issue of the highest order. To pick one example, perhaps the most provocative: Friedrich Schlegel's notion of the novel as the ideal romantic poetic form, a *Progressives Gedicht* that can become the "mirror of the whole circumambient world, an image of the age."[11] Embedded in Schlegel's claim is the transcending, in some sense, of traditional literary genres and questions about genre: *die Romantik*, he says, is the only kind of poetry that is "more than a kind."[12] Part of Schlegel's hope for the romantic novel rested on its ability to encompass theoretical reflection on itself – to combine in some sense philosophy and poetry: "a theory of the novel would have to be itself a novel. . . ."[13]

Schlegel's notion of a novel capable of containing its own theory within it had a correlate in his novelistic practice: in his *Lucinde,* which has frequently been taken to play a role in the background of Hegel's section on the beautiful soul, an "Allegory of Impudence" presents a *contest* among the novel-types that might shape the ensuing work. In the course of that contest, Impudence yanks on the face of a figure called "Beautiful Soul" and calls her a hypocrite – thus suggesting the lines of a Schlegelian criticism of the Jacobian "beautiful soul" novel we have mentioned as lying behind Hegel's thought about the beautiful soul.

Putting these two claims together – the first about the overall narrative importance of Jacobi to Hegel's account and the second about the

conscience and the beautiful soul was first made by Otto Pöggeler, *Hegels Kritik der Romantik* – although Pöggeler also took into consideration in his view the important other figures besides Jacobi involved in the section. See the following discussion and the account in Speight, "The Beautiful Soul and the Language of Forgiveness," in *Die Metaphysik der Praktischen Welt,* ed. C. Jamme and A. Grossmann (Amsterdam: Rodopi, 2000), 238–245.

11. Schlegel, *Athenäumsfragment* #116 (in Friedrich Schlegel, *Philosophical Fragments,* trans. Peter Firchow [Minneapolis: University of Minnesota Press, 1991]). See the discussion of this and related fragments in Simon Critchley, *Very Little . . . Almost Nothing: Death, Philosophy, Literature* (London: Routledge, 1997), 86.

12. *Athenäumsfragment* #116.

13. "Dialogue on Poetry," in *German Romantic Criticism,* ed. Leslie Willson (The German Library, vol. 21) (New York: Continuum, 1982), 109.

sort of Schlegelian contest among various novel-types that may be under way – suggests a way of reading the *PhG* section with two strong advantages. First, it opens up the possibility of considering the various novelistic claims about the beautiful soul within the section not as a series of mere allusions but as part of an ongoing Romantic "conversation" involving public claims of conscience, counterclaims, confessions, and (ultimately) the possibility of forgiveness. The central lines of that contest, for Hegel, lie between Schlegelian irony and incompletion on the one hand and Jacobian conscience and forgiveness on the other hand, but one may see a wider contest of the beautiful soul – between Goethe and Novalis, for example, or Hölderlin and Hegel.[14]

The second advantage is that it might help us to see Hegel not merely as a moralistic critic of the essentially aesthetic claims of Schlegelian irony – the dull end of the silly "Hegel and Schlegel" poem that Friedrich's brother August wrote in later years – but as an opponent who took Schlegel more seriously than is often thought.[15] Hegel had nothing but contempt for the notion of a fusion of poetry and philosophy that Schlegel suggested; yet seeing what Hegel gains from looking at the beautiful soul in terms of a Schlegelian "contest" may point up one concern that they shared: a concern with the status of art in modernity, if earlier genres (such as the dramatic) must now be regarded as essentially connected to the ancient world.

On this reading, then, the nature of the "beautiful soul" and its conscientious claims will be seen as deeply connected to the essentially *literary* issues of an appropriate form of modern art for the claims of authority and authenticity associated with the literary artist. Having suggested important ways in which we will see that the form of Hegel's own narrative is shaped by figures such as Jacobi and Schlegel, it is important to add one crucial caveat: it is, of course, *Hegel's* own narrative

14. Novalis came to have a quite critical attitude toward *Wilhelm Meister:* "It is at bottom a fatal and foolish book – so pretentious and precious – unpoetic to the highest degree, so far as the spirit is concerned. . . . [it] is actually a Candide directed against poetry" ("Last Fragments," in *Novalis: Philosophical Writings,* trans. Margaret Mahony Stoljar [Albany: State University of New York Press, 1997], 158–9 and 184, n. 6). His own *Heinrich von Ofterdingen* is viewed as something of a counternarrative.

15. "Schlegel predigt gegen Hegel, / Für den Teufel schiebt' er Kegel. / Hegel spottet über Schlegel / Sagt, er schwatzt' ohn' alle Regel / Schlegel spannt der Mystik Segel; / Hegel fasst der Logik Flegel. / Kommt, ihr Deutschen, Kind und Kegel, / Von der Saar bis an den Pregel! / Schaut, wie Schlegel kämpft mit Hegel! / Schaut, wie Hegel kämpft mit Schlegel!"

that is working itself out; and while he derives a notion of reconciling forgiveness from Jacobi, and a notion of a "contest" of novels from Schlegel, those notions will have their own Hegelian construction and defense. That narrative will, in the end, present a recapitulatory figure who will go through, rather than "escape," the important Hegelian concerns with retrospectivity and theatricality in action.

In what follows, we will examine first the range of attempts to simply get *beyond* the issues of theatricality and retrospectivity that Hegel saw in the claims of morality and conscience, and then look more closely at the evolving shape of the beautiful soul. The chapter will conclude with an exploration of Hegel's notion of forgiveness as it sets up the contours for the project of his later philosophy of agency.

1. From the Categorical Imperative to the Beautiful Soul:
Kantian and Post-Kantian Attempts at Escaping
Retrospectivity and Theatricality

The final section of the "Spirit" chapter – "Morality," or "Spirit That is Certain of Itself" – may be understood to be concerned with the possibility of getting beyond the problems of retrospectivity and theatricality in action. The question that emerges at this point in Hegel's narrative of agency is whether an agent's reasons for acting can somehow be ones that allow him to take his actions as *his own,* without the sorts of conflict that proved irresoluble in the tragic picture of the world and without the divided self that is implicit in "comic" agency.

The notion of rational and free agency as that in which the agent can see actions as genuinely his own lies behind what Hegel categorizes as the "moral view of the world," a Kant- and Fichte-inspired moral scheme that attempts to avoid the issues of retrospectivity and theatricality by means of a formal scheme of justification concerned only with purity of intention.[16] The concern with what is "one's own" within this view of morality has the shape of a notion of an agent's *autonomy:* an agent is autonomous if he acts on a maxim that could be tested by the rational standard of an imperative derived from self-given law. Attempting to act on such an imperative, however, involves an agent in a familiar set of oppo-

---

16. For discussion of Hegel's critique here, see particularly Harris, *Hegel's Ladder,* II, 413–456; Kenneth Westphal, "Hegel's Critique of Kant's Moral World View," *Philosophical Topics* 19:2 (1991): 133–76; and Jonathan Robinson, *Duty and Hypocrisy in Hegel's "Phenomenology of Mind"* (Toronto: University of Toronto Press, 1977), 30–97.

sitions – morality versus nature, specific versus pure duty – that Hegel argues make agency and any notion of a (nonduplicitous) *self* impossible.

With the emergence of the post-Kantian notion of *conscience,* which no longer involves the gap between judgment and deed that made the moral consciousness duplicitous, there is both self and agency, but also consequently the issues of retrospectivity and theatricality that beset action to begin with. The concern of conscience with what is "one's own" is a concern with *authenticity:* if an agent could never be assured of acting on pure duty, he could at least be convinced of the individual aims that were authentically his. Such a standard of authenticity Hegel calls "conscience," which is both a specific and a general term for the shape of consciousness that he considers in the final section of "Spirit."

The specific form of conscience, in a Fichtean sense, is just that immediate conviction that no longer is concerned with an opposed notion of pure duty: "There is, then, no more talk of good intentions coming to nothing, or of the good man faring badly" (§640), because what is one's duty-as-conviction is simply what one *claims* it to be. Conscience, on the other hand, is "in its contingency completely valid in its own sight" (§632): what an action *is* is only as conscience *knows* it (§635). Because the conscientious agent claims that his action is only what he himself recognizes in a given deed, he can view himself in his action as free of contingent circumstances that he may not have foreseen (or which, indeed, were unforeseeable).

What is implied in this new figure, as not in Kant, is a certain demand for *recognition.* Because the person who claims to act for conscience need not acknowledge any specific action as dutiful, the opposition between universal consciousness and individual self has been put by. What becomes crucial now is not any specific *deed* but rather the *utterance* of the claim that he is acting on conscience: "whoever says he acts in such and such a way from conscience, speaks the truth, for his conscience is the self that knows and wills. But it is essential that he *say* so . . ." (§654)

The Romantic search for modes of recognition that allow for mutual assurance of the claims of conscientious authenticity takes many forms – in the elevation of love and friendship, for example, and more broadly, in the aspiration toward a new sort of community where the claims of all consciences could be equally respected. To be taken myself as conscientious involves, so Hegel's analysis runs, an acknowledgment of space for the conscientiousness of others.

Yet, as Hegel will show, these Romantic attempts at such self-assuring community are subject to inherent contradictions that appear when attention is paid to how members of such a community must speak. And it is this attention to the *language* of conscience that begins to uncover oppositions inherent in the Romantic project:

> [T]he language in which all reciprocally acknowledge each other as acting conscientiously, this universal identity, falls apart into the non-identity of individual being-for-self: each consciousness is just as much simply reflected out of its universality into itself. As a result, the antithesis of individuality to other individuals, and to the universal, inevitably comes on the scene . . . (§659)

Hegel sketches, in all, five specific attempts at the project of conscientious community: first, the simple (apparently Fichtean) claim to act on one's own conviction; second, the notion of a "moral genius"; and finally, three species of "beautiful soul." All of these forms that Hegel takes up following the first Fichtean notion of individual conviction involve precisely some sort of opposition because of the role of recognition and the other. The "moral genius," a figure often associated with Jacobi, thinks of itself as having the gifts of an artist in moral matters and thus opposes itself to conventional moral norms. The further forms of conscience are three possible shapes that Hegel thinks the notion of the *beautiful soul* can take. The first such form is that of a *withdrawn* beauty that "lacks the power to externalize itself, the power to make itself into a Thing" and that thus "lives in dread of besmirching the splendor of its inner being by action and an existence":

> Its activity is a yearning which merely loses itself as consciousness becomes an object devoid of substance, and rising above this loss, and falling back on itself, finds itself only as a lost soul. In this transparent purity of its moments, an unhappy, so-called 'beautiful soul,' its light dies away within it, and it vanishes like a shapeless vapor that dissolves into thin air. (§658)

Hegel follows the sketch of this type of beautiful soul with that of an opposition between two other forms of the beautiful soul that do not simply withdraw but that find themselves opposed to one another: an *acting consciousness* that, because it insists on the particular in its deed, can find itself criticized by a universal or *judging consciousness*.

The acting consciousness, on its side, "knows itself to be free" of any claims that can be made about its specific duty: "it is positively aware that it, as *this particular* self, makes the content" of its claims conscientious (§659).

For the consciousness which holds firmly to duty [the judging conscious-
ness], the first consciousness [the acting consciousness] counts as *evil*,
because of the disparity between its *inner being* and the universal; and
since, at the same time, this first consciousness declares its action to be
in conformity with itself, to be duty and conscientiousness, it is held by
the universal consciousness to be *hypocrisy*. (§660)

Yet the judging consciousness is itself not free from hypocrisy:

Just as little is the persistence of the universal consciousness in its judgment an unmasking and abolition of hypocrisy. In denouncing hypocrisy
as base, vile and so on, it is appealing in such judgment to its *own* law, just
as the evil consciousness appeals to *its* law. . . . It has, therefore, no supe-
riority over the other law . . . (§663)

The opposition here is, of course, familiar not just to the Romantics
but to any ethics of conscientious conviction more generally: on the one
hand, your claim that you have acted conscientiously cannot be denied,
since no one but you has access to your conscience in this sense; on the
other hand, my interpretation of your action as stemming from an un-
charitable motive (greed, ambition) *also* cannot be denied, since it, too,
is dependent on an introspection that cannot be communicable.

What sort of resolution of these two competing interpretations is
possible? As Hegel points out, any hypocrisy behind such claims cannot
be borne out by the counterclaims of either side. Something further will
be required if we are to get beyond the position of competing interpretations of an action – or to "unmask" the hypocrisy, if it exists. This
further step is what is involved, Hegel thinks, in the act of forgiveness.
The agent who claims to have acted on conscience sees now in the
harshness of the judgment of the other something similar to himself
and *confesses* that what he has done is wrong. The judge does not immediately respond to this confession, which the agent regards as a
hardness of heart. What allows there to be an ultimate reconciliation
between the two, however, is the judge's forgiveness of the deed of the
agent. Thus there is a reconciliation at the end of this opposition that
betokens something that Romanticism seemed to be after in the religious
side of its project:

The reconciling *Yea*, in which the two 'I's let go their antithetical *existence*,
is the *existence* of the 'I' which has expanded into a duality, and therein
remains identical with itself, and in its complete externalization and op-
posite, possesses the certainty of itself: it is God manifested in the midst
of those who know themselves in the form of pure knowledge. (§671)

The sources for Hegel's sketch of these forms of conscience – particularly the varieties of the beautiful soul – have been widely disputed: from Kojève's conviction, in an earlier era of Hegel interpretation, that Hegel was presenting a recognition and reconciliation between the acting consciousness of Napoleon and Hegel himself as author/judge, to the attempts to link the beautiful soul with specific figures of the numerous eighteenth-century literary portraits of the "beautiful soul," from Rousseau to Goethe and Schiller. Most of the discussion, however, has focused on the issue of what specific referents for these figures in earlier Romantic literature might be teased out of Hegel's text rather than on what might be termed the narrative structure of their relationships and the ultimate movement of this section toward its conclusion.[17] Such a focus is not unwarranted, of course: the description of the withdrawn beautiful soul's "vanishing" (*schwinden*), for example, seems quite clearly to be a reference the Romantic figure Novalis, whose own early death by consumption (*Schwindsucht*) seems to be in Hegel's imagination here. Yet seeing the larger picture requires a more careful look at Hegel's act of literary appropriation in this third of his "Spirit" chapter's literary reconstructions.

There are, I claim, among the numerous figures and works lying "behind" the text, two crucial points of reference for understanding Hegel's literary borrowing here. The first is the peculiar and not widely recognized importance of one text for the ultimate shape of the *resolution* or denouement of Hegel's "plot" for this section: Friedrich Heinrich Jacobi's philosophical novel *Woldemar*. Jacobi's novel is usually discussed only in connection with the claims of the "moral genius" in this section. Yet its importance as a literary prototype for this section rivals that of Sophocles' *Antigone* and Diderot's *Rameau's Nephew* for their respective parts of the *Phenomenology*. Although Hegel does not name his source explicitly in this case (as he does the *Antigone*) or quote directly from the text (as he does in the case of both *Rameau* and *Antigone*), his reliance on Jacobi's novel here is just as striking. Gustav Falke in fact

---

17. The notion of the beautiful soul itself has a rich tradition in the centuries prior to the publication of the *Phenomenology*, beginning chiefly with Shaftesbury's appropriation of the notion of *kalokagathia* from the Greeks and running through Schiller's "Anmut und Würde," Goethe's "Confessions of a Beautiful Soul" in *Wilhelm Meisters Lehrjahre*, Jacobi's *Woldemar* and *Allwill*, and Novalis's *Heinrich von Ofterdingen*. See Schmeer, *Der Begriff der 'schönen Seele' besonders bei Wieland und in der deutschen Literatur des 18 Jahrhunderts*, and Norton, *The Beautiful Soul: Aesthetic Morality in the Eighteenth Century*.

goes so far as to claim that the "beautiful soul" section must be read *only* as an adaptation of *Woldemar,* a claim that underplays the strong resonances throughout the section with other Romantic authors and characters and does not adequately account for one or two curious plot twists in Hegel's reconstruction.[18] Yet Falke is certainly right to claim that the structure of Hegel's section, read as a plot, corresponds in substantial ways to that of Jacobi's novel. Otto Pöggeler attempts to bring together the underlying Jacobian structure of the section's development with the strong Hegelian references to other Romantic figures by suggesting that Hegel read *Woldemar* as somehow prefiguring all the other significant figures of German Romanticism that he came to treat in this part of the *Phenomenology.*[19]

In general, Pöggeler's suggestion combining an organizing role for the *Woldemar* with references to the other Romantics seems to get us closer to what Hegel is doing in this section. From the perspective of the *Phenomenology*'s task, I shall claim, it is not that Jacobi's novel "prefigured" various of the Romantics, but that it suggests, in its appropriation of forgiveness, the highest form of mutual self-assurance possible in the Romantic project of the beautiful soul. The notion of forgiveness is thus a sort of "vantage point" from which the various Romantic claims can be seen.

Central to the emergence of this vantage point is the importance of language for understanding the project of the beautiful soul. Why did Hegel turn to a novel (and one concerned with this particular sort of character) in order to examine the Romantic project? Hegel's attempt to sketch his own version of the eighteenth century's literary figure of the beautiful soul is not, however, concerned to offer one more claim about what makes such a soul beautiful, but rather is directed to the question of what kind of language of assurance a community of beautiful souls gives rise to. Hegel's claim is that other Romantic attempts at such language – the language of beautiful withdrawal in Novalis, the language of unmasking and confession in Friedrich Schlegel, the language of confession and transparency in Rousseau – point toward the language of forgiveness in Jacobi's *Woldemar.* It is only the *Woldemar,* of

18. Gustav Falke, "Hegel und Jacobi," 129–142. See also the more recent discussion by Falke, *Begriffne Geschichte,* 318–330, and some criticism in Dietmar Köhler, "Hegels Gewissendialektik," 127–141.
19. Otto Pöggeler, *Hegels Kritik der Romantik,* 52–56. Harris, despite his wider literary reading of the section, also seems to agree.

the many productions of the Romantic period, that Hegel thought presented a notion of forgiveness that could be an adequate standard for resolving the contradictions inherent in post-Kantian ethics. For Hegel, the highest form of mutual self-assurance through the language of Romantic community – and really the transition from Romantic community to a higher form of community – lies in a mutual renunciation of claims by judge and agent in the act of forgiveness.[20] And the conclusion of Jacobi's novel provides a similar moment of forgiveness in its denouement, framed by the two quotations with which Jacobi concludes the novel ("Judge not!" and "Trust love").

The second important point of reference for the structure of Hegel's presentation of the beautiful soul is the presence of Friedrich Schlegel, and particularly of his novel *Lucinde*. If Jacobi's picture of the beautiful soul in *Woldemar* lies behind whatever *unity* Hegel's plot has – and most particularly the denouement toward which that plot heads (for it is in the most important sense a "forgiveness" plot) – then it is perhaps Schlegel's sketch of the beautiful soul that gives Hegel the idea of presenting a *diversity* of claims about who the beautiful soul is. Schlegel's idea, after all, is not just that of a plot that presents a number of literary *characters* over the course of its development, but one which, self-reflectively, opens up the question of which possible paths it might take: a "plot" that offers, in other words, a *contest of possible plots or novels* within itself. Such a self-reflective literary structure – and here the Schlegelian claim about the novel as a modern "Socratic dialogue" may come to mind[21] – suggests perhaps the inescapability of the issue of theatricality within the context of even this most inward of shapes of consciousness.

One does not have to listen very closely, for example, to hear echoes of the world of the younger Rameau in Schlegel's review of the beautiful soul portrait that Goethe gives in the sixth book of *Wilhelm Meisters Lehrjahre*: "her inwardness shapes the stage on which she is *at the same time actor and spectator,* and also concerned with the intrigues behind-scenes."[22] However the beautiful soul of Goethe's sketch attempts to unite her roles, Schlegel says,

---

20. Pinkard (*Hegel's "Phenomenology,"* 219) has called this new form of community that forgiveness gives rise to "absolute" – as opposed to "romantic" – community.

21. Along with, of course, Socrates' claim in Plato's *Symposium* that the best tragic playwright will also write comedy – an interestingly similar self-reflective claim about that dialogue's own inclusion of both tragic and comic performances.

22. Friedrich Schlegel, *Kritische Schriften*, ed. Wolfdietrich Rasch (Munich: Hanser, 1970), 467 (stress mine).

[f]undamentally, she also *lives theatrically*.. . . . She stands continually before the mirror of conscience and is busy washing and decorating (*putzen
und schmucken*) her disposition. In her the most *external* measure of inwardness is reached . . .[23]

Schlegel's probing of Goethe's version of the beautiful soul in this
review corresponds, in fact, to a moment in his own novel *Lucinde* at
which a figure named "beautiful soul" is unmasked – the famous "Allegory of Impudence" scene. This perspective on the beautiful soul we
might link more generally with Schlegel's own notion of *irony;* it contrasts in its frankness and impudence with the underlying seriousness
of the earlier form of universal judging that does not act. Can there be
a "beautiful soul" that is successfully at one with itself in what it does
and is, that most fully could unite the perspectives of agent and judging
spectator? I will turn first to the "contest" among the novelistic claims
about the beautiful soul and then to the issue of that contest's possible
"resolution."

2. The Contest of Conscientious Agent and Conscientious Judge

Hegel presents, as we have seen, an opposition between an acting consciousness and a judging "beautiful soul." This *contest* represents in effect the culmination of the Romantic pursuit of the question, "Who is
the beautiful soul?" For Hegel, this question about the character of the
"*genuine* beautiful soul" – as both Goethe and Hegel come to speak of
the issue – is a question concerned with the possibility of a free and rational agent emerging from the two previous moments of "Spirit," one
that would neither carry the "mask" of a (naturally given) character worn
by ancient tragic heroes nor be the inauthentic master of social pantomimes that Rameau was.

The contest in this final section of the *PhG* between an acting and
a judging beautiful soul is one that is sketched, as is usually thought, by

23. Ibid.; stress mine. This is in fact the point of unity Schlegel sees in Goethe's inclusion
    of the "Confessions of the Beautiful Soul" within the context of the "theatrical mission"
    of the young Wilhelm. (In my discussion, I have taken it for granted that Goethe's por-
    trayal of the "beautiful soul" lies behind Hegel's account – but only in the background,
    as a point of reference for the more pointed portraits in writers like Jacobi and Schlegel.
    For a reading of Hegel's "beautiful soul" section that hears more of a resonance with
    Goethe's version than my account suggests, see Benjamin Sax, "Active Individuality and
    the Language of Confession: The Figure of the Beautiful Soul in *Lehrjahre* and the
    Phänomenologie," *Journal of the History of Philosophy* 21:4 [1983]: 437–66.)

means of allusions to representative figures from the "beautiful soul" literature: for the acting soul, the scene of confession and unmasking of the beautiful soul that occurs in the "Allegory of Impudence" in Schlegel's *Lucinde;* for the judging soul, Jacobi's *Allwill* or *Woldemar* – or perhaps more often the poet Hölderlin is thought to be the model. On the reading of this section that I will propose, however, Hegel's intention is not simply to allude to figures within these novels, but rather – on a meta-narrative level – to consider these moments as the *claims of different sorts of novels themselves.* The contest of this section, in other words, is between an *"ironist"* or fallibilist conception of the novel that we may associate with Schlegel and what we might call the "forgiveness novel," of the sort that Jacobi attempts in *Woldemar.*

How does a consideration of this section in terms of a contest of novels make it different? Let us briefly consider the two novel types in question and how Hegel appropriates them for his own "beautiful soul" narrative.

The Ironist's Confession. In the "Allegory of Impudence," a figure named Wit offers to a first-person narrator a choice among four "true novels" that appear in the allegory in various poses. Scholars have attempted to read this allegory in terms of Schlegel's own intentions for various novels that he wished to write;[24] in any case, the first "novel" – shown initially naked, then clothed, then playing with a mask – seems to have yet another choice before him, one between Impudence and Delicacy. Other young women are around Delicacy: figures with names like Morality (*Sittlichkeit*), Modesty (*Bescheidenheit*), and Beautiful Soul. Beautiful Soul claims to have more feeling than Morality, and Modesty claims to be jealous of Beautiful Soul – but the exchange is interrupted by Impudence, who seizes Beautiful Soul's face and claims to have hold of only a mask. In the end, the first novel goes off with Impudence.

What Schlegel achieves with this scene is a sort of self-commentary on the novel that he is writing – a move that critics like Lacoue-Labarthe and Nancy read as part of Schlegel's own self-construal of the Romantic project of the novel as one of irony and essential *incompletion.*[25] It is such a view of the novel's project that, I would claim, lies behind what most

24. See Rudolf Haym, *Die Romantische Schule: Ein Beitrag zur Geschichte des deutschen Geistes* (Berlin: Weidmann, 1906), 496.
25. Philippe Lacoue-Labarthe and Jean-Luc Nancy, *The Literary Absolute,* trans. P. Barnard and C. Lester (Albany: State University of New York Press, 1987).

readers have taken to be the Schlegelian moment of Hegel's narrative – the "confession" of the "evil" agent.

Such a construal of the confession of fallibility as part of a *novelistic* project gives us something of a different perspective on one of the shopworn tropes of Romantic criticism: that Hegel's famous attack on Schlegelian irony missed Schlegel's point because Hegel could focus only on the *ethical,* as opposed to the artistic, issues the novel raises.[26] I wish to suggest that both Hegel and Schlegel are clear about the *connection* between the ethical and the artistic here, and that Hegel's means of appropriating Schlegel's challenge is to let his own narrative of the beautiful soul become at least for a moment a Schlegelian contest of sorts – but one that, on its own terms, could not lead to a satisfactory sort of resolution.[27] The reason why the claims of the *ironic* "beautiful soul" novel are in the end insufficient has to do with a challenge it faces from the direction of a different sort of "confession": the demand of a judge who uses universal standards to enforce a sort of confessional *transparency.*

The "Hard Heart" of the Judge. The other figure is more difficult to identify with a particular novelistic approach to the figure of the beautiful soul.

26. Hegel criticized Schlegel's notion of irony severely in his later *Philosophy of Right* (§140R). On the fundamental opposition between the two, see Ernst Behler, "Friedrich Schlegel und Hegel," *Hegel-Studien* 2 (1963): 203–250, and Judith Norman, "Squaring the Romantic Circle: Hegel's Critique of Schlegel's Theories of Art," in *Hegel and Aesthetics,* ed. William Maker (Albany: State University of New York Press, 2000), 131–144.

27. My reading of Schlegel as particularly concerned with the "confessional" moment in Hegel's beautiful soul story is rooted in the interpretation of Emmanuel Hirsch. Harris has suggested that it is unfair to follow Hirsch and read *Lucinde* as the locus primarily of the "confessional" figure of the beautiful soul, the voice that says "Ich bin's." *Lucinde,* Harris claims, presents rather the full range of motion that we see in Hegel's account – from confession all the way to forgiveness – since it includes a playful forgiveness scene between the two lovers. Harris makes clear, however, that the forgiveness in *Lucinde,* precisely because of its playful nature, is not the essentially public moment that characterizes the end of the *PhG* treatment.

Harris's reading is suggestive, but even if we accept it, there is still no reason to deny that it is the *Woldemar* that comes much closer to providing the plot form of Hegel's account, since Jacobi's account includes something like the "hard heart" (in Woldemar's rage at the "insult") that has such impediments to its serious forgiveness of the other. (The "public" character of what is at issue between Woldemar and Henriette – the gossip of neighbors, etc. – does not, of course, go all the way toward what Harris wants in the "public" moment of forgiveness, since he has in mind much more the Frankfurt-essay Jesus who takes up the fate of opposing the way things are. But my claim is not that Hegel is simply presenting the *Woldemar,* but rather that its plot is the most embracing or resonant of the various beautiful soul plots that were to hand.)

The secluded madness that overcomes the unreconciled "hard" heart has suggested to some the poet Hölderlin, but Hegel's language suggests a different sort of relationship: a figure who insists on the universality of claims as the guarantee of conscientious mutual self-assurance and who consequently cannot deign to acknowledge the particularity of desire and character that the "evil" agent insists upon.

Pinkard has offered the suggestion that such a judging figure – who remains in opposition to his time while having to live within it – is more reminiscent of Rousseau than of any single figure in German Romanticism. Rousseau's concern with the beautiful soul in *La Nouvelle Héloïse* bears, as we saw in the previous chapter, a striking connection to the dialectic exhibited here in the aspirations for conscientious community pursued by the "judging" figure of Wolmar.

But if we see *La Nouvelle Héloïse* as the model here, we have a problem: while it is not essential to Hegel's project that an exact chronological relationship exist among figures within a given "shape of consciousness," it does seem odd not to have a contemporaneous source. More problematically, we are left from Rousseau's novel with no resources to imagine how the "hard heart" might come to be sympathetic toward the confessing agent. What we need, in other words, is a contemporary account of how the hard heart comes to reconcile. We have one: Jacobi's Woldemar, whose name and whose desire for a kind of confessional transparency as the hallmark of the beautiful soul both seem to have been modelled on Rousseau's Wolmar, but who is part of a general plot structure that moves toward a forgiveness and reconciliation that is present only in a certain other-worldliness (that is to say, finally, in an unsuccessful way) in Rousseau's novel.

The claims of this "forgiveness" novel are somewhat harder to pick out literarily than those of Schlegel's claims to irony. For Jacobi, the background of this novel-type seems to involve assumptions about immediacy and religion that will need further examination before we can see how Hegel might appropriate from such a novel-type a notion of forgiveness.

3. Jacobi's *Woldemar* and the Narrative Language of Forgiveness

The title character of Jacobi's *Woldemar* – referred to by others in the course of the novel as a "beautiful soul" – is sketched as a figure of both deep interiority and peculiar social traits. Like the figures of conscience in Hegel's account, he experiences no Kantian opposition between universal moral claims and his own desires, but "every feeling [*Empfindung*] in him becomes thought, and every thought feeling. . . . What attracted him, he followed with his whole soul; therein he lost himself every time."[28]

Few critics of the novel have perhaps come closer to the source for Woldemar's character than Friedrich Schlegel, who suggests that there is much of Jacobi himself in his character. Woldemar's ability to "lose himself" in the other reflects, for example, Jacobi's overriding philosophical concern with the other (experienced as connection with other people, the world, and God) in his attack on what he construes as the subjectivistic basis of German idealism. Woldemar, Jacobi tells us, experienced a characteristic melancholy concerning himself and his projects and remained uncertain about the ends of human striving until he saw, waking from a dream, a figure who reminded him of the ethical importance of the other: "not the I, but the 'more than I,' the 'better than I' – someone entirely other," Jacobi has Woldemar say in a passage that he quotes in full in his own voice in the famous *Letter to Fichte*. The connection of the individual to this other is, for Jacobi, not to be found in the analysis of subjective impressions or in the transcendental ego, but rather in an immediacy of conviction that he calls faith. And it is that conviction that, he claims, is essential for all ethical motivation if it is to be at all ethical: conventions and social norms are mere constraints for an individual who is in touch with the feelings that connect him to the immediacy of his ethical concerns.

Perhaps the chief dramatic element of the novel is the relation between Woldemar, as he expresses such views, and the circle of somewhat more conventional people who surround him. He has come to stay in a small town where his brother is married to the youngest daughter of a conservative businessman named Hornich, who finds Woldemar's reliance on his own convictions immoral. It is in fact this antipathy that makes for the main dramatic turn in the novel, which otherwise Jacobi devoted more and more over successive revisions[29] to a series of

---

28. Friedrich Heinrich Jacobi, *Werke* (Leipzig: Fleischer, 1820), V, 14. Further references from the novel are to page numbers in this edition.

29. Jacobi originally published *Woldemar* in 1777 under the title "Freundschaft und Liebe: Eine wahre Geschichte, von dem Herausgeber von Eduard Allwills Papieren," in Wieland's *Teutscher Merkur;* the novel first appeared under the title of its chief character in 1779, when it was published as *Woldemar: Eine Seltenheit aus der Naturgeschichte, Theil I.* Jacobi also published in that year a piece entitled "Ein Stück Philosophie des Lebens und der Menschheit: Aus dem zweiten Bande von Woldemar," in the *Deutsches*

philosophical conversations among the small circle of family-related friends – Woldemar's brother and his wife, his brother's friend and his wife (the eldest of Hornich's daughters), and Hornich's middle daughter, Henriette, who remains unmarried but develops a sort of spiritual friendship with Woldemar.

Hornich has watched with ill humor the relation of Woldemar and Henriette and, on his deathbed, extracts a promise from Henriette that she will not marry Woldemar. Although Hornich does not know it, the promise is unnecessary: Henriette has no intention of trading her *Seelenfreundschaft* with Woldemar for marriage, and professes herself happy to see Woldemar married to her best friend, Allwina.

Woldemar happens to hear of the promise Henriette made, however, and – seeing her action as an injury – begins to withdraw his affections. His expression of grief at Henriette's promise shows up clearly the importance of the recognition of the other to Jacobi's notion of the hyper-sentimental beautiful soul: "So that was a deception then that we felt one in everything – one heart, one soul? I must go out of myself, as from a stranger, . . . Henriette is to me someone other, she is *against me*" (328–9).

Henriette, meanwhile, who does not know that Woldemar has learned of her promise, experiences his "hard heart" against her. Trying to come to terms with this, she thinks that part of what may have estranged him is the local gossip reflecting surprise that Woldemar married Allwina instead of her. She decides to confess to Woldemar what she hears people are saying – the first of her two important confessions in the novel – but that does not change Woldemar's evident distance from her.

When Henriette finally finds out what has made Woldemar angry, however, her reactions run in the same sentimental vein as his: "Woldemar was injured; she herself was at fault" (369). Her sense of identity with him gets the better of her: "Fearfully must the first slight feeling of a doubt about me have unsettled the man! He felt a wound which of itself could never be healed!" (387)

Her sense of having caused a wound leads her to a confession, which in turn prompts the change in Woldemar's hard heart to an act of forgiveness. The act, as Woldemar expresses it, sounds like a mutual one: "If

---

Museum. The 1794 and 1796 revisions contain both of the earlier parts, as well as important new material: for the full account, see Frida David, *Friedrich Heinrich Jacobis "Woldemar" in seinen verschiedenen Fassungen* (Leipzig: Voigtländer, 1913).

you could see me as I see myself, you could not forgive me. But you do forgive me, and I accept your forgiveness. You thereby become yet more heavenly!" (461–2)

The novel concludes with the characters' drawing a moral from quotations that stand on their respective walls – on Woldemar's wall the scriptural command "Judge not!" and on Henriette's, a quotation from Fenelon, "Trust love. It takes all, but gives all." (482)

4. Hegel and Jacobi

What did Hegel see in Jacobi's (somewhat peculiar) sketch of this (somewhat peculiar) romantic hero? As with his attitude toward the Romantics in general, Hegel's stance toward the kind of beautiful soul that Jacobi sketches and the language of reconciliation that is possible for him is complicated, involving both acceptance and criticism.

Hegel's explicit assessments of Jacobi's philosophical project and its claims of immediate faith in conviction – from his early Jena criticism of Jacobi's subjectivism to his later *Encyclopedia* attack on the "immediate" attitude toward knowing that he found in both Jacobi and Descartes – are, it might be pointed out, so harshly negative that any "appropriation" of something Jacobian here might be thought surprising.[30] Yet Hegel's interest in Jacobi's novelistic praxis seems to have been in some tension with his assessment of the theoretical worth of Jacobian philosophizing.

30. Hegel's stance toward Jacobi's philosophical project and its claims of immediate faith in conviction is in the main rather harshly critical, from his early treatment of it as a philosophy of subjective yearning (see *Glauben und Wissen*, translated as *Faith and Knowledge* by Walter Cerf and H. S. Harris [Albany: State University of New York Press, 1977], 97–152) to his later criticisms in the *Encyclopedia* (Hegel's *Logic*, trans. William Wallace [Oxford: Oxford University Press, 1873], 95–112) and the *Lectures on the History of Philosophy* (trans. E. S. Haldane and Frances H. Simson [London: Kegan Paul, 1896], 410–422). It does not appear that Hegel always made clear (as in his *Aesthetics* criticism of the plot of *Woldemar*) that the Jacobian presentation of "beautiful soul" figures was itself meant to be critical. It is perhaps true, as Falke claims (*Begriffne Geschichte*, 325), that Hegel's appropriation of Jacobi's novel as "interpretive praxis" was simply keener than his aesthetic theory's criticism of the work; certainly this distinction is relevant when comparing Hegel's appropriation of Sophocles' *Antigone* in the *Phenomenology* to his less inspired account of the play in the *Aesthetics* lectures. Also, as George diGiovanni has suggested (in his translation of Jacobi, *The Main Philosophical Writings and the Novel "Allwill"* [Montreal: McGill-Queen's University Press, 1994], 165), it appears that Hegel began to appreciate (clearly by the time of his 1817 review of Jacobi's *Werke*) the implicit rationality of natural societies and the possibilities for social and historical reconciliation that Jacobi had articulated.

To begin with, *Woldemar* was part of Hegel's reading – from the editions of the 1770s, which he read in Tübingen with Hölderlin and other friends, to the last revision in 1796, which he reread before writing the *Phenomenology*.[31] It is not difficult to see what attracted particularly the younger Hegel to Jacobi's work: from his Frankfurt essay on, Hegel shows an affinity with Jacobian claims about "subjective freedom" as the heart of what must be justified in accounts of post-Kantian conscience. The Frankfurt essay, in addition to trying to understand the meaning of the Gospel command "Judge not," features an exegesis derived from Jacobi of the Gospel passage in which Jesus eats grain on the Sabbath.

This stress on the subjective side of human freedom is a *leitmotif* in the philosophical conversations that Jacobi weaves (not so artistically) through *Woldemar*. Woldemar, for example, gets a rise out of Henriette when he quotes her favorite author, Hemsterhuis, to the effect that there are times when an ethical person must act entirely on his own thoughts and feelings, in contradiction to what public opinion might demand. Brutus, he says, may have committed a crime against his society, but not from the perspective of the good.

Jacobi, of course, put all of these speeches in the mouth of a hero whom its author wanted to "follow to the grave" in the conflicts and madnesses he endured – a critical stance that Hegel's own explicit discussions of Jacobi do not always appreciate. Yet the dialectic of conscience that emerges from this consideration of the subjective side of freedom encapsulates much of what seems to be between the sorts of novels Schlegel and Rousseau, respectively, are writing. And it is Jacobi's ability to capture the oppositions involved in the language expressive of such notions of conscience – as well as the possible grounds for their resolution – that caught Hegel's narrative eye.

The issue that caught Schlegel's eye – the conflict between the subjective claim of conscience and public opinion – can be seen in *Woldemar* in Henriette's first confession, as well as in the continuing *contretemps* between Woldemar and traditional villagers like Hornich. The agentive attitude that goes along with conscience's side here is one that looks to the particular demands of an individual's subjectivity. In *Lucinde*, this concern with the particular meant a confessional claim of "evil" against the universal, apparently tidy order of "Decency," "Morality," and "Beauty of Soul." The action that brings Henriette into conflict in *Woldemar*, while

31. Or so claims Falke.

not flagrantly against convention in the sense that Schlegel's novel cel-
ebrated, nonetheless involves a similar sort of particular-against-universal
claim. The action with which Woldemar finds fault is, on her claim,
done out of a specific concern for her father.

Meanwhile, it is the dual *Bildung* that we have seen in the communi-
tarian project of Rousseau's Wolmar – a beautiful soul's rising above
common prejudices by trusting her own heart and then rising above the
particularity of her own desire by acting only according to universally
recognizable standards – that appears in Woldemar's perspective on what
Henriette has done. Yet this conscientious judging according to universal standards leaves Woldemar devastatingly alone with his own exclama-
tions of having been abandoned by his friend's particular motives.

The language of confession – if it involves only the particularist, fallibilist expression of itself as separable from universal claims, or the un-
relenting judging of particular motives by a universal standard – can offer no resolution of the oppositions to which it gives rise. The language
of forgiveness that Jacobi suggests points to a way in which the two sides
can recognize one another under a new conception of agency.

For Jacobi, of course, this grounds for reaccepting the other is, like
sense perception, a matter of immediate connection. God, the world,
and others are to be taken, so Jacobi claims, as a matter of *faith* or trust –
the peculiar successor claim of "givenness" that we have seen nonetheless emerges in the post-Kantian world. For Hegel, no such immediate
grounds are adequate for a modern conception of agency. What is required, however, is to find the spiritual equivalent – that is to say, the
self-conscious, recognitive equivalent – of this immediate and affecting
act of forgiveness.

5. Hegel's Appropriation of Forgiveness: From the Reconciliation of Spirit to the Possibility of Modern Ethical Agency

The act of forgiveness at this moment in the "Spirit" chapter must represent, of course, something more than an act of ordinary forgiveness
for a particular misdeed of the sort that we have seen between characters
in the novelistic account of the beautiful soul. Since what Hegel sketches
is a forgiveness between the figures of "universal" and "acting" consciousness, we have before us a moment in which, as Jay Bernstein has
put it, "what is forgiven is not this or that transgression, but *transgression*

as such."[32] As such, we move within the *PhG* narrative *beyond* a consideration of agency – and the necessary opposition between judging and acting that it represents.[33]

But we may also read this moment of forgiveness in the context of another transition that seems to be required by Hegel's project. By the end of the "Spirit" chapter, the *PhG* has sketched a way to understand modern agency in terms that acknowledge both a universal demand for a self-grounding account of agency and a particular set of connections for an individual agent through which he may see his identity within a form of life. It has set up the demand for such a reconciliation by examining the (historically insufficient) attempts, in tragic *amor fati* and comic pantomime, that do not allow for such reconciled agency.[34] In the context of the *PhG*, this project of reconciliation remains, however, very much *just* a project, since Hegel moves directly to the consideration of "religion" without beginning to work out the institutions or prac-

32. Bernstein, "Conscience and Transgression," 67. See also Harris on *PhG* §670: "the process of what Hegel calls *Verzeihung* is not that of ordinary 'forgiveness' at all. In essence, we are dealing with a logical forgiveness, exchanged between the agent and the observer, for the inevitable one-sidedness of being agent and observer" (Harris, *Hegel's Ladder,* II, 503).

33. As Harris has pointed out, this means a move to a perspective in "religion" from which we can watch an unfolding of historical moments that are not most properly assessed in terms of our usual moral judgments. It is important to add that this does not imply, as many of Hegel's readers seem to have thought, that "all is forgiven" before the bar of history. Such an interpretation – unfortunately suggested by Hegel's own language concerning the *Weltgericht* that is implicit in *Weltgeschichte* – ignores the careful way in which Hegel addresses such issues as the judgments that can be made in later times about practices, such as slavery, that are no longer in accordance with the notion of ethical freedom. Hegel's point, as expressed in his discussion of slavery and freedom in the *Philosophy of Right* (§57R), is that the judgment that insists on contemporary moral standards and the judgment that attempts to exonerate the practitioners of such a practice are both one-sided.

  The relation of forgiveness and history, as well as the symmetry or asymmetry involved in Hegel's forgiveness scene, are discussed in Robert Bernasconi's perceptive comparison of Hegelian forgiveness and Levinasian pardon ("Hegel and Levinas: The Possibility of Forgiveness and Reconciliation," *Archivio di Filosofia* 54 [1986]: 325–46).

34. One of the ongoing questions about the *PhG* has been how to assess the relative places of (modern, Kant-inspired) morality and (ancient, Greek-inspired) *Sittlichkeit*. Wood claims that morality is "historically" but not "systematically" superior, but Pinkard has argued well that, while the *PhG* account presents the notion of "morality" as a higher claim within its dialectic, nevertheless something about the context of *Sittlichkeit* is required for our access to that notion (Pinkard, *Hegel's "Phenomenology,"* 269–270 and 417–18, n. 2). Both an agent's freedom and his "identification" with what he does are required in Hegel's view of modern agency.

tices that would be required for agency along these lines. Hegel does turn to carry out this project of giving an account of agency within the institutions of modern ethical life some dozen years after the *PhG*, but, as Hegel's readers know well, the context of that account giving is different in important ways. Hegel's new *Logic* and the philosophical system that he publishes in its wake require a different consideration of a number of issues in the account of agency he will give in his lectures on the *Philosophy of Right:* most strikingly, Hegel will develop a notion of *Sittlichkeit* that now emerges from contradictions inherent in morality and that is distinctly modern in its various institutions.

The road from the *PhG* to the *Philosophy of Right* is a complicated one. In the following chapter, I will argue that the narrative concerns with agency that we have seen develop from a reading of the *PhG* are indeed present within the specific project of the *PR*. Before we leave the context of this last chapter on the *PhG*, however, I should like to emphasize how forgiveness – as the recapitulatory moment in the *PhG* that comes to terms with both the retrospectivity and theatricality of action – indicates something about the conditions that will hold for the account of agency and institutions that we will get in the *PR*. There are three issues for Hegel's later account that forgiveness seems particularly to set up: the questions of judgment and responsibility, the acceptability of agent-relative reasons for action, and the recognitive structure underlying claims of conscience.

1. The imperative "Judge not," which so influences Hegel and Jacobi, does not for Hegel (nor, I think, for Jacobi) mean that ordinary moral judgment of one's own and others' actions is something that is no longer ethically acceptable. Rather, the appeal to the Gospel command suggests that forgiveness is concerned with what possible authorization there may be for *correct* judging – a judging that must acknowledge the retrospective and theatrical sides of agency that we have seen. That is to say, forgiveness establishes certain standards for judgment by requiring the forgiver to be concerned precisely with *those conditions that can be involved for an agent in any action.* As a *revision of judgment,* forgiveness would seem to be first of all a move to assess an action from an *impersonal* perspective – one that, unlike the hard heart's initial judgment, is free of personal considerations that a judge may pretend he has escaped. Like Butler in his account of forgiveness, Hegel thinks that forgiveness may be based on a consideration of an agent's *fallibility* – the inadvertence that may attach to an action or simply an agent's

mistakenness.[35] When I forgive you, I look thus from an impersonal perspective that takes these facets of your action into consideration.[36]

2. The "impersonal" perspective important for forgiveness does not mean that only agent-neutral reasons for action can count, however. We may, for example, have a reason to forgive not only in cases where an action we thought malicious can be understood as mistaken or inadvertent, but also in cases where an apparently malicious action can be understood to stem from an agent's "self-love" or particular self-interest. As we have seen, Hegel's presentation of the "beautiful soul" makes quite sharp the issue of forgiving self-interested action: the "judging" beautiful soul does not even allege particular maliciousness on the part of the agent, but points simply to the apparent interestedness of the agent and claims that *that* is precisely what is wrong with the action. Forgiveness is thus a form of ethical judgment under which an agent's claim to indi-

35. Cf. the classic account in Joseph Butler, *Fifteen Sermons Preached at the Rolls Chapel* (London: Botham, 1726), Sermon VIII, "Upon Resentment," and Sermon IX, "Upon Forgiveness of Injuries," as well as recent discussion in Jeffrie G. Murphy and Jean Hampton, *Forgiveness and Mercy* (Cambridge: Cambridge University Press, 1988); Aurel Kolnai, "Forgiveness," in *Ethics, Values and Reality: Selected Papers of Aurel Kolnai* (Indianapolis: Hackett, 1978); Norvin Richards, "Forgiveness," *Ethics* 99 (October 1988): 77–97; David Novitz, "Forgiveness and Self-Respect," *Philosophy and Phenomenological Research* 58: 2 (June 1998): 299–315; R. J. O'Shaughnessy, "Forgiveness," *Philosophy* 42 (Oct. 1967): 336–352; H. J. N. Horsbrugh, "Forgiveness," *Canadian Journal of Philosophy* 4 (1974): 269–282; Martin P. Golding, "Forgiveness and Regret," *Philosophical Forum* 16 (Fall–Winter 1984–5): 121–137; Elizabeth Beardsley, "Understanding and Forgiveness," in *The Philosophy of Brand Blanshard,* ed. Paul Arthur Schilpp (LaSalle, Illinois: Open Court, 1980), 247–257; Klaus-M. Kodalle, "Der 'Geist der Verzeihung': Zu den Voraussetzungen von Moralität und Recht," in *Recht, Macht, Gerechtigkeit,* ed. Joachim Mehlhausen (Gutersloh: Kaiser, 1998), 606–624; and Joram Graf Haber, *Forgiveness* (Savage, Maryland: Rowman and Littlefield, 1991).

36. This move to the impersonal cannot mean, however, the sort of impersonality that exonerates the agent because of facts of the case that show that, all things considered, he acted involuntarily. Impersonality in this sense – what Thomas Nagel talks about in terms of the "objective disengagement" that might temporarily allow us to view even heinous crimes without anger – cannot be forgiveness, since it is not at all clear that forgiveness is always concerned with the kind of complete exoneration of agent for deed that the "impersonal view" on this interpretation permits. But, on Hegel's view, impersonality also cannot mean what Butler thinks it does: assessing responsibility only in terms of the agent's – supposedly nonmalicious – intention (as opposed to the consequences that ensue). As we have seen in the examination of retrospectivity, Hegel's "tragic" perspective on action would lead him to ask whether cases of moral luck – i.e., cases in which an agent is in fact responsible for certain unintended consequences of his deed – can be forgiven on this perspective. If an agent is to be forgiven in such cases of moral luck, how can that forgiveness stem from the imputation of an intention divorced from consequences (however nonmalicious an intention it may be) to the agent in question?

vidual satisfaction in an action is not to be held against him, but is to be at least compatible with the account we give of the norms for which he can be said to act. Forgiveness, then, involves the issue of particular motivation as well as that of justification; it allows that there may be acceptable agent-relative reasons for an action. A successful reason for action, as Hegel will come to elaborate in the *Philosophy of Right*, can be neither a purely moral imperative nor a purely prudential reason for action, but must involve both an *ethical* connection to an other and some sense that I myself *desire* that connection.

3. The argument of the last section of "Spirit," as we have seen, is that the authority of conscience is for Hegel finally something that depends on its setting in a recognitive structure like forgiveness. While "conscience" will have a somewhat different place within the structure of ethical institutions in the *PR*, it will still require in order to be operative the context of various forms of ethical recognition of the sort that forgiveness provides – that is, those in which the *particular* interest of an individual agent (one's "right," for example) is compatible with a larger ethical norm (one's "duty").

Forgiveness is, then, crucial not only as the moment in which the retrospective and theatrical sides of action can be recognized, but also as a sort of standard that will be implicit in Hegel's ultimate treatments of issues such as justification, motivation, and the ethical ground of conscientiousness. If I am right that Hegel's recapitulatory notion of forgiveness in the *PhG* sets up important conditions for his ultimate account of agency in the *PR*, it may open the possibility for understanding that project, as well, in the context of the moments of agency that we have developed. In the following chapter, I will examine how the central concept of Hegel's *PR* – that of the rational and free will – might be linked to the concerns of retrospectivity, sociality, and forgiveness, and what light that connection might shed on the project of an Hegelian understanding of modern ethical life.

FROM THE *PHENOMENOLOGY* TO THE *PHILOSOPHY OF RIGHT:* HEGEL'S CONCEPT OF THE WILL AND THE POSSIBILITY OF MODERN ETHICAL LIFE

The path that we have taken in the previous chapters requires some assessment. Someone interested in Hegel's philosophy of agency – in the questions of what it would mean, on his account, for an agent to have desires or to act for reasons, or for an agent to be free – might object that our reading of the *Phenomenology*'s treatment of these topics has been pursued in a somewhat tangential manner, drawing as it does on a consideration of such issues as the relations among literary genres like tragedy, comedy, and the romantic novel. If it is a *theory* of agency that is supposed to emerge from an engagement with these literary texts, does such a theory not have conceptual grounds that can be set out on their own, apart from their evocative connections with literary genres? And further, if Hegel's ultimate system could present the elements of agency that we have identified as all deriving from, say, a conception of rational will, what then are we to say of the literary approach that opened up these elements in the first place? Does Hegel, as might seem evident from a quick comparison of the *PhG* to his later works, simply leave such concerns behind when he moves to his mature system?

The mature Hegel did, of course, present a philosophy of agency in the context of his system's eventual *Philosophy of Spirit*. Within the context of his systematic *Encyclopedia*, Hegel sketched a transition in the *Philosophy of Subjective Spirit* from "theoretical" to "practical spirit" – where the shaping of agency from the side of the individual is considered – and then showed how practical spirit itself leads to the further notion of "free spirit." Under this latter notion, which Hegel presented first in the *Philosophy of Objective Spirit* and then in greater detail in his *Philosophy of Right,* freedom and agency are rooted in an account of the central institutions of what Hegel calls "ethical life" (the family, civil society, and the state).[1]

The problems with connecting the *PhG*'s treatment to Hegel's later *Philosophy of Spirit* are also, of course, well known: shifts in the underlying logic, in the relation of the *PhG* to the system as a whole, not to mention evident changes to and additional elements present in Hegel's ethical and political philosophy between 1807 and 1821.[2] A full study of this relationship would require a book of its own, but I believe that, in the scope of a final chapter, it is possible to see how the three elements of agency that we have seen emerge in the *PhG* can be shown to derive from Hegel's distinctive concept of the rational and free will that anchors the *PR* and is presented in its initial paragraphs.

In what follows, I will focus on Hegel's exposition of the concept of the will in the Introduction to the *Philosophy of Right,* a discussion placed at the transition point within Hegel's ultimate system that interests us the most in connection with the notion of agency: the move from the "subjective" side of spirit and the account of what makes an individual agent to the grounding of the rational and free will in the institutions of ethical life.[3] I hope to show that an examination of the three elements

1. In the context of the present chapter, I will not be concerned to give an account of the various textual differences between the *Philosophy of Objective Spirit* and the *Philosophy of Right,* or between the two published works and the lecture notes. I have, where useful, drawn on the lecture material – which, as I will suggest, gives an important window onto Hegel's continuing use of especially tragic literature for (at least the oral) exposition of his philosophy of agency.

   References in what follows are to the *Philosophy of Right* by paragraph number, or refer to the Remarks (R) or Additions (A) thereto in Hegel, *Elements of the Philosophy of Right,* ed. Allen W. Wood, trans. H. B. Nisbet (Cambridge: Cambridge University Press, 1991). The lecture series material from which the additions were drawn is referred to in the text as follows: *VPR* 1–4: *Vorlesungen über Rechtsphilosophie, 1818–1831,* ed. Karl-Heinz Ilting, 4 vols. (Stuttgart: Frommann Verlag, 1973); *VPR* 17: *Die Philosophie des Rechts: Die Mitschriften Wannenmann (Heidelberg 1817/18) und Homeyer (Berlin 1818/19),* ed. Karl-Heinz Ilting (Stuttgart: Klett-Cotta, 1983); and *VPR* 19: *Philosophie des Rechts: Die Vorlesung von 1819/ 1820 in einer Nachschrift,* ed. Dieter Henrich (Frankfurt: Suhrkamp Verlag, 1983).

2. After the publication of the *Phenomenology,* Hegel's view of his system undergoes a number of significant changes. Among the scholarly issues that a fuller account of the move from the *PhG* to the *PR* would need to address are the status of the *PhG* in this later system, and the various issues in Hegel's own political and ethical philosophy that came to require a different treatment (a notable example is the relation of "morality" and "conscience" to "ethical life," which is quite different on *PhG* and *PR* versions).

3. The claims of Hegel's ethical and political philosophy in the *Philosophy of Right* have been the subject of a number of recent studies: Allen Wood, *Hegel's Ethical Thought* (Cambridge: Cambridge University Press, 1990); the essays in Robert Pippin, *Idealism as Modernism*

central to the "literary" opening out of the problem of agency in the *PhG* can give us a way of approaching three crucial sets of questions for the *PR*'s account of the will:

1. What is the nature of will and how can we understand it to be *free?*
2. What is the status of *reason* and *desire* on such an account of freedom?
3. To what *ends* in the social and ethical world do an agent's desires and reasons connect and how are such institutions conditions for one's agency?

I will consider in turn how each of these central questions for the *PR* is rooted in the exposition of agency we have explored in the more literary moments of the *PhG,* concluding with a brief discussion of the status of literature in Hegel's post-*PhG* view of agency.

1. Retrospectivity and Hegel's Concept of the Will

In Chapter 2, we saw that Hegel developed the notion of action's retrospectivity in the *Phenomenology of Spirit* from a reading of Greek tragedy, in particular of the Sophoclean *Antigone.* In that context, Hegel looked to Greek tragedy as making clear the "original" notion of action in the sense of a "breaking open" of something that is implicit but "silent" in an action until it is done.

In the Introduction to the *Philosophy of Right,* Hegel offers a brief but pregnant account of the will that sheds some light on why action has such a retrospective character. Hegel's analysis of the concept of will in these well-known paragraphs (§5–7) involves an exploration of two opposed moments observable in our willing: (1) the moment of "pure indeterminacy" – the will's ability, as Hegel puts it, "to free myself from everything, to renounce all ends, and to abstract from everything"; and (2) the moment of "finitude or particularization," concerned with the fact that "I do not merely will – I will *something.*"

The will is, Hegel says, "the *unity* of both these moments," a unity that

(Cambridge: Cambridge University Press, 1997); Robert Williams, *Hegel's Ethics of Recognition* (Berkeley: University of California Press, 1997); Paul Franco, *Hegel's Philosophy of Freedom* (New Haven: Yale University Press, 1999); Alan Patten, *Hegel's Idea of Freedom* (Oxford: Oxford University Press, 1999); Steven B. Smith, *Hegel's Critique of Liberalism: Rights in Context* (Chicago: University of Chicago Press, 1989); Mark Tunick, *Hegel's Political Philosophy: Interpreting the Practice of Legal Punishment* (Princeton: Princeton University Press, 1992); and Michael Hardimon, *Hegel's Social Philosophy: The Project of Reconciliation* (Cambridge: Cambridge University Press, 1994).

he fleshes out in part by means of a play on the German expressions for resolution or decision: on the one hand is the expression *etwas beschliessen,* which means literally "to *close* something," to restrict the will's indeterminacy to a specific content; on the other hand is the expression *sich entschliessen,* which means literally "to *un*close *oneself,*" a phrase that suggests that decisive action is an opening out of a person's indeterminate will. Hegel's explication of these two expressions for decisive willing suggests an important resemblance to the language of action's tragic "breaking open": "the indeterminacy of the will itself, as something neutral yet infinitely fruitful, the original seed of all existence *(Dasein),* contains its determinations and ends within itself, and merely *brings them forth* from within" *(PR* §12R).

The position that Hegel sketches here is, at least in formula, fairly clear: against the indeterminacy and empty formalism associated most strongly in his mind with the Kantian–Fichtean will, on the one hand, and a more positivist account of particularist willing on the other hand, a full and adequate account of the will must somehow bring these two sides of the will together. It is with this "somehow," of course, that the more difficult questions for Hegel's account start to arise. The two sides of the will are contained in a famous Hegelian "third":

> What is properly called the will contains both the preceding moments [of universal and particular will]. . . . [T]he third moment is that 'I' is with itself in its limitation; as it determines itself, it nevertheless still remains with itself and does not cease to hold fast to the universal. *(PR* §7A)

On what Hegel calls this "concrete concept of freedom," an agent must be able to understand his will as freely present *in* what he wills, or find himself – on Hegel's distinctive formula for freedom – "by himself *in* another." The underlying notion of Hegel's brief discussion of the will seems to be, then, that it is not possible to give an account of the will and its freedom in general that is divorced from the particular commitments that a will has made.

This inseparability of universal and particular wills has an obvious connection to the inseparability of intention and result that we discussed in Chapter 2. On neither account can an agent's will be understood in terms of a sort of introspectible prior "intention" that caused the action.[4] In the sense that it avoids Cartesian claims of the introspectible

4. The *PR*'s consideration of this topic within the context of an account of the rational and free will, however, involves certain demands that were not present in the *PhG*'s tragic

mental and a mind/body dualism, Hegel's ultimate view of agency thus may be characterized as generally compatibilist, but his actual position is somewhat more distinctive, and in fact eschews compatibilist reliance on the causal.[5]

As we saw in Chapter 2, what is at issue is part of a larger Hegelian claim about how action and the mental are to be regarded. A proper treatment of the question of agency involves for Hegel a concern with *spirit,* rather than nature – and hence a move to considerations of action that cannot be understood simply in causal terms. It is not that Hegel thinks that causal accounts are to be dispensed with, but rather that a causal treatment of *agency* – and of how an agent is connected to what he does – would involve a misapplication of categories.[6]

How best to characterize Hegel's approach to agency in the *PR?* In Chapter 2, we suggested that Hegel's view of the relation between intention and result had much in common with Aristotle's view of agency, and that connection seems even stronger on examining Hegel's *PR* contextualization of the question of agency within the larger realm of spirit. In fact, without offering the reader any explanation of his appeal to these terms, Hegel seems – from the very first paragraphs of the *PR* Introduction onward – to appropriate the Aristotelian language of body and soul (*PR* §1A)[7] and of "second" nature (*PR* §4)[8] for the task of grounding the concept of will in the realm of the "spiritual."

situations. For one thing, Hegel will be required to show how it is that an account of intention and responsibility *can* be given that confirms our intuitions that intention must somehow be marked off from result as well as being considered in its light. This is the task of Hegel's explicit *Handlungstheorie* in the initial paragraphs of the "Morality" section. For helpful accounts of this section, see the discussion in Michael Quante, *Hegels Begriff der Handlung,* and the account of Hegel's treatment of moral luck in Wood, *Hegel's Ethical Thought,* 142–4.

5. For a sketch of Hegel's position on this issue, see Robert Pippin, "Naturalness and Minded-ness: Hegel's Compatibilism," *European Journal of Philosophy* 7:2 (August 1999): 194–212.

6. In a well-known passage in the *Science of Logic,* Hegel criticizes the "inadmissible appli-cation" of the notion of cause for relations within organic and spiritual life: the "com-mon jest," for example, that in history great effects can arise from small causes may be "an instance of the conversion which spirit imposes on the external; but for this very rea-son, this external is not *cause in the process,* in other words, this conversion itself sublates the relationship of causality" (*Hegel's Science of Logic,* trans. A. V. Miller [Atlantic Highlands, NJ: Humanities Press International, 1989], 562).

7. On Hegel's appropriation of the language of body and soul, see James Dodd, "The Body as 'Sign and Tool' in Hegel's *Encyclopedia,*" *International Studies in Philosophy* 27:1 (1995): 21–32, and John Russon, *The Self and Its Body in Hegel's "Phenomenology of Spirit"* (Toronto: University of Toronto Press, 1997).

8. Hegel refers to Aristotle's notion of "second nature" both in his discussion of habit in

Hegel's appeal to these Aristotelian terms for an elaboration of his own notion of spirit rests on his discussion of their usefulness in the preceding *Philosophy of Subjective Spirit.*[9] What seems most important about the notion of spirit developed there is that it provides a way around the usual metaphysical representations of the soul–body "problem" that view soul or spirit as a separate (material or immaterial) "thing." In his Aristotelian orientation, Hegel looks rather to a notion of spirit as the *form* or activity of body. For Hegel, this form cannot be understood as something "supervenient" on natural causality since it is *spirit* that is prior to (and considered as the "truth of") nature and on its own terms "free."

As the move from soul as *form* of body to spirit as *truth* of nature might suggest, Hegel's working out of the notion of spirit cannot be understood merely as the carrying-out of an Aristotelian project.[10] The non-Aristotelian side of Hegel's approach can likewise be seen in the sort of "generative" or developmental account that Hegel gives of the relation between the "lower" but nonetheless purposive elements of our organic being (desires, impulses) and reason.[11] In this account, as we will see in the next section, Hegel both appropriates the Aristotelian notion of "second nature" and adapts it for his own distinctive sense of *Bildung*.

"subjective spirit" – where Hegel says that it is "through . . . habit that I first exist for myself as a thinking being" (*Philosophy of Subjective Spirit,* §410) – and in his description of the institutions of ethical life in the *PR*. As Wolff points out, there is for Hegel no mental activity that is not in some way habit, or something that has taken on the form of habit (Wolff, *Das Körper-Seele Problem,* 178–182).

9. Hegel's famous claim that "Aristotle's books on the soul . . . are still by far the best or even the sole work of speculative interest on this general topic" (*Hegel's Philosophy of Subjective Spirit,* ed. M. J. Petry [Dordrecht: Reidel, 1978], §378) has frequently been ignored in the scholarly literature, but has recently attracted a deserved consideration. See Alfredo Ferrarin, *Hegel and Aristotle* (Cambridge: Cambridge University Press, 2001); Michael Wolff, *Das Körper-Seele Problem* (Frankfurt: Klostermann, 1992); and Willem A. deVries, *Hegel's Theory of Mental Activity* (Ithaca: Cornell University Press, 1988). For treatments of Hegel's philosophy of subjective spirit, see Adriaan Peperzak, *Selbsterkenntnis des Absoluten* (Stuttgart and Bad Cannstatt: Frommann-Holzboog, 1987); and the collections *Hegels Theorie des subjektiven Geistes,* ed. Lothar Eley (Stuttgart and Bad Cannstatt: Frommann-Holzboog, 1990), and *Psychologie und Anthropologie oder Philosophie des Geistes,* ed. Franz Hespe and Burkhard Tuschling (Stuttgart and Bad Cannstatt: Frommann-Holzboog, 1991).

10. For one thing, the roots of the Aristotelian "psychology" are much more closely tied in the *de Anima* to the Aristotelian philosophy of nature. For a careful discussion of the issue as a whole, see Ferrarin, *Hegel and Aristotle,* Chapter 8.

11. Unlike Aristotle, who distinguishes the cognitive aspect of soul from its other functions, Hegel looks for rationality and subjectivity as already present in the more basic moments of organic life, such as in animal purposiveness.

2. Reason, Desire, and Sociality:
Hegel's Generative Account of the Will

To claim that desire and reason must be taken together in an account of the free will may be the sort of claim that makes it tempting to charge Hegel with some philosophical version of the sin of "having and eating." Exactly how does Hegel think that these two sides of the will can cohere in a single unified concept of the will?

One form of this objection may be found, for example, in Alan Patten's recent treatment of Hegel's idea of freedom, which asks whether Hegel's account here should be considered on the whole a Kantian one. On the one hand, Hegel seems quite Kantian in his theory of *justification,* insisting that claims of right can be grounded only on what is rational and independent of contingently given desires and inclinations. On the other hand, when it comes to the particular side of willing and *motivation,* Hegel seems clearly *anti-*Kantian, since he gives an un-Kantian role to our motivating desires and impulses in action, and the individual agent must find his *satisfaction* in the action (as Hegel says at one point in the *Philosophy of Subjective Spirit,* "nothing great has been, nor can be accomplished without passion" [EG §474]). How do Hegel's accounts of justification and motivation go together, then?[12]

We have already seen in Chapters 2 and 3 some ground for suspecting that Hegel's account of the relation between my rational reflectivity and my desires will – despite its justificatory appeal to the rational – avoid the usual Kantian dichotomy between reason and desire. If we accept Hegel's notion of action's retrospectivity, to begin with, the account that we will give of desire must involve facets of an action that sometimes emerge only within the action itself: an agent may not fully be able, for example, to characterize his desire(s) until he reflects upon them after he has acted. Moreover, as was claimed in Chapter 3, the contingency or givenness of desires seems to require a more thoroughgoing account of desire formation than is often allowed by many theories of agency: while my desires might seem to be among those things that are most "my own," they are nonetheless subject to the theatrical set of relations that make us social beings.

In both the *PhG* and the *PR,* a crucial term in Hegel's answer to the question concerning the relation of reason and desire is that of *Bildung.* In the *PhG,* we saw that this notion involved both a general project of

---

12. Patten, *Hegel's Idea of Freedom,* 53.

education and a specific concern with the theatrical elements of culture, where the experience of desire is socially mediated. Hegel's mature formulation of the issue in the *PR* – reaching back in some sense to his pre-*PhG* attempt at Frankfurt to sketch a more unified picture of human action that avoids the separation between reason and desire (as well as that between positive law and moral duty) in Kantian ethics – offers the following sketch of the relation between desire and reason: first, Hegel begins not with an assessment of maxims, but with an acknowledgment of the existence of desires[13] themselves as leading toward action and as having a directedness that may already have an implicit rational character; second, my attempt to *satisfy* or to act on a desire involves of necessity the application of some principle of rationality,[14] usually at first an hedonic calculus aiming at the general satisfaction of my impulses (in happiness); but finally, if I am to be fully satisfied in my action – in my regard that it is my own – the rationality principle that I apply must not be conditional on a contingent end like happiness (which may depend on some view of desire preference that I can't be sure is my own, since others may have influenced my selection of it). Rather, the principle of my action must involve my willing that I be present in my action as a free agent. This revision of my reason for acting involves an identification with my end or object as one in which the freedom and rationality of my agency is thus to be recognized; it is the

---

13. In the *Philosophy of Spirit*, Hegel distinguishes the more immediate character of *desire* (*Begierde*), which is always for something single, from *impulse* (*Trieb*), which "embraces a series of satisfactions" (*Philosophy of Subjective Spirit*, §473A; further text references are by paragraph number to *EG*); in the *Philosophy of Right*, however, Hegel does not appear to differentiate between the two (*PR* §11). In what follows, I have followed the latter usage and referred to desire and impulse as virtually synonymous.

14. "The subject *is* the activity of the formal rationality of satisfying impulses" (*Philosophy of Subjective Spirit* §475, stress mine); more fully, in the Introduction to the *Philosophy of History*:

> [Man] places the ideal, the realm of thought, *between* the demands of the impulse and their satisfaction. In the animal, the two coincide; it cannot sever their connection by its own efforts – only pain or fear can do so. In man, the impulse is present before it is satisfied and independently of its satisfaction; in controlling or giving rein to his impulses, man acts in accordance with *ends* and determines himself in the light of a general principle. It is up to him to decide what end to follow; he can even make his end a universal one. In so doing, he is *determined* by whatever conceptions he has formed of his own nature and volitions. It is this which constitutes man's independence: for he knows what it is that determines him. (Hegel, *Lectures on the Philosophy of World History: Introduction [Reason in History]*, trans. H. B. Nisbet [Cambridge: Cambridge University Press, 1975], 49–50; the word "ends" is stressed in the translation, but the other stresses are my own.)

burden of Hegel's account of agency to show how such rational ends correspond to the institutions of ethical life in which I may see my agency embodied.

The process Hegel sketches here, which he calls not only the *Bildung* (*PR* §20) of impulses, but also their *Aufheben* (or *Erheben, PR* §21R) or "purification" (*Reinigung, PR* §19), is the process by which the implicitly free natural will, acting to satisfy its impulses, becomes universal will, will "by itself" or genuinely free (*PR* §21, §23). The process reveals that the universal ethical commitments that are the objects of a genuinely free will correspond on the level of content to objects of the natural will's impulses – desires for property, family, economic corporations and so forth – that have now been invested with a rational form, or understood to be rational ends. Thus, the impulses themselves[15] have only an implicit (*an sich* or *formelle*)[16] rationality distinct from genuine rationality, in which the ethical agent "wills his own freedom" in association with the attachments of ethical life – for example, to property, family, and city.[17]

What "continuity" of reason and desire means for Hegel, then, is that

15. Hegel speaks here of those impulses that become, in the attempt of natural will to satisfy them, the various duties associated with ethical life. He does allow that the natural will can involve irrational impulses: the natural will would not even be "formally" free if all of its impulses were bound of necessity to "complete" themselves as ethical duties. But such irrational impulses are, Hegel thinks, inherently incapable of leading to satisfaction on any rational principle, and hence not those impulses with which an account of free and rational agency must primarily concern itself. "Not all impulses are rational, but all rational determinations of the will also exist as impulses. As natural, the will can also be irrational, partly against reason, partly contingent. But these do not concern us; only those impulses have interest for us which are posited through rational development." (*VPR* 4, 128)

16. Cf. *EG* §474 and *PR* §11.

17. Hegel's actual working out of this sketch of the process of "purification" is complicated by its application for three different but related purposes: on a "subjective" level, to show how an individual natural will rises from the level of impulse to that of free will; on an "objective" level, to show how a will that is free "in itself" comes to identify itself with the ends associated with the institutions of right (property, morality, ethical life); and on an "historical" level, how the various ethical institutions that are commitments of the free and rational agent have come to be taken as such. These three tasks are addressed, respectively, in the treatment of "practical spirit" in the *Philosophy of Spirit;* in the development from natural will to ethical will in the *Philosophy of Right* and the section on "objective spirit" in the *Philosophy of Spirit;* and in the progressions from the "actualization of rational self-consciousness through its own activity" to "spirit" in the *Phenomenology of Spirit.* Although each of these applications represents a different fundamental task and is therefore slightly different from the others – with the *Phenomenology* account giving the most colorful range of "revisions" to principles of action – there are in each of these parallel processes similar determinate features.

impulses are not eradicated (*ausgerottet*) but rather given a new form (*aufgehoben*).[18] The "*rational shape of the impulses*" – that is, what we can take to be rational in them, what a rationality principle can consistently find in them to take as an end – remains "in the ethical system of the whole" in its "true determination of their being graded in respect of one another."[19] Hegel says *both* that "nothing is ever accomplished without impulse" *and* that the free will is something "without impulse":[20] to deny desires satisfaction is, Hegel claims, a "monkish practice,"[21] but likewise, for an agent to have only an impulsive attachment to ethical ends cannot be sufficient for a coherent account of modern agency.

It is an account precisely of such *ends* in our agency that Hegel's approach to the question of the relation of desire and reason requires as a next step. What are the social structures and institutions that make action – and the recognition of an agent in his action – possible? I will consider this issue in the next section.

3. Recognitive Identity and Reconciliation in the Institutions of Ethical Life

Hegel has, by means of the notion of *Bildung*, linked together universal and impersonal standards of judgment with the particular side of individual satisfaction in a way that would give an individual a "reason" to act that could be classified neither merely as a Kantian moral reason on the one hand nor merely as a prudential (Aristotelian) reason on the other. What ends or goals would an agent have, then, on such "ethical reasons"?

The elaboration of such institutions as the "objective" structure of freedom is, in fact, the largest part of the project of the *PR*. The realm of *Sittlichkeit*, or ethical life, consists of institutions in which individuals are connected to ends in which they can recognize their identity as agents.

In his connections to family, civil society, and the state, an individual may, for example, see his action as at once universally valid and individually satisfactory. Bringing together or reconciling these two sides of agency in the *PhG* involved a consideration of the practice of forgiveness

18. *Philosophy of Subjective Spirit* §480A, cf. *VPR* 4, 134.
19. *Philosophy of Subjective Spirit* §480A.
20. *Philosophy of Subjective Spirit* §475, *VPR* 4, 129; *Philosophy of Subjective Spirit* §482.
21. *VPR* 19, 64.

on which the impersonal and the agent-relative sides of action were recognized. In the *PR,* the notion of reconciliation may be said to offer the
underlying structure of the institutions of ethical life.[22]

   This notion of a reconciliation of impersonal and agent-relative sides
of action is visible both in the structure of the *PR* as a whole and in the
nature of the reasons that connect any agent to the particular moments
of ethical life itself. In its structure, the *PR* unites two famous pieces of
what we might call the holy grail of post-Kantian moral and political
thought: a comprehensive ethics that unites the claims of both *right*
and *morality.*[23] On the level of individual reasons for action within particular moments of ethical life, the *PR* is always concerned with showing how every genuinely ethical relation is at once one of *duty* and of
right: "in the process of fulfilling his duty, the individual must somehow
attain his own interest and satisfaction or settle his own account" (*PR*
§261R). The mediating term for this account of individual obligation
to the ethical whole is the articulated structure of that whole: an ethical duty looks less like something sacrificial, and is more my own, when
it is a part of my membership in a smaller ethical unit, such as the family or a corporation. Hegel's example of such a reconciling structure
when he introduced the "concrete" concept of freedom was that of
familial love and friendship, in which we are "not one-sidedly within
ourselves, but willingly limit ourselves with reference to an other, even
while knowing ourselves in this limitation as ourselves" (*PR* §7R). An

22. Among Hegel's early readers, the notion of political and social reconciliation was turned
    into a charge of accommodationism with regard to the Prussian reaction; later readings
    tended to understand this tendency in the light of Hegel's perceived interest in his-
    torical theodicy. Following the postwar trend in Hegel scholarship that has in the main
    defended Hegel on the score of his relations to Prussian authority, and in the wake of
    serious recent examinations of Hegel's ethical and political philosophy which have chal-
    lenged previous understandings of the role of history in Hegel, there has been a reex-
    amination of the purpose and importance of reconciliaiton in Hegel's political thought.
    See particularly T. M. Knox, "Hegel and Prussianism," in *Hegel's Political Philosophy,* ed.
    Walter Kaufman (New York: Atherton Press, 1970), 13–29; Shlomo Avineri, *Hegel's
    Theory of the Modern State* (Cambridge: Cambridge University Press, 1972); and most re-
    cently, Michael Hardimon, *Hegel's Social Philosophy: The Project of Reconciliation.*
23. The project of reconciling the claims of right and morality in the wake of Kant's moral
    philosophy was a "Kantian" problem even before the appearance of Kant's own *Recht-
    slehre* in 1797: see Wolfgang Kersting, "Sittengesetz und Rechtsgesetz – Die Begründung
    des Rechts bei Kant und den frühen Kantianern," in *Rechtsphilosophie der Aufklärung,* ed.
    Reinhard Brandt (Berlin: Walter de Gruyter, 1982), 148–177. On Hegel's early attempt
    at Frankfurt to wrestle with this question and how that attempt is visible still within the
    PR, see my article "The *Metaphysics of Morals* and Hegel's Critique of Kantian Ethics,"
    History of Philosophy Quarterly 14:4 (October 1997): 379–402.

agent's reasons for acting on behalf of his family thus are not prudential calculations of self-interest, nor are they derived from an impersonal moral imperative. He does not perform an ethical duty with the
thought of "giving up" something that is his, but rather with a sense of
having already come to *identify* his own interests and desires with those
of ethical duty.

Being able to recognize oneself *in* one's agency may thus be taken to
be the object of freedom in the *PR* – a principle which Hegel even claims
should govern the most difficult tasks of reconciliation within society,
such as that of a criminal with his punishment. In other words, nothing, says Hegel, in an interesting turn of phrase, should be ultimately
experienced by an agent as a merely "external fate" (*PR* §228R). Hegel's
appeal to a notion of reconciled fate is curious, precisely because the
PR seems to have left behind the more embedded tragic account of action that we considered in the *PhG*. As a final question, it is worth considering what has become of the literary structures of tragedy and the
other genres in Hegel's final philosophy of agency.

4. Farewell to Literature? The Use of Literary Modes in the Project of Modern Ethical Life

The *PhG* is, with good reason, often thought to mark within Hegel's life
a sort of Prospero's farewell to the employment of literary and imaginative arts. The specific philosophical tasks of the *PhG*, which required
so much attention to culturally and literarily rich "forms of spirit," are,
of course, different from the tasks associated with the systematic exposition of subjective and objective spirit. Stylistically, too, Hegel's post-*PhG*
philosophical system must be conducted in a different voice, a "strict
style," and the various artistic forms are now, it would seem, of interest
only with respect to their "pastness": the *Aesthetics* speaks, in a well-
known passage, of the end of art,[24] and the *PR* itself makes clear that
the world of modernity cannot in any sense be like the conflictual world
of Antigone and Greek tragedy.[25]

What, then, are we to make of the fact that nonetheless something

---

24. For a discussion of various meanings of Hegel's claim, see Stephen Bungay, *Beauty and
Truth: A Study of Hegel's Aesthetics* (Oxford: Oxford University Press, 1984), 76–89.

25. Hegel writes about the ethical whole in the *Philosophy of Right*, for example, as if tragic
conflict is something that is primarily past: "[T]he ethical Idea, *without such unfortunate
collisions* and the downfall of the individuals caught up in this misfortune, is *actual* and
present in the ethical world . . ." (*PR* §140R [footnote]).

of the narrative character of action that literature opened up seems again present in the *PR*'s account of freedom, and that the moments of retrospectivity, sociality, and recognitive identity seem central, as well, within Hegel's ultimate account of the rational will and modern ethical life?

Hegel's stylistic and philosophical changes notwithstanding, it is a striking fact that – particularly in the *lectures* that he gave at Berlin using the *PR* as text – literary works and genres remain for Hegel important modes of access to the notion of agency.[26] It is also striking that the richest set of references in the *PR* and the lecture series are those that concern tragedy and the issue of retrospectivity, whereas the more distinctively modern experiences of the world of *Bildung* and the recognitive structure of identity in comedy and the novel work through the *PR* in a somewhat more diffuse way.[27] What resonance these notions may have for our own time – what bearing, for example, they may have on a set of social structures quite different from the Berlin of 1821 – is an issue that clearly might bear exploration in terms of an attention to the literary and artistic forms that developed more fully after Hegel's death – for example, in the great novels of the nineteenth century or in film.[28] Hegel's achievement with respect to literature and the notion of agency can best be judged, however, by a consideration of the questions that

26. Even though Hegel makes clear that the time of tragedy's artistic sway is past, it is still ancient tragedy to which Hegel appeals when he wants to explain concepts such as responsibility and moral luck. Hegel's references to tragedy in the published text of the *Philosophy of Right* (see paragraphs 101A, 118R, 140R [footnote], 166R, 257R) are given context by the larger discussion of tragedy in the lecture series concerning the philosophy of right (see especially *VPR* 4, 319–323; *VPR* 17, 78–79; and *VPR* 19, 93–94; and the "Randbemergunken" in Hegel's own hand in Hoffmeister's edition [*Grundlinien der Philosophie des Rechts* (Hamburg: Meiner, 1955), 380–2]).

27. The discussion of *Bildung* in the *PR* refers, as did the *PhG*'s, to the problem of wealth and the criticism of it by figures like Diogenes (cf. *PR* §195 and *PhG* §524). The "Conscience" section in the *PR* makes reference back to the *PhG*'s treatment of the beautiful soul, but the structure of the *PR* discussion of conscience itself – as well as its place within the organization of the *PR* – has changed in a significant way: for an account of the differences between *PhG* and *PR* treatments of conscience, see Dietmar Köhler, "Hegels Gewissendialektik," *Hegel-Studien* 28 (1993): 127–141; on the structure of the *PR* account and the interpretive difficulties it has posed for readers, see Daniel Dahlstrom, "The Dialetic of Conscience and the Necessity of Morality in Hegel's *Philosophy of Right*," *The Owl of Minerva* 24:2 (Spring 1993): 181–189.

28. One relevant issue here is the emergence of a novelistic form, unlike those that Hegel considers in the *PhG*, that is *non*romantic. The issues of retrospectivity and sociality or dependence on others loom large in Robert Pippin's recent *Henry James and Modern Moral Life* (Cambridge: Cambridge University Press, 2000).

would animate such an exploration. If the central, even inescapable questions discernible in the products of modern literary artists are ones that concern the account we give of our freedom as modern agents – and understanding such freedom seems to be bound up with the questions of norms we have come to take and relations that characterize our social lives – then a distinctly "Hegelian" approach to the question of agency and literature may have a wider relevance for contemporary ethical life, as well.

SELECTED BIBLIOGRAPHY

WORKS BY HEGEL

1. Collected Works

Gesammelte Werke. Edited by the Rheinisch-Westfälischen Akademie der Wissenschaften. Hamburg: Felix Meiner, 1968– .

Sämtliche Werke: Jubiläumsausgabe in zwanzig Bänden. Edited by Hermann Glockner. Stuttgart: Frommann, 1941.

Werke: Theorie Werkausgabe. Edited by Eva Moldenhauer and Karl Markus Michel. Frankfurt: Suhrkamp Verlag, 1969– .

2. Individual Works

Aesthetics: Lectures on Fine Art. Translated by T. M. Knox. Oxford: Clarendon Press, 1975.

Early Theological Writings. Translated by T. M. Knox, with an introduction and fragments translated by Richard Kroner. Chicago: University of Chicago Press, 1948.

Elements of the Philosophy of Right. Edited by Allen W. Wood, translated by H. B. Nisbet. Cambridge: Cambridge University Press, 1991.

Encyclopedia of the Philosophical Sciences in Outline and Critical Writings, ed. Ernst Behler. (The German Library, Vol. 24). New York: Continuum, 1990.

Faith and Knowledge. Translated by Walter Cerf and H. S. Harris. Albany: State University of New York Press, 1977.

Grundlinien der Philosophie des Rechts. Edited by J. Hoffmeister. Hamburg: Meiner, 1955.

Hegel on Tragedy. Edited by Anne and Henry Paolucci. New York: Harper and Row, 1975; reprint, Westport, CT: Greenwood Press, 1978.

Hegel's Philosophy of Mind. Translated by William Wallace and A. V. Miller. Oxford: Clarendon Press, 1971.

Hegel's Philosophy of Subjective Spirit. Edited and translated by M. J. Petry. Dordrecht: D. Reidel, 1978.

Hegels Theologische Jugendschriften. Edited by Herman Nohl. Tübingen: Mohr, 1907.

Lectures on the Philosophy of Religion. Translated by E. B. Speirs and J. Burdon Sanderson. London: Routledge and Kegan Paul, 1962; reprint, New York: The Humanities Press, 1974.

Lectures on the Philosophy of Religion. Edited by Peter C. Hodgson. Berkeley: University of California Press, 1984.

Lectures on the Philosophy of World History: Introduction (Reason in History). Translated by H. B. Nisbet. Cambridge: Cambridge University Press, 1975.

Natural Law. Translated by T. M. Knox. Philadelphia: University of Pennsylvania Press, 1975.

Phänomenologie des Geistes. Edited by J. Hoffmeister. Hamburg: Felix Meiner Verlag, 1955.

Phänomenologie des Geistes. Edited by Hans-Friedrich Wessels and Heinrich Clairmont. Hamburg: Meiner, 1988.

Phenomenology of Spirit. Translated by A. V. Miller. Oxford: Oxford University Press, 1977.

Die Philosophie des Rechts: Die Mitschriften Wannenmann (Heidelberg 1817/18) und Homeyer (Berlin 1818/19). Edited by Karl-Heinz Ilting. Stuttgart: Klett-Cotta, 1983.

Philosophie des Rechts: Die Vorlesung von 1819/1820. Edited by Dieter Henrich. Frankfurt: Suhrkamp Verlag, 1983.

Philosophy of Right. Translated by T. M. Knox. London: Oxford University Press, 1952.

Three Essays: 1793–1795. The Tübingen Essay, Berne Framgents, The Life of Jesus. Edited and translated by Peter Fuss and John Dobbins. Notre Dame: University of Notre Dame Press, 1984.

Vorlesungen über Rechtsphilosophie. Edited by Karl-Heinz Ilting. Stuttgart and Bad Cannstatt: Frommann-Holzboog, 1974.

3. Letters

Briefe von und an Hegel. Edited by J. Hoffmeister and R. Flechsig. Hamburg: Felix Meiner, 1961.

Hegel: The Letters. Translated by Clark Butler and Christiane Seiler. Bloomington: Indiana University Press, 1984.

OTHER WORKS CITED

Allison, Henry. "We Can Act Only Under the Idea of Freedom." *Proceedings of the American Philosophical Association* 71:2 (November 1997): 39–50.

Avineri, Shlomo. *Hegel's Theory of the Modern State.* Cambridge: Cambridge University Press, 1972.

Axelos, C. "Zu Hegels Interpretation der Tragödie." *Zeitschrift für philosophische Forschung* 19 (1965): 654–667.

Baum, Manfred, and Meist, Kurt. "Hegel's 'Prometheische Confession': Quellen für vier Jenaer Aphorismen Hegels." *Hegel-Studien* 7 (1972): 79–90.

Behler, Ernst. "Freidrich Schlegel und Hegel." *Hegel-Studien* 2 (1963): 203–250.

Benjamin, Walter. *The Origin of German Tragic Drama*. Frankfurt: Suhrkamp, 1977.

Bergel, Lienhard. "Cervantes in Germany." In *Cervantes Across the Centuries*, ed. Angel Flores and M. J. Benardete, 315–352. New York: Dryden Press, 1948.

Bernasconi, Robert. "Hegel and Levinas: The Possibility of Forgiveness and Reconciliation." *Archivio di Filosofia* 54 (1986): 325–46.

Bernstein, J. M. *The Philosophy of the Novel: Lukács, Marxism and the Dialectics of Form*. Minneapolis: University of Minnesota Press, 1984.

The Fate of Art: Aesthetic Alienation from Kant to Derrida and Adorno. University Park: Pennsylvania State University Press, 1992.

"Conscience and Transgression: The Persistence of Misrecognition." *Bulletin of the Hegel Society of Great Britain* 29 (Spring–Summer 1994): 55–70.

Bird, Graham. "McDowell's Kant: *Mind and World*." *Philosophy* 71 (1996): 219–243.

Boey, Koen. "De literatur en haar betekenis in Hegels 'Phänomenologie.' In *Om de waarheid te zeggen. Opstellen over filosofie en literatuur aangeboden aan Ad Peperzak*, ed. K. Boey et. al., 67–78. Nijmegen: Kampen, 1992.

Bowra, C. M. *Sophoclean Tragedy*. Oxford: Clarendon Press, 1944.

Boyle, Nicholas. *Goethe: The Poet and the Age*. Vol. 1: *The Poetry of Desire (1749–1790)*. Vol. 2: *Revolution and Renunciation (1790–1803)*. Oxford: Clarendon Press, 1991– .

Bradley, A. C. *Shakespearean Tragedy*. London: Macmillan, 1964.

"Hegel's Theory of Tragedy." In *Hegel on Tragedy*, ed. Anne and Henry Paolucci, 367–388. New York: Harper and Row, 1975; reprint, Westport, CT: Greenwood Press, 1978.

Brandom, Robert. "Freedom and Constraint by Norms." *American Philosophical Quarterly* 16 (1979): 187–196.

Making It Explicit: Reasoning, Representing and Discursive Commitment. Cambridge, MA: Harvard University Press, 1994.

"Some Pragmatist Themes in Hegel's Idealism: Negotiation and Administration in Hegel's Account of the Structure and Content of Conceptual Norms." *European Journal of Philosophy* 7:2 (August 1999): 164–189.

Articulating Reasons: An Introduction to Inferentialism. Cambridge, MA: Harvard University Press, 2000.

Bungay, Stephen. *Beauty and Truth: A Study of Hegel's Aesthetics*. Oxford: Oxford University Press, 1984.

Butler, Joseph. *Fifteen Sermons Preached at the Rolls Chapel*. London: Botham, 1726.

Butler, Judith. *Subjects of Desire*. New York: Columbia University Press, 1987.

Chytry, Josef. *The Aesthetic State: A Quest in Modern German Thought*. Berkeley: University of California Press, 1989.

Critchley, Simon. *Very Little . . . Almost Nothing: Death, Philosophy, Literature*. London: Routledge, 1997.

Dahlstrom, Daniel. "Die Quelle der Sittlichkeit in Hegels 'Phänomenologie des Geistes'." *Hegel-Jahrbuch* 1987: 256–261.

"Die 'schöne Seele' bei Schiller und Hegel." *Hegel-Jahrbuch* 1991: 147–156.

"The Dialectic of Conscience and the Necessity of Morality in Hegel's *Philosophy of Right*." *The Owl of Minerva* 24:2 (Spring 1993): 181–189.

David, Frida. *Friedrich Heinrich Jacobis "Woldemar" in seinen verschiedenen Fassungen.* Leipzig: Voigtländer, 1913.

Derbolav, Josef. "Hegels Theorie der Handlung." *Hegel-Studien* 3 (1965): 209–223.

Desmond, William. *Beyond Hegel and Dialectic.* Albany: State University of New York Press, 1992.

deVries, Willem A. *Hegel's Theory of Mental Activity.* Ithaca and London: Cornell University Press, 1988.

Dickey, Laurence. *Hegel: Religion, Economics and the Politics of Spirit, 1770–1807.* Cambridge: Cambridge University Press, 1987.

Diderot, Denis. *Rameau's Nephew and Other Works.* Translated by Jacques Barzun and Ralph Bowen. Indianapolis: Library of Liberal Arts, 1956.

Dodd, James. "The Body as 'Sign and Tool' in Hegel's *Encyclopedia.*" *International Studies in Philosophy* 27:1 (1995): 21–32.

Donougho, Martin. "Die Theorie der Tragödie bei Hölderlin und Hegel." In *Jenseits des Idealismus: Hölderlins letzte Homburger Jahre (1804–06),* ed. Christoph Jamme and Otto Pöggeler, 55–82. Bonn: Bouvier, 1988.

"The Woman in White: On the Reception of Hegel's *Antigone.*" *The Owl of Minerva* 21:1 (Fall 1989): 65–89.

Eley, Lothar, ed. *Hegels Theorie des subjektiven Geistes.* Stuttgart and Bad Cannstatt: Frommann-Holzboog, 1990.

Falke, Gustav-H. H. "Hegel und Jacobi." *Hegel-Studien* 22 (1987): 129–142.

Begriffne Geschichte. Berlin: Lukas, 1996.

Ferrarin, Alfredo. *Hegel and Aristotle.* Cambridge: Cambridge University Press, 2001.

Fichte, J. G. *Werke.* Edited by I. H. Fichte. Berlin: W. de Gruyter, 1971.

The Science of Knowledge. Translated by Peter Heath and John Lachs. Cambridge: Cambridge University Press, 1982.

Flay, Joseph C. *Hegel's Quest for Certainty.* Albany: State University of New York Press, 1984.

Fleischacker, Samuel. *A Third Concept of Liberty: Judgment and Freedom in Kant and Adam Smith.* Princeton: Princeton University Press, 1999.

Forster, Michael. *Hegel and Skepticism.* Cambridge, MA: Harvard University Press, 1989.

Hegel's Idea of a Phenomenology of Spirit. Chicago: University of Chicago Press, 1998.

Franco, Paul. *Hegel's Philosophy of Freedom.* New Haven: Yale University Press, 1999.

Frankfurt, Harry. "Freedom of the Will and the Concept of a Person." *The Journal of Philosophy* 68:1 (January 1971): 5–20.

Fried, Michael. *Absorption and Theatricality: Painting and Beholder in the Age of Diderot.* Berkeley: University of California Press, 1980.

Friedman, Michael. "Exorcising the Philosophical Tradition: Comments on John McDowell's *Mind and World.*" *Philosophical Review* 105:4 (1996): 427–67.

Fuss, Peter, and John Dobbins. "The Silhouette of Dante in Hegel's *Phenomenology.*" *Clio* 11 (1982): 387–413.

Gellrich, Michelle. *Tragedy and Theory: The Problem of Conflict since Aristotle.* Princeton: Princeton University Press, 1988.

Giusti, Miguel. "Bemerkungen zu Hegels Begriff der Handlung." *Hegel-Studien* 22 (1987): 51–72.

Goethe, Johann Wolfgang von. *Faust.* Translated by Walter Arndt, edited by Cyrus Hamlin. New York: W. Norton, 1976.

Gram, Moltke. "Moral and Literary Ideals in Hegel's Critique of 'The Moral World-View.'" *Clio* 7:3 (1978): 375–402.

Griswold, Charles. *Adam Smith and the Virtues of Enlightenment.* Cambridge: Cambridge University Press, 1999.

Haber, Joram Graf. *Forgiveness.* Savage, MD: Rowman and Littlefield, 1991.

Haering, T. "Die Entstehungsgeschichte der Phänomenologie des Geistes." In *Verhandlungen des dritten Hegelkongresses,* ed. B. Wigersma. Tübingen: Mohr, 1934.

Hardimon, Michael. *Hegel's Social Philosophy: The Project of Reconciliation.* Cambridge: Cambridge University Press, 1994.

Harris, H. S. *Hegel's Development: Toward the Sunlight, 1770–1801.* Oxford: Clarendon Press, 1972.

Hegel's Development: Night Thoughts (Jena 1801–1806). Oxford: Clarendon Press, 1983.

Hegel's Ladder. Vol. 1: *The Pilgrimage of Reason.* Vol. 2: *The Odyssey of Spirit.* Indianapolis: Hackett, 1997.

Hartmann, Klaus. "Hegel: A Non-Metaphysical View." In *Hegel: A Collection of Critical Essays,* ed. Alasdair MacIntyre, 101–124. Notre Dame, IN: University of Notre Dame Press, 1976.

Haym, Rudolf. *Hegel und seine Zeit.* Berlin: Rudolph Gaertner, 1857.

Die Romantische Schule: Ein Beitrag zur Geschichte des deutschen Geistes. Berlin: Weidmann, 1906.

Henrich, Dieter. "Hölderlin über Urteil und Sein." *Hölderlin Jahrbuch* 16 (1965–6): 73–96.

"Beauty and Freedom: Schiller's Struggle with Kant's Aesthetics." In *Essays in Kant's Aesthetics,* ed. Ted Cohen and Paul Guyer, 237–257. Chicago: University of Chicago Press, 1982.

Hespe, Franz, and Tuschling, Burkhard, eds. *Psychologie und Anthropologie oder Philosophie des Geistes.* Stuttgart and Bad Cannstatt: Frommann-Holzboog, 1991.

Hinchman, Lewis. *Hegel's Critique of the Enlightenment.* Gainesville: University Presses of Florida, 1984.

Hirsch, E. "Die Beisetzung der Romantiker in Hegels Phänomenologie: Ein Kommentar zu dem Abschnitte über die Moralität." In *Materialen zu Hegels "Phänomenologie des Geistes,"* ed. H.-F. Fulda and Dieter Henrich, 245–275. Frankfurt: Suhrkamp, 1973.

Hölderin, Friedrich. *Sämtliche Werke.* Edited by F. Beissner and A. Beck. Stuttgart: Cotta, 1943– .

Hösle, Vittorio. *Die Vollendung der Tragödie im Spätwerk des Sophokles: Ästhetisch-historische Bemerkungen zur Struktur der attischen Tragödie.* Stuttgart and Bad Cannstatt: Frommann-Holzboog, 1984.

Houlgate, Stephen. *Hegel, Nietzsche and the Criticism of Metaphysics.* Cambridge: Cambridge University Press, 1986.

Hulbert, James. "Diderot in the Text of Hegel: A Question of Intertextuality." *Studies in Romanticism* 22 (1983): 267–291.

Hundert, E. J. "A Satire of Self-Disclosure: From Hegel through Rameau to the Augustans." *Journal of the History of Ideas* 47 (1986): 235–248.

Hyppolite, Jean. *Genesis and Structure of Hegel's 'Phenomenology of Spirit'*. Translated by Samuel Cherniak and John Heckman. Evanston: Northwestern University Press, 1974.

Jacobi, F. H. *Werke*. Leipzig: 1820.

The Main Philosophical Writings and the Novel "Allwill." Translated by George diGiovanni. Montreal: McGill–Queen's University Press, 1994.

Jamme, Christoph. *Ein ungelehrtes Buch: die philosophische Gemeinschaft zwischen Hölderlin und Hegel in Frankfurt, 1797–1800*. Bonn: Bouvier, 1983.

Jauss, Hans Robert. "The Dialogical and the Dialectical *Neveu de Rameau;* or, The Reciprocity between Diderot and Socrates, Hegel and Diderot." In Jauss, *Question and Answer: Forms of Dialogic Understanding*, trans. Michael Hays, 118–147. Minneapolis: University of Minnesota Press, 1989.

Jones, John. *On Aristotle and Greek Tragedy*. New York: Oxford University Press, 1962.

Jurist, Elliot L. "Hegel's Concept of Recognition." *The Owl of Minerva* 19:1 (Fall 1987): 5–22.

"Tragedy In/And/Of Hegel." *Philosophical Forum* 25:2 (Winter 1993): 151–172.

Kainz, Howard P. *Hegel's Phenomenology*. Athens: Ohio University Press, 1976 and 1983.

Kant, Immanuel. *Gesammelte Schriften*. Edited by the Königlich Preussischen Akademie der Wissenschaften. Berlin and Leipzig: de Gruyter, 1922.

Critique of Judgment. Trans. J. H. Bernard. New York: Hafner, 1951.

Kaufmann, Walter. *Hegel: Texts and Commentary*. Garden City, NY: Doubleday, 1965.

Kelly, G. A. *Hegel's Retreat from Eleusis*. Princeton: Princeton University Press, 1970.

"Notes on Lordship and Bondage." In *Hegel: A Collection of Critical Essays*, ed. Alasdair MacIntyre. Garden City, NY: Anchor Books, 1972.

Kersting, Wolfgang. "Sittengesetz und Rechtsgesetz – Die Begründung des Rechts bei Kant und den frühen Kantianern." In *Rechtsphilosophie der Aufklärung*, ed. Reinhard Brandt, 148–177. Berlin: Walter de Gruyter, 1982.

Klinger, F. M. *Fausts Leben, Taten und Höllenfahrt*. Frankfurt: Insel, 1964.

Knox, T. M. "Hegel and Prussianism." In *Hegel's Political Philosophy*, ed. Walter Kaufman, 13–29. New York: Atherton Press, 1970.

Kodalle, Klaus-M. "Der 'Geist der Verzeihung': Zu den Voraussetzungen von Moralität und Recht." In *Recht, Macht, Gerechtigkeit*, ed. Joachim Mehlhausen, 606–624. Gutersloh: Kaiser, 1998.

Köhler, Dietmar. "Hegels Gewissendialektik." *Hegel-Studien* 28 (1993): 127–141.

Kojève, Alexandre. *Introduction to the Reading of Hegel: Lectures on the 'Phenomenology of Spirit'*. Edited by Allan Bloom, translated by James H. Nichols, Jr. Ithaca and London: Cornell University Press, 1983.

Kolnai, Aurel. "Forgiveness." In *Ethics, Values and Reality: Selected Papers of Aurel Kolnai*. Indianapolis: Hackett, 1978.

Königson, Marie-Jeanne. "Hegel, Adam Smith et Diderot." In *Hegel et le Siècle des Lumières*, ed. Jacques D'Hondt, 51–70. Paris: Presses Universitaires de France, 1974.

Korsgaard, Christine. *Sources of Normativity*. Cambridge: Cambridge University Press, 1996.

Lacoue-Labarthe, Philippe, and Jean-Luc Nancy. *The Literary Absolute*. Translated by P. Barnard and C. Lester. Albany: State University of New York Press, 1987.

Lauer, Quentin. *A Reading of Hegel's "Phenomenology of Spirit."* New York: Fordham University Press, 1976.

Lear, Jonathan. "Katharsis." *Phronesis* 33:3 (1988): 297–326.

Lukács, Georg. *The Theory of the Novel: A Historico-Philosophical Essay on the Forms of Great Epic Literature*. Translated by Anna Bostock. Cambridge, MA: MIT Press, 1971.

The Young Hegel: Studies in the Relations between Dialectics and Economics. Translated by Rodney Livingstone. Cambridge, MA: MIT Press, 1975.

McDowell, John. *Mind and World*. Cambridge, MA: Harvard University Press, 1994.

McGinn, Colin. *Ethics, Evil and Fiction*. Oxford: Clarendon Press, 1997.

MacIntyre, Alasdair. *After Virtue*. Notre Dame: University of Notre Dame Press, 1981.

Marshall, David. *The Figure of Theater: Shaftesbury, Defoe, Adam Smith and George Eliot*. New York: Columbia University Press, 1986.

The Surprising Effects of Sympathy: Marivaux, Diderot, Rousseau, and Mary Shelley. Chicago: University of Chicago Press, 1988.

Marx, Karl. *Surveys from Exile: Political Writings*, Vol. II. Edited by David Fernbach. New York: Vintage, 1974.

Marx, Werner. *Hegel's Phenomenology of Spirit: A Commentary on the Preface and Introduction*. Translated by Peter Heath. New York: Harper and Row, 1975.

The Philosophy of F. W. J. Schelling. Translated by Thomas Nenon. Bloomington: Indiana University Press, 1984.

Menegoni, Francesca. *Soggetto e struttura dell'agire in Hegel*. Trento: Verifiche, 1993.

Menke-Eggers, Christoph. *Tragödie im Sittlichen: Gerechtigkeit und Freiheit nach Hegel*. Frankfurt: Suhrkamp, 1996.

Mortier, Roland. *Diderot en Allemagne (1750–1850)*, 254–263. Paris: Presses Universitaires de France, 1954.

Murphy, Jeffrie G., and Jean Hampton. *Forgiveness and Mercy*. Cambridge: Cambridge University Press, 1988.

Nagel, Thomas. *Mortal Questions*. Cambridge: Cambridge University Press, 1979.

The View from Nowhere. Oxford: Oxford University Press, 1986.

Nietzsche, Friedrich. *The Birth of Tragedy and the Case of Wagner*. Translated by Walter Kaufmann. New York: Vintage Books, 1967.

Norman, Judith. "Squaring the Romantic Circle: Hegel's Critique of Schlegel's Theories of Art." In *Hegel and Aesthetics*, ed. William Maker, 131–144. Albany: State University of New York Press, 2000.

Norton, Robert. *The Beautiful Soul: Aesthetic Morality in the Eighteenth Century*. Ithaca: Cornell University Press, 1995.

Novalis [Friedrich von Hardenberg]. *Philosophical Writings*. Translated by Margaret Mahony Stoljar. Albany: State University of New York Press, 1997.

Novitz, David. "Forgiveness and Self-Respect." *Philosophy and Phenomenological Research* 58:2 (June 1998): 299–315.

Nussbaum, Martha C. *The Fragility of Goodness*. Cambridge: Cambridge University Press, 1986.

O'Grady, William. *Theory and Practice in Hegel's 'Phenomenology'*. Ph.D. dissertation, University of Chicago, 1970.

Olson, Alan. *Hegel and the Spirit: Philosophy as Pneumatology*. Princeton: Princeton University Press, 1992.

Patten, Alan. *Hegel's Idea of Freedom*. Oxford: Oxford University Press, 1999.

Peperzak, Adriaan. *Selbsterkenntnis des Absoluten*. Stuttgart and Bad Cannstatt: Frommann-Holzboog, 1987.

Pillau, Helmut. *Die fortgedachte Dissonanz: Hegels Tragödientheorie and Schillers Tragödie. Deutsche Antworten auf die Französische Revolution*. Munich: Wilhelm Fink Verlag, 1981.

Pinkard, Terry. *Hegel's "Phenomenology": The Sociality of Reason*. Cambridge: Cambridge University Press, 1994.

Hegel: A Biography. Cambridge: Cambridge University Press, 2000.

Pippin, Robert. *Hegel's Idealism: The Satisfactions of Self-Consciousness*. Cambridge: Cambridge University Press, 1989.

Modernism as a Philosophical Problem. Oxford: Blackwell, 1991.

"'You Can't Get There from Here': Transition Problems in Hegel's *Phenomenology of Spirit*." In *The Cambridge Companion to Hegel*, ed. Frederick Beiser, 52–85. Cambridge: Cambridge University Press, 1993.

"Hegelianism as Modernism," *Inquiry* 38:3 (September 1995): 305–327.

Idealism as Modernism: Hegelian Variations. Cambridge: Cambridge University Press, 1997.

"Hegel on Historical Meaning: For Example, The Enlightenment." *Bulletin of the Hegel Society of Great Britain* 35 (Spring–Summer 1997): 1–17.

"Naturalness and Mindedness: Hegel's Compatibilism." *European Journal of Philosophy* 7:2 (August 1999): 194–212.

Henry James and Modern Moral Life. Cambridge: Cambridge University Press, 2000.

Pöggeler, Otto. *Hegels Kritik der Romantik*. Bonn: Bouvier, 1956.

"Zur Deutung der Phänomenologie des Geistes." *Hegel-Studien* 1 (1961): 255–294.

"Hegel und die griechische Tragödie." *Heidelberger Hegel-Tage* (Hegel-Studien, Beiheft 1 [1964]): 285–305.

"Hegels Jenaer Systemkonzeption." In Pöggeler, *Hegels Idee einer Phänomenologie des Geistes*. Freiburg and Munich: Alber, 1973.

"Die Komposition der Phänomenologie des Geistes." In *Materialen zu Hegels 'Phänomenologie des Geistes'*, ed. Hans Fulda and Dieter Henrich, 329–389. Frankfurt: Suhrkamp, 1973.

Price, David W. "Hegel's Intertextual Dialectic: Diderot's *Le Neveu de Rameau* in the *Phenomenology of Spirit*." *Clio* 20:3 (1991): 223–233.

Quante, Michael. *Hegels Begriff der Handlung*. Stuttgart and Bad Cannstatt: Frommann-Holzboog, 1993.

"Personal Autonomy and the Structure of the Will." In *Right, Morality, Ethical Life: Studies in G. W. F. Hegel's Philosophy of Right*, ed. Jussi Kotkavirta, 75–92. Jyvaskyla: University of Jyvaskyla, 1997.

Redding, Paul. *Hegel's Hermeneutics*. Ithaca: Cornell University Press, 1996.

Redfield, James. *Nature and Culture in the Iliad: The Tragedy of Hector*. Chicago: University of Chicago Press, 1975.

Richards, Norvin. "Forgiveness." *Ethics* 99 (October 1988): 77–97.

Ricoeur, Paul. *Oneself as Another.* Translated by Kathleen Blamey. Chicago: University of Chicago Press, 1992.

Robinson, Jonathan. *Duty and Hypocrisy in Hegel's 'Phenomenology of Mind': An Essay in the Real and Ideal.* Toronto and Buffalo: University of Toronto Press, 1977.

Roche, Mark. *Tragedy and Comedy: A Systematic Study and a Critique of Hegel.* Albany: State University of New York Press, 1998.

Rose, Gillian. *Hegel contra Sociology.* London: Athlone, 1981.

Rosen, Stanley. *G. W. F. Hegel: An Introduction to the Science of Wisdom.* New Haven: Yale University Press, 1974.

Rosenberg, Jay. *The Thinking Self.* Philadelphia: Temple University Press, 1986.

Rosenkranz, Karl. *Georg Wilhelm Friedrich Hegel's Leben.* Berlin: Duncker and Humblot, 1844.

Rosenmeyer, Thomas G. *The Art of Aeschylus.* Berkeley: University of California Press, 1982.

Rosenzweig, Franz. *Hegel und der Staat.* Munich and Berlin: Oldenbourg, 1920.
Der Stern der Erlösung. Frankfurt, 1921.

Rousseau, J. J. *Politics and the Arts: Letter to M. D'Alembert on the Theatre.* Translated by Allan Bloom. Ithaca: Cornell University Press, 1968.

Royce, Josiah. *Lectures on Modern Idealism.* New Haven: Yale University Press, 1919.

Russon, John. *The Self and Its Body in Hegel's "Phenomenology of Spirit."* Toronto: University of Toronto Press, 1997.

Sax, Benjamin. "Active Individuality and the Language of Confession: The Figure of the Beautiful Soul in *Lehrjahre* and the *Phänomenologie.*" *Journal of the History of Philosophy* 21:4 (1983): 437–66.

Scheier, Claus-Artur. *Analytischer Commentar zu Hegels Phaenomenologie des Geistes.* Freiburg-Munich: Alber, 1980.

Schelling, Friedrich Wilhelm Joseph. *Sämmtliche Werke.* Edited by Karl Schelling. Stuttgart and Augsburg: Cotta, 1859.
System of Transcendental Idealism (1800). Translated by Peter Heath. Charlottesville: University of Virginia Press, 1978.

Schiller, Friedrich. *Naive and Sentimental Poetry and On the Sublime.* Translated by Julius A. Elias. New York: Frederick Ungar, 1966.
The Robbers and Wallenstein. Translated by F. J. Lamport. New York: Penguin, 1979.
Friedrich Schiller: Werke und Briefe. Edited by Klaus Harro Hilzinger et. al. Frankfurt: Deutscher Klassiker Verlag, 1988.

Schlegel, Friedrich. "Dialogue on Poetry." In *German Romantic Criticism,* ed. Leslie Willson. (The German Library, Vol. 21). New York: Continuum, 1982.
Philosophical Fragments. Translated by Peter Firchow. Minneapolis: University of Minnesota Press, 1991.

Schmeer, Hans. *Der Begriff der 'schönen Seele' besonders bei Wieland und in der deutschen Literatur des 18 Jahrhunderts.* Berlin: Ebering, 1926.

Schmidt, James. "The Fool's Truth: Diderot, Goethe and Hegel." *Journal of the History of Ideas* 57:4 (1996): 625–44.

Schulte, Michael. *Die "Tragödie im Sittlichen": Zur Dramentheorie Hegels.* Munich: Fink, 1992.

Sedgwick, Sally. "McDowell's Hegelianism." *European Journal of Philosophy* 5:1 (1997): 21–38.

Sellars, Wilfrid. *Empiricism and the Philosophy of Mind.* With an introduction by Richard Rorty and study guide by Robert Brandom. Cambridge: Harvard University Press, 1997.

Shapiro, Gary. "An Ancient Quarrel in Hegel's *Phenomenology.*" *The Owl of Minerva* 17:2 (Spring 1986): 165–180.

Shattuck, Roger. *Forbidden Knowledge: From Prometheus to Pornography.* New York: St. Martin's Press, 1996.

Siep, Ludwig. *Anerkennung als Prinzip der praktischen Philosophie.* Freiburg and Munich: Karl Alber, 1979.

Smith, Adam. *The Theory of Moral Sentiments.* Edited by A. L. Macfie and D. D. Raphael. Oxford: Clarendon Press, 1976.

Smith, John H. *The Spirit and Its Letter: Traces of Rhetoric in Hegel's Philosophy of "Bildung."* Ithaca: Cornell University Press, 1988.

Smith, Steven B. *Hegel's Critique of Liberalism: Rights in Context.* Chicago: University of Chicago Press, 1989.

Solomon, Robert. *In the Spirit of Hegel: A Study of G. W. F. Hegel's "Phenomenology of Spirit."* New York: Oxford University Press, 1983.

Sophocles. *Antigone.* Translated by Elizabeth Wyckoff. Chicago: University of Chicago Press, 1954.

Speight, Allen. "The *Metaphysics of Morals* and Hegel's Critique of Kantian Ethics." *History of Philosophy Quarterly* 14:4 (October 1997): 379–402.

——— "The Beautiful Soul and the Language of Forgiveness." In *Die Metaphysik der Praktischen Welt,* ed. C. Jamme and A. Grossmann, 238–245. Amsterdam: Rodopi, 2000.

Starobinski, Jean. *Jean-Jacques Rousseau: Transparency and Obstruction.* Translated by Arthur Goldhammer. Chicago: University of Chicago Press, 1988.

Steinberger, Peter. *Logic and Politics: Hegel's Philosophy of Right.* New Haven: Yale University Press, 1988.

Steiner, George. *Antigones.* Oxford: Clarendon Press, 1984.

Stepelevich, Lawrence S., and Lamb, David. *Hegel's Philosophy of Action.* Atlantic Highlands, NJ: Humanities Press, 1983.

Stern, Robert. "Going Beyond the Kantian Philosophy: On McDowell's Hegelian Critique of Kant." *European Journal of Philosophy* 7:2 (August 1999): 247–269.

Szondi, Peter. "Hegels Lehre von der Dicthung." In Szondi, *Poetik and Geschichtsphilosophie,* Vol. 2, 269–511. Frankfurt: Suhrkamp, 1974.

Taylor, Charles. *Hegel.* Cambridge: Cambridge University Press, 1975.

——— "Hegel and the Philosophy of Action." In *Hegel's Philosophy of Action,* ed. Lawrence Stepelevich and David Lamb, 1–18. Atlantic Highlands, NJ: Humanities Press, 1983. (A later version of this paper appears as "Hegel's Philosophy of Mind" in Taylor, *Human Agency and Language: Philosophical Papers I,* 77–96. Cambridge: Cambridge University Press, 1985.)

Theunissen, M. *Sein und Schein. Die kritische Funktion der Hegelschen Logik.* Frankfurt: Suhrkamp, 1978.

Thomas, Alan. "Kant, McDowell and the Theory of Consciousness." *European Journal of Philosophy* 5:3 (1997): 283–305.

Trilling, Lionel. *Sincerity and Authenticity.* Cambridge, MA: Harvard University Press, 1972.

Tunick, Mark. *Hegel's Political Philosophy: Interpreting the Practice of Legal Punishment.* Princeton: Princeton University Press, 1992.

[Unger, Friederike Helene.] *Bekenntnisse einer schönen Seele von ihr selbst geschrieben.* Berlin: Unger, 1806.

Verene, Donald Phillip. *Hegel's Recollection.* Albany: State University of New York Press, 1985.

Vierhaus, Rudolf. *"Bildung."* In *Geschichtliche Grundbegriffe: Historisches Lexikon zur politisch-sozialen Sprache in Deutschland,* ed. Otto Brunner, Werner Conze, and Reinhart Koselleck, 508–551. Stuttgart: Klett, 1972.

von Fritz, K. *Antike und moderne Tragödie.* Berlin: W. de Gruyter, 1962.

Waszek, Norbert. *The Scottish Enlightenment and Hegel's Account of "Civil Society."* Dordrecht: Kluwer, 1988.

Westphal, Kenneth. "Hegel's Critique of Kant's Moral World View." *Philosophical Topics* 19:2 (1991): 133–76.

Wiehl, Reiner. "Über den Handlungsbegriff als Kategorie der Hegelschen Ästhetik." *Hegel-Studien* 6 (1971): 135–170.

Wildt, Andreas. *Autonomie und Anerkennung: Hegels Moralitätskritik im Lichte seiner Fichte-Rezeption.* Stuttgart: Klett-Cotta, 1982.

Williams, Bernard. *Moral Luck.* Cambridge: Cambridge University Press, 1981.
Ethics and the Limits of Philosophy. Cambridge: Harvard University Press, 1985.
Shame and Necessity. Berkeley: University of California Press, 1993.

Williams, Robert. *Hegel's Ethics of Recognition.* Berkeley: University of California Press, 1997.

Wolff, Michael. *Das Körper-Seele Problem.* Frankfurt: Klostermann, 1992.

Wood, Allen. *Hegel's Ethical Thought.* Cambridge: Cambridge University Press, 1990.

INDEX

Absolute Knowledge, 40
action, *see* agency
Active Reason (literature in *PhG* section
  on, *see* Cervantes; Goethe; Schiller),
  20, 21, 24, 25, 27, 28–9, 31, 34, 35;
  narrative shape of *PhG* section, 20–3;
  as transition from Reason to Spirit, 21
actor, dramatic, 79, 82, 83
Aeschylus, 74
aesthetics, 17, 52
agency (*see also* forgiveness; narrativity;
  retrospectivity; theatricality), 1–10,
  30, 32, 36–7, 40, 92, 119; as
  appearance, 34; causal account of, 44,
  45, 126; comic, 30–1, 34, 40, 69,
  71–5; compatibilist view of, 126;
  corrigibilist view of, 4, 13, 28, 43, 45;
  expressivity of, 46, 71; first-person
  perspective of, 94; free and rational,
  102, 109, 125 n4; in Greek life, 64;
  ideal type of, 53; impersonal and
  personal sides of, 56, 102–5, 113, 118;
  intentionalist account of, 44; modern
  notion of, 8 n9, 10, 17, 35, 43, 53, 54
  n25, 56 n29, 64, 65 n38, 92, 94, 117,
  119, 121, 131, 135; nonvoluntarist
  account of, 55; philosophy of, 3, 43–4,
  71, 95, 102, 122, 123 nl; poetics of,
  46–50; in the *PR*, 121, 122, 124;
  praxical presuppositions of, 61;
  qualitative approach to, 44;
  reconciliation and, 95; social
  conditions of, 92, 130; teleological
  character of, 38, 44; third-person
  perspective of, 94; three-part claim,
  45 n6, 53–4, 56, 59, 60, 64; tragic, 27,
  30, 34, 36, 39, 40, 42, 47, 55, 59, 61,
  65–7, 72; voluntarist account of, 4, 5,
  44–5, 55, 59

agent (*see also* agency), 3–6, 33, 45, 46;
  evil, 111, 112, 116; of the heart, 28;
  identification with an action, 53, 54;
  identity of, 38, 45, 54; self-expression
  of, 37
alienation, 25, 75, 77
Allison, Henry, 2 n3
Antigone (*see also* Sophocles), 28, 35, 36,
  40, 50–67, 70, 72, 73, 97, 133
Aristophanes, 74, 75, 77, 79, 83, 84, 86;
  Clouds, 74, 76 n10, 84, 86; *Frogs*, 74
Aristotle, 44, 46–50, 66, 68 nl, 77, 126–7,
  131; *De Anima*, 127 n10; *Nicomachean
  Ethics*, 48; *Poetics*, 46–7
art, 37, 101, 111, 133
Art-Religion, 18, 38, 40–1, 73, 75 n9, 96
authenticity, 71, 88, 90, 95, 103
autonomy, 92, 102

Baum, Manfred, 26 n26
Beardsley, Elizabeth, 120 n35
beautiful soul, 7, 8, 18, 37, 38, 41, 49, 50,
  65, 94–121, 134 n27
Behler, Ernst, 111 n26
Benjamin, Walter, 42–3
Bergel, Lienhard, 30 n34
Bernasconi, Robert, 118 n33
Bernstein, J. M., 8 n9, 17 n15, 48 n15, 99
  n9, 117, 118 n32
Bildung, see Culture
Bildungsroman, 1, 12
Bird, Graham, 2 n3
Boey, Koen, 18 n16
Bradley, A. C., 50 n19
Brandom, Robert, 3 n5, 4 n7, 13 n4
Brandt, Reinhard, 132 n23
Bungay, Stephen, 17 n15, 133 n24
Butler, Joseph, 119, 120 n35
Butler, Judith, 12 n3, 69

Cartesian, *see* Descartes
categorical imperative, 102
Cervantes (*Don Quixote*), 23, 29–32, 40
Christianity, 40, 96
civil society, 123, 131
comedy (*see also* theatricality), 1, 7–8, 28, 32, 34–5, 41, 68–93, 96, 118, 122, 134; and agency, 99, 102, 118; and *Bildung*, 39; comic actor, 70, 73; comic actor as spectator, 70; as completion of tragedy, 68; Greek, 74–5; moment of, 19, 25, 36, 37, 75; *PhG* as, 12, 15, 17
community, 103, 104, 107–8, 112
confession, 110–11, 112, 114, 116–17
conscience, 7, 35 n43, 65, 95, 97, 98, 103, 104–6, 116, 119, 121, 123 n2, 134 n27; Antigone and, 51–2, 65; the beautiful soul and, 8, 98, 101–2, 106; language of, 104
consciousness, 25; acting, 104–5, 109, 118; judging, 104–5, 108, 109, 111–12, 118, 120; perverted or simple, 85–7; shapes of, in the *PhG*, 6, 12, 14, 108
corporations, 130, 132
corrigibility, 3–6, 76; and agency, 3–6; and epistemology, 3, 13, 19, 43
Critchley, Simon, 100 n11
culture, 25 n25, 75, 82, 85, 92, 97
Culture (*Bildung*), 7, 14–15, 19, 32, 35, 36–7, 39, 68, 86, 88, 91 n40, 92, 93, 117, 127, 131; comedy and, 75; in the *PR*, 128–9, 134; Spirit and, 75–7; theatricality and, 71, 86

Dahlstrom, Daniel, 64 n37, 97 n3, 98 n7, 134 n27
Dante, 13 n3
David, Frida, 114 n29
Descartes, René, 3, 14 n6, 43, 87 n31, 115, 125
desire, 4 n7, 5, 25, 53, 56, 61, 63, 67, 68, 77, 80, 93, 112, 113, 122, 124, 127, 128, 130, 133; desire-based agency, 44; epistemic access to, 70–1, 82; first- and second-order, 44; internal account of, 44, 45; social and historical conditions of, 45, 129
Desmond, William, 12 n3
deVries, Willem A., 127
Diderot, Denis, *Paradox of Acting*, 68, 79 n18, 81; *Rameau's Nephew*, 7, 18, 32 n41, 36, 37, 40, 41, 68, 75 n10, 78–84, 91–2, 97, 106, 108, 109
DiGiovanni, George, 115 n30
Dobbins, John, 13 n3
Dodd, James, 126 n7

Don Quixote (*see also* Cervantes), 23, 29–34; as comic, 30; as tragic, 30
drama (*see also* comedy; tragedy), 7 n8, 47–8, 66, 72, 74, 88, 96
duty, 103, 105, 121, 130 n15, 133

emotion, epistemic access to, 89–90
Enlightenment, 76, 84, 86, 88
epistemology, social character of, 3, 13, 19, 43
Ethical Life/Ethical Order (*Sittlichkeit*), 53, 62, 118 n34, 119, 123, 130–2; Greek, 7, 37, 38; modern, 122, 133, 134; in the *PhG*, 19, 33 n35, 55 n26, 57; in the *PR*, 131–35
ethics, 43, 48, 49 n17, 95, 105, 111, 113, 132; rationalist, 33
Euripides, 74

faith, 29, 113, 117
Falke, Gustav-H.H., 9 n10, 26 n26, 29 n31, 97 n3, 106–7, 115 n30, 116 n31
family, 123, 130, 131, 132, 133
fate, 8, 34, 49, 67, 94, 133
Faust, 23–32, 34, 36, 40, 41
Ferrarin, Alfredo, 127 nn9–10
Fichte, Johann Gottlieb, 20, 95, 102, 103, 125
Flay, Joseph, 61 n33
Force and the Understanding, 19 n17
forgiveness (*see also* novel), 1, 6, 8, 19, 35, 37, 40, 93–121, 131; and history, 118 n33; language of, 112–15, 117; moment of, 19, 40; as recognition, 38
Forster, Michael, 3 n4, 14, 22 n20, 29 n31, 38 n47
Franco, Paul, 124 n3
Frankfurt, Harry, 44 n4
Frederick the Great, 29 n31
freedom, 10, 134; of an action, 53, 95; of an agent, 44, 65, 92, 104, 116, 118 n34, 122, 125, 129, 131, 135; and property, 71; of spirit, 127; of the will, 128, 131
French Revolution, 7, 92
Freud, Sigmund, 81
Fried, Michael, 71 n6
Friedman, Michael, 2 n3
friendship, 103, 132
Fritz, K. von, 47 n11
Fulda, Hans Friedrich, 11 n1
Fuss, Peter, 13 n3

Gellrich, Michelle, 47, 50 n19, 52 n21
German idealism, 113
Geuss, Raymond, 10 n12
Given, Myth of the, 2–3, 14, 43

givenness, 2–3, 5, 53, 64–5, 70, 72, 73, 76, 77, 81, 128
Goethe, J. W. von, 9, 20, 23–5, 34, 78 n15, 82 n24, 83 n26, 98, 101, 106 n17, 108, 109; *Faust*, 13 n4, 18, 19, 23–9; *Wilhelm Meister,* 30 n35, 98, 101 n14, 106 n17, 108
Goldhammer, Arthur, 10 n12
Golding, Martin P., 120 n35
Gram, Moltke, 97 n3
Greece, ancient, 9, 35, 73, 106 n17; Greek comedy, 18, 74–5, 77; drama, 7 n8; epic, 18, 72; ethical life 7, 35, 37, 41, 59, 64; religion, 38–9, 40; tragedy, 8, 18, 42, 46, 47, 50, 73, 75 n9, 124, 133
Griswold, Charles, 10 n12, 89 n35, 90
Gruber, Johann Gottfried, 26 n26

Haakonssen, Knud, 89 n35
Haber, Joram Graf, 120 n35
Haering, T., 12, 21, 22 n30
Hamlet, 23–4, 37, 40, 75 n9
happiness, 129
Hardimon, Michael, 124 n3, 132 n22
Harris, H. S., 13 n3, 18 n16, 24 n23, 29 n29, 32 n40, 37, 40 n50, 68 nl, 74 n7, 76, 79 n17, 82 n24, 83, 87, 97 n3, 98 n6, 102 n16, 107 n19, 111 n27, 118 n32
Haym, Rudolf, 11, 12
Hegel, Georg Wilhelm Friedrich: Frankfurt years, 49, 50, 55 n26, 78; 111 n27, 116, 129, 132 n23; Jena years, 49 n18, 98 n7, 115; political philosophy of, 123, 132; and post-Kantian philosophy, 2, 7; Tübingen years, 78, 116
Elements of the Philosophy of Right, 46 n8, 48, 54 n25, 56 n29, 111 n26, 118 n33, 119, 121, 122–35
Encyclopedia of the Philosophical Sciences, 115
Lectures on Aesthetics, 7 n8, 29, 31, 38 n45, 39, 47, 50, 52, 53 n23, 68, 69 n2, 79 n18, 96, 97, 115 n30, 133
Lectures on the History of Philosophy, 115 n30
Phenomenology of Spirit (*see also* Active Reason; Art-Religion; Culture; Ethical Life/Ethical Order; Force and the Understanding; Morality; Observing Reason; Reason; Religion), as anthropological, 12, 13, 15; as *Bildungsroman,* 1, 12, 16, 17; as comedy, 1, 12, 13, 16, 69; culture in, 15, 76, 77; epistemological project of,

2–3, 13–15, 43; history in, 15, 35; history of, 11 n1, 12; literary project of, 15–16; literature and, 6–10, 17, 18, 20–41, 94, 96; logical significance of, 13, 15; metaphysical project of, 14, 15; narrative shape of, 11–41; as novel, 27, 134 n28; as palimpsest, 12, 13, 15, 21, 22 n20; pedagogical project of, 14, 15, 76; practical project of, 14; purpose/project of, 7, 9, 14, 15, 18, 21, 22, 37, 99; recollective character of, 41; relation to Hegel's later works, 11–12, 15, 52, 63 n36, 115 n30, 121, 123; as tragedy, 1, 12, 13, 16, 75; unitary readings of, 13, 15, 21, 22
Philosophy of Religion, 52
Science of Logic, 11, 119
Henrich, Dieter, 11 n1
Herder, Johann Gottfried von, 76
Hinchman, Lewis, 88 n32
Hirsch, Emanuel, 97 n3, 98 n6, 111 n27
Hölderlin, Friedrich, 9, 20, 49 n18, 98, 101, 110, 112, 116
Horsbrugh, H. J.N., 120 n35
Hösle, Vittorio, 47, 96 n1
Hulbert, James, 78 n15
Hume, David, 4 n7, 14 n6
Hundert, E. J., 78 n15
hypocrisy, 83, 100, 105
Hyppolite, Jean, 23, 32 n40

immediacy, 57–9, 60, 61, 113, 115
individual, 32, 33, 37, 40 n49, 64, 85, 88
institutions, 119, 121, 123–4, 130–3
intention, 4, 28, 34, 44, 53–60, 120 n36, 125, 126
irony, 9, 10, 101, 109–11

Jacobi, Friedrich Heinrich, 35 n43, 98, 100–4, 106, 107, 108, 109 n23, 110, 113, 117; *Allwill,* 98, 106 n17, 110; *Woldemar,* 98, 99, 106–8, 110, 111 n27, 112, 115, 116, 117
Jamme, Christoph, 49 n18
Jauss, Hans Robert, 78 n15, 82 n24
Jones, John, 48 n12
judgment, ethical, 119–20, 131
Jurist, Elliott, 13 n3
justification, 5, 6, 121, 128

Kant, Immanuel, 2, 20, 33, 38, 51, 53, 57, 92, 95, 102, 112, 118 n34, 125, 128, 129, 131
Karl Moor, 23, 27–8, 36, 40
Kaufmann, Walter, 25 n25, 132 n22
Kersting, Wolfgang, 132 n23

Klinger, F. M., 34, 35 n43; *Fausts Leben, Taten und Höllenfahrt*, 26–7
Knight of Virtue, 23, 27–32
Knox, T. M., 132 n22
Kodalle, Klaus-M., 120 n35
Köhler, Dietmar, 97 n3, 107 n18, 134 n27
Kojève, Alexandre, 106
Kolnai, Aurel, 120 n35
Königson, Marie-Jeanne, 78 n15
Korsgaard, Christine, 10 n12

Lacoue-Labarthe, Philippe, 110
language, 96–7, 104, 107–8, 125; of forgiveness, 112–15
law, 30–5, 38, 55, 57–9, 62, 97, 102, 105; masculine and feminine, 64
Law of the Heart, 23, 27–8
Lear, Jonathan, 49 n16
literature (*see also* comedy; novel; tragedy), 1, 6–10, 17, 19, 20, 22, 34, 37–41; philosophy of, 9, 16
love, 103
Lukács, Georg, 38 n47, 99 n9

Macbeth, 75 n9
McDowell, John, 2, 3 n6, 13, 43, 76–7
McGinn, Colin, 98 n7
Machiavelli, Niccolò, 29 n31
MacIntyre, Alisdair, 49 n17
Mandeville, Bernard de, 29 n31
Marshall, David, 71 n6, 89 n34
Marx, Karl, 68, 69
mask, 64–7, 70–1, 73, 76 n10, 79–82, 94, 105, 109–10
Meist, Kurt, 26 n26
Mendelssohn, Moses, 76
Menke-Eggers, Christoph, 42 n1
Molière, 90, 92
moral genius, 104, 106
moral luck, 4, 10, 45, 46–50, 55, 120 n36, 126 n4, 134 n26
moral sentiment, 89
morality, 92, 102–3, 119
Morality, in the *PhG*, 19, 54, 92, 95, 119, 123 n2, 126 n4; in the *PR*, 130 n17, 132
Mortier, Roland, 78 n15
motivation, 57, 59, 77, 80, 121, 128; epistemic access to, 70; social conditions of, 71

Nagel, Thomas, 10 n12, 120 n36
Nancy, Jean-Luc, 110
Napoleon, 106
narrativity, 1, 6, 11, 134; philosophical, 40
nature, 103, 126–7
necessity, 25, 27–8, 33–4, 36

Nehamas, Alexander, 17
Norman, Judith, 111 n26
norms, 4–6, 14, 41, 76–7, 104, 113, 121, 135
Norton, Robert, 98, 106 n17
Novalis, 98, 101, 106, 107
novel (*see also* forgiveness), 15, 17, 41, 99, 107, 110, 134; romantic, 1, 7, 8, 19, 37, 40, 65 n38, 93, 100, 122
Novitz, David, 120 n35
Nussbaum, Martha, 42 n1, 49 n16, 50 n19, 52 n20, 61 n35

Observing Reason, 21, 23
Oedipus, 36, 46, 49, 53–5, 65 n38, 70, 75, 96
Orestes, 75 n9
O'Shaughnessy, R.J., 120 n35

Palissot de Montenoy, Charles de, 86
particular, 93, 104, 112, 118, 124
Patten, Alan, 124 n3, 128
Peperzak, Adriaan, 127 n9
personality, 75
perspective, impersonal, 35, 120
philosophy of action, *see* agency
phrenology, 23, 40
physiognomy, 23
Pietism, 76, 77
Pinkard, Terry, 3 n4, 14, 15, 17, 19 n17, 22 n21, 29 n31, 35, 38, 45 n6, 53, 61 n33, 64, 76 n11, 108 n20, 112, 118 n34
Pippin, Robert, 3 n4, 13 n4, 15, 17, 22, 77 n14, 79 n17, 91 n41, 123 n3, 126 n5, 134 n28
Plato, 16, 68 n1, 78 n16, 108 n21
pleasure, 25, 27
plot, 99, 100
poetry, 16, 47, 100, 101
Pöggeler, Otto, 11 n1, 12, 42 n1, 97 n3, 100 n10, 107
post-Kantian philosophy, 2, 7, 35, 51, 102–3, 108, 116, 117, 132
poverty, 71
practical identity, 5–6, 10, 61, 65, 66, 118; recognitive, 8, 134
pragmatism, 4
Price, David W., 78 n15
property, 71, 130
punishment, 133

Quante, Michael, 44 n5, 60, 71 n5, 126 n4

Rameau's Nephew, see Diderot
rationalist expressivism, 4 n7
Reason, 7, 8, 21, 22 n20, 31, 33 n42, 35–7,

40–1, 51, 85, 93, 124, 127, 128–30; summary of *PhG* section, 33; transition to Spirit, 59

reasons for belief and action, 6, 38, 53, 102, 122, 131, 132, 133; agent-neutral, 120; agent-relative, 119, 121, 132; impersonal, 6, 35

receptivity, 2

recognition, 36, 49, 64, 65 n38, 94, 119, 121; identity and, 5–6; of the other, 103–4, 114, 117; tragic, 28, 36, 94

recollection, 40–1

reconciliation, 35, 50, 105–6, 112, 118; dramas, 96, 99; language of, 115; moment of, 95; society and, 132–3

Redding, Paul, 91 n41

Redfield, James, 48 n12, 49 n17

reflectiveness, 43

regret, 45, 55–6, 71

religion, 38, 39, 52, 112

Religion, in the *PhG*, 8, 18, 19, 20 n18, 22, 35, 37, 40, 41, 73, 75, 118

responsibility, 45, 55, 119, 126 n4

retrospectivity (*see also* tragedy), 8, 19, 42–67, 94, 96, 102–3, 120 n36, 128, 134; of action, 1, 4, 6, 8 n9, 53, 54, 72; and forgiveness, 119, 121; tragic moment of action, 94; and the will, 124

Richards, Norvin, 120 n35

Ricoeur, Paul, 42, n42

Rieger, Max, 26 n26

right, 75, 121, 128, 132

Robinson, Jonathan, 102 n16

Roche, Mark, 7 n8, 68 n1

Romantics, 9, 16, 29–35, 38, 40 n49, 51, 93, 97, 99, 101, 103–9, 111, 112

Rome, 75

Rorty, Richard, 17

Rosenberg, Jay, 14 n7

Rosenkranz, Karl, 26 n26

Rosenzweig, Franz, 42, 43 n2

Royce, Josiah, 12, 23, 29 n33

Rousseau, Jean-Jacques, 10 n12, 71, 84, 89, 90–3, 98, 106, 107, 112, 116

Russon, John, 126 n7

Sache selbst, die, see Thing-in-Itself

satire, 79

Sax, Benjamin, 109 n23

Schelling, Friedrich Wilhelm Joseph, 9, 20, 30 n35

Schiller, Friedrich, 18, 20, 23, 27, 29–30, 41 n51, 98 n7, 106

Schlegel, August Wilhelm, 101

Schlegel, Friedrich, 9, 16, 20, 30, 34, 39, 94, 100–2, 107, 108–9, 110–11, 113,

116, 117; *Lucinde*, 98, 108–9, 110–11, 116

Schmeer, Hans, 98 n7, 106 n17

Schmidt, James, 76 n11, 78 n15, 79 n18, 85 n28

Schulte, Michael, 33 n42, 42 n1, 52, 53 n23, 63 n36

science, 76

second nature, 126–7

Sedgwick, Sally, 2 n3

self-awareness, 70

self-consciousness, 66, 72, 74

Self-Consciousness, in the *PhG*, 25

self-knowledge, 10, 70, 95; sociality of, 68; theatricality of, 70

self-reflectiveness, 71

Sellars, Wilfrid, 13

Sense-Certainty, 19

Shaftesbury, Anthony Ashley Cooper, earl of, 29 n31, 106 n17

Shapiro, Gary, 12 n3, 68 n1

Shattuck, Roger, 31 n39

Sittlichkeit, see Ethical Life/Ethical Order

skepticism, 3, 13, 14 n6, 43, 67

slavery, 7

Smith, Adam, 10 n12, 71, 84, 89–91

Smith, John, 18 n16

Smith, Steven B., 124 n3

Socrates, 108

Sophocles (*Antigone*), 7, 18, 33, 35, 37, 41, 45, 46, 106, 115 n30, 124

soul-body problem, 126–7

space of concepts, 2

space of reasons, 14–15, 76

spectacle, 94

spectator, 42, 50–1, 66, 70–4, 79, 82–3, 88–91, 94; impartial, 89, 90

Speight, Allen, 100 n10, 132 n23

Spirit, 6–8, 15, 18, 19, 21–5, 28, 31–8, 40, 50–51, 57, 65 n38, 68 n1, 75, 77, 85, 86, 92, 93, 94–6, 97, 99, 103, 118, 121, 126, 127; culture in, 76, 77; forgiveness as a moment in, 40; literature in *PhG* section on, 35–7, 40–1, 78, 94; as normative realm, 15; objective, 130 n17, 133; practical, 122, 130 n17; recollection of, 41; as social space, 15; subjective, 133; theoretical, 122, 130 n17; tragic conflict in, 75; transition from Reason, 59; transition to Religion, 38

spontaneity, 2

Starobinski, Jean, 10 n12, 90, 91 n40, 92 n43, 93

Steiner, George, 33 n42, 50 n19, 52

Stern, Robert, 2 n3

stoicism, 67

Taylor, Charles, 44, 47
theatricality (*see also* comedy), 10, 19, 68–96, 108, 128; of action, 1, 6, 8, 10, 66, 71, 82, 88, 90, 95–6, 102–3, 119, 121; overcoming of, 84
Thing-in-Itself, 31–2, 37
Thomas, Alan, 2 n3
Tieck, Ludwig, 19 n17, 30
tragedy (*see also* Greece, ancient; retrospectivity), 1, 7, 8, 10, 12, 17, 19, 23, 26–8, 34–5, 39, 41, 43, 69, 96, 99, 102, 118, 120 n36, 122, 123 n1, 133, 134; action in, 45, 47, 74; of active reason, 25; as imitation of action, 48; relation to comedy, 68, 70, 92, 99; relation to ethics, 48–9; tragic hero, 66, 72, 82, 94, 109
transparency, 93, 111, 112
Trilling, Lionel, 78 n15, 81
Tunick, Mark, 124 n3

Unger, Friederike Helene, 98 n7
universal, 32, 33 n42, 87, 92, 104, 105, 116, 118
universal self, 88

Vernant, J.-P., 46
Verene, Donald Phillip, 18 n16
Vierhaus, Rudolf, 76 n11

Waszek, Norbert, 91 n41
Weil, Eric, 92 n43
Westphal, Kenneth, 102 n16
Wieland, C.M., 98
will, 4, 10, 48–9, 122–5, 128; general, 92; indeterminacy of, 124–5; natural, 130; particular, 124–5; rational/free, 121–3, 130–1 134; universal, 125, 130
Williams, Bernard, 10 n12, 46
Williams, Robert, 124 n3
Wolff, Michael, 127 n9
Wood, Allen, 26 n27, 46 n8, 118 n34, 123 n3, 126 n4